Weaving the Tapestry

A Journey Exploring Women of Valor Through History

by Nechama Dina Wasserman Laber

JGU PRESS

Weaving the Tapestry:
A Journey Exploring Women of Valor Through History
ISBN: 978-0-9841624-9-9
Second Edition — Cheshvan 5784 / October 2023

Copyright © 2023 by JGU Press

Jewish Girls Unite
12 Thompson Hill Rd
Rensselaer NY, 12144
www.JewishGirlsUnite.com

ALL RIGHTS RESERVED
No part of this book may be reproduced in any form without written permission from the copyright holder.

Design & Layout by Carasmatic Design
www.CarasmaticDesign.com
Cover art by Miriam Leah Herman
Interior art by Chana Cotter

Printed in the USA

DEDICATED IN LOVING MEMORY OF

Henya Federman OB"M

Henya Federman, ob"m was an exceptional woman who embodied the qualities of a true Aishes Chayil from Alef to Tav.

Henya was a devoted wife, mother, and Chabad Shlucha in the Virgin Islands. Her home was a haven of exuding warmth and hospitality, welcoming everyone with open arms.

Her enduring legacy and impact on the world will continue to inspire and uplift for generations to come.

Dedicated by the Federman family

OUR MISSION

Jewish Girls Unite is a global community that empowers girls and women through innovative education and technology. Our mission is to inspire pride in our heritage, foster spiritual and emotional growth, and encourage girls and women to shine their inner light to create positive change in the world. We believe in expressing Judaism through the arts and supporting women to grow as leaders in their homes, communities, and the world.

We offer a diverse range of initiatives, including **JGR retreats** for girls, women, and leaders at our **Jewish Greenbush Retreat** campus, as well as **JGU** online programs. Additionally, our **GROW Connection Network** has evolved over two decades of connecting with the souls of Jewish girls and empowering them with leadership principles. Our global network has expanded to connect women through various channels, such as **JGU Press** publications, the **GROW Method** of Prayer, **GROW Circles**, coaching, and training. We invite you to join our mission in empowering and uplifting the next generation of Jewish women!

JewishGirlsUnite.com

GROWconnectionNetwork.com

JewishGirlsRetreat.com

GreenbushRetreat.com

TABLE OF CONTENTS

Author's Note	10
Aishes Chayil	12
Weaving Shabbos Into the Week	17
Woman Warrior	26
Shabbos Hamalka	26
As the Sun is Setting Low	27
Challah Power	29
Welcoming Shabbos Without Stress	30
What the NY Times Got Right About Shabbos Candles	32
א *A Thread of Self Discovery*	35
I Am a Jewish Girl, An *Aishes Chayil*	38
Aishes Chayil	38
Four Generations, Their Stories Intertwined	40
א *A Thread of Pearls of Wisdom*	45
Women of the Future	48
Diving into a Sea of Pearls in the Hospital	50
ב *A Thread of Trust*	53
Shine Your Inner Light	57
A Beautiful Partnership	58
ג *A Thread of Loyalty*	61
GLOW	64
Bubby Dina & Roza's Devotion	66
A Mother's Lesson	69
ד *A Thread of Leadership*	73
Unraveled	76
A Mother's Prayer	78
Legacies Intertwined	79
Unwinding	81
ה *A Thread of Empathy*	83
Mama Rochel	86
Be Good and Be Kind!	88
ו *A Thread of Nourishment*	91
Stretch Out Your Hand	95
Copper Mirrors	95
Hidden Bread	98
Diving into Kosher	100
ז *A Thread of Planting*	103
Looking Back	107
L'Saken Olam	107
Without a Title, an Institution of Her Own	109
ח *A Thread of Readiness*	113
Bezchut Nashim	116
Got Tambourines!	117
The Face of a Believer	119
ט *A Thread of Faith*	123
Vatispalel Chana	128
Be A Warrior, not a Worrier!	130

🌱 GROWing Through Prayer	132
י A Thread of Feminine Strength	135
🎵 One More Light	140
🌱 My Bubby's Life Guides Me	142
כ A Thread of Tzedakah	145
🎵 Silent Prayer	148
🌱 Tzedakah Saves from Death	150
🌱 In Business to Feed the Hungry	151
🌱 A Legacy of Tzedakah	152
ל A Thread of Courage	155
🎵 Light Up A Candle	158
🌱 A Fearless Mother	160
🌱 The Shabbos That Kept Rose	163
מ A Thread of Modesty	167
🎵 Three *Malachim* Came	170
🌱 A Private Life of Public Service	172
נ A Thread of Influence	175
🎵 Rebbetzin Chana	177
🌱 Influence with Ink	180
ס A Thread of Resourcefulness	183
🎵 Heaven on Earth	186
🌱 Perfect Porridge	188
ע A Thread of Optimism	191
🎵 *Ashira* (I Will Sing)	195
🌱 Dancing Through Life	197
פ A Thread of Communication	201
🎵 *Psach Libi* — I Want to Grow	204
🌱 My Mom's Love	206
צ A Thread of Action	209
🎵 Brick by Brick	212
🌱 The Rebbe's Birthday Gift	214
ק A Thread of Thanks	217
🎵 My Dear *Ima*	219
🌱 Mother's Praise	221
🌱 My Dearest Mother	222
🌱 Dare to Dream	224
ר A Thread of Success	227
🎵 The Princess	229
🎵 The Crown of Creation	230
🌱 Through Higher Channels	232
ש A Thread of True Beauty	237
🎵 Deep in the Ground	243
🎵 Eternally Bright	243
🎵 I Will Go Where You Will Go	244
🌱 One Mitzvah Overcomes Total Darkness	246
🌱 Bubbe's Challah	248
🌱 Miracle at Sea	251
ת A Thread of Redemption	255
🎵 The Secret	257
🎵 Welcome to our Garden	257
🌱 She is You!	259
Glossary	264
Acknowledgments	268
About the Author	271
About the GROW Method	272

AUTHOR'S NOTE

"*Aishes Chayil* — A Woman of Valor" is a cherished Jewish song sung every Friday night before the festive Shabbos meal. Its twenty-two verses beautifully express gratitude and recognition for the remarkable qualities of a woman of valor. In each chapter of this book, we encounter captivating portraits of seemingly ordinary women leading extraordinary lives. This song celebrates the everyday tasks performed by an *Aishes Chayil* in her home and business, where she reveals the divine within the physical realm.

With skill and grace, she weaves the sacred threads of faith, courage, prayer, kindness, leadership, and the three mitzvos entrusted to Jewish women into the intricate tapestry of her life. From the glow of her Shabbos candles to the preparation of nourishing challah and food, she forges a profound connection between her family and G-d, creating a *Dira Btachtonim*, a sacred dwelling for His presence in her heart and home.

Welcome to the empowering journey of growing as a Woman of Valor. From the moment of your birth, you were chosen by G-d to be His *Aishes Chayil*, with a unique purpose. Together, let us embark on a path of self-discovery, intricately weaving the twenty-two verses of the *Aishes Chayil* into the very fabric of our minds and hearts.

By immersing ourselves in these verses and delving into the lives of women who exemplify their virtues, we will find inspiration to reveal the Woman of Valor within us. Each verse represents a distinct trait, serving as a thread that artfully weaves together our unique tapestry of character and strength.

Stitch by stitch and thread by thread, we each contribute to the grand tapestry alongside women of valor, both past and present, enhancing the beauty of G-d's world. We are connected with Jewish women across the globe, transcending generations back to our first Matriarch, Sarah. We warmly invite you to share your unique strengths and talents, joining our collective endeavor of "Weaving The Tapestry" and uniting our efforts towards the fulfillment of our ultimate wish — the redemption.

Each chapter begins with thought-provoking **Digging Deeper** questions, offering insightful explanations of verses based on commentaries from our Sages. We also delve into the lives of **Women in the Torah** who exemplify the traits highlighted in each verse. Throughout the chapters, you will discover **Meaningful Melodies**, **Pearls of Wisdom** — a collection of inspiring quotes — and heartfelt **Aishes Chayil stories and tributes** that resonate with the essence of the verse.

To deepen your personal growth, each chapter concludes with a **GROW as an *Aishes Chayil*** reflection, rooted in the GROW Method of Prayer (see page 272 for details), empowering you to integrate the lessons into your daily life.

May we embrace our role as "the cloth in the weaver's hand," allowing G-d to intertwine our unique tapestries with countless others throughout history, ultimately completing the magnificent tapestry of creation with the final redemption.

For further connection and inspiration, we invite you to join our global community for girls at **JewishGirlsUnite.com** and women at **GROWconnectionNetwork.com**, where you can connect with other women of valor.

May your journey be blessed as you embrace your inherent strengths to weave your tapestry and join the esteemed lineage of women who have left an indelible mark on the world.

With gratitude and blessings,

Nechama Dina Laber
JGU Founder & Director

P.S. To listen to the songs in each chapter, visit jewishgirlsunite.com/tapestrysongs.

Aishes Chayil

א	A Woman of Valor, who can find? Her worth is far beyond pearls.	אֵשֶׁת חַיִל מִי יִמְצָא, וְרָחֹק מִפְּנִינִים מִכְרָהּ	א
ב	Her husband's heart trusts in her and he shall lack no fortune.	בָּטַח בָּהּ לֵב בַּעְלָהּ, וְשָׁלָל לֹא יֶחְסָר	ב
ג	She repays him with good and not evil all the days of her life.	גְּמָלַתְהוּ טוֹב וְלֹא רָע, כֹּל יְמֵי חַיֶּיהָ	ג
ד	She seeks out wool and linen, and her hands work willingly	דָּרְשָׁה צֶמֶר וּפִשְׁתִּים, וַתַּעַשׂ בְּחֵפֶץ כַּפֶּיהָ	ד
ה	She is like the merchant's ships bringing her bread from afar.	הָיְתָה כָּאֳנִיּוֹת סוֹחֵר, מִמֶּרְחָק תָּבִיא לַחְמָהּ	ה
ו	She rises while it is still nighttime, and gives food to her household and a portion to her maids.	וַתָּקָם בְּעוֹד לַיְלָה, וַתִּתֵּן טֶרֶף לְבֵיתָהּ, וְחֹק לְנַעֲרֹתֶיהָ	ו
ז	She considers a field and acquires it; from the fruit of her hands, she plants a vineyard.	זָמְמָה שָׂדֶה וַתִּקָּחֵהוּ, מִפְּרִי כַפֶּיהָ נָטְעָה כָּרֶם	ז
ח	She girds her hips with might and strengthens her arms.	חָגְרָה בְעוֹז מָתְנֶיהָ, וַתְּאַמֵּץ זְרוֹעֹתֶיהָ	ח
ט	She senses that her trade is profitable, so her lamp is not extinguished at night.	טָעֲמָה כִּי טוֹב סַחְרָהּ, לֹא יִכְבֶּה בַלַּיְלָה נֵרָהּ	ט
י	She stretches forth her hands to the spindle, and her palms support the distaff.	יָדֶיהָ שִׁלְּחָה בַכִּישׁוֹר, וְכַפֶּיהָ תָּמְכוּ פָלֶךְ	י

כ She spreads out her palm to the poor and extends her hands to the needy.	כַּפָּהּ פָּרְשָׂה לֶעָנִי, וְיָדֶיהָ שִׁלְּחָה לָאֶבְיוֹן
ל She has no fear of the snow for her household, for all her household is dressed in scarlet wool.	לֹא תִירָא לְבֵיתָהּ מִשָּׁלֶג, כִּי כָל בֵּיתָהּ לָבֻשׁ שָׁנִים
מ Bedspreads she makes for herself; linen and purple wool are her clothing.	מַרְבַדִּים עָשְׂתָה לָּהּ, שֵׁשׁ וְאַרְגָּמָן לְבוּשָׁהּ
נ Her husband is known in the gates, where he sits with the elders of the land.	נוֹדָע בַּשְּׁעָרִים בַּעְלָהּ, בְּשִׁבְתּוֹ עִם זִקְנֵי אָרֶץ
ס Linens she makes and sells, and she delivers a belt to the peddler.	סָדִין עָשְׂתָה וַתִּמְכֹּר, וַחֲגוֹר נָתְנָה לַכְּנַעֲנִי
ע Strength and splendor are her clothing, and she looks smilingly towards the future.	עֹז וְהָדָר לְבוּשָׁהּ, וַתִּשְׂחַק לְיוֹם אַחֲרוֹן
פ She opens her mouth with wisdom, and the teaching of kindness is on her tongue.	פִּיהָ פָּתְחָה בְחָכְמָה, וְתוֹרַת חֶסֶד עַל לְשׁוֹנָהּ
צ She looks after the conduct of her household and does not eat the bread of laziness.	צוֹפִיָּה הֲלִיכוֹת בֵּיתָהּ, וְלֶחֶם עַצְלוּת לֹא תֹאכֵל
ק Her children rise and celebrate her; and her husband, he praises her.	קָמוּ בָנֶיהָ וַיְאַשְּׁרוּהָ, בַּעְלָהּ וַיְהַלְלָהּ
ר Many daughters have attained valor, but you have surpassed them all.	רַבּוֹת בָּנוֹת עָשׂוּ חָיִל, וְאַתְּ עָלִית עַל כֻּלָּנָה
ש Charm is false and beauty is vain; [but] a G-d-fearing woman, she should be praised.	שֶׁקֶר הַחֵן וְהֶבֶל הַיֹּפִי, אִשָּׁה יִרְאַת ה׳ הִיא תִתְהַלָּל
ת Give her the fruit of her hands, and let her deeds praise her at the gates.	תְּנוּ לָהּ מִפְּרִי יָדֶיהָ, וִיהַלְלוּהָ בַשְּׁעָרִים מַעֲשֶׂיהָ

Digging Deeper

Who composed the song "Aishes Chayil"?

Our forefather Avraham wrote *"Aishes Chayil"* as a tribute to his wife, Sarah, after her passing. Centuries later, King Shlomo, son of King David, included the song in the closing section of *Mishlei*, his book of Proverbs, which is one of the twenty-four holy books of the Torah.[1]

Why is the "Aishes Chayil" song written alphabetically, each verse beginning with a different Hebrew letter?

The *Alef-Beis* format used by Shlomo is a way of comparing the numerous positive qualities of a righteous woman to the completeness of the entire alphabet.

An *Aishes Chayil* is someone who embodies the truth contained in our holy language, from *alef* at the beginning, to *mem* in the middle, to *tav* at the end. These three letters form the word *"emes,"* meaning truth.

G-d creates the world with ten statements made up of the letters of the *Alef-Beis*. As the letters are the building blocks of creation, so too, Jewish women are the builders of the Jewish nation.

G-d gave the Jews the Torah through the twenty-two letters of the *Alef-Beis*, and similarly He praises the Jewish woman with twenty-two letters.[2]

1. In his youth, Shlomo wrote Shir Hashirim. In mid-life, he wrote Mishlei. In his old age, he wrote Kohelet.
2. Yalkut Shimoni on Mishlei

What does the word "chayil חיל" mean?

"Chayil" means strength, power, wealth, virtue, honesty, courage, success, accomplishment, and literally, a "warrior." An *Aishes Chayil* utilizes her *aishes*, referring to her "feminine abilities," to be a warrior conquering the darkness in the world to usher in the light of redemption.

She is a Warrior of Light!

What are the tools of an Aishes Chayil?

In Hebrew, נשק *"neshek"* means weapon and is an acronym for *"Neiros Shabbos Kodesh — The Holy Sabbath Candles,"* a powerful tool to dispel darkness. They also symbolize the power of Torah and mitzvos to illuminate the world. As King Shlomo states, "A mitzvah is a candle and Torah is light."[3]

The Lubavitcher Rebbe stated this mission as follows: It is imperative that every Jew know that he is an emissary of the Master of all, charged with the mission, wherever he may be, of bringing into reality G-d's will and intention in creating the universe, namely, to illuminate the world with the light of Torah and *avoda* [service]. This is done through performing practical mitzvos and implanting in oneself fine character traits.[4]

3. Mishlei 6:23
4. Hayom Yom for Adar I, 8

What is significant about recognizing an Aishes Chayil's everyday tasks within her home and business, rather than praising her spiritual greatness?

The *Aishes Chayil* skillfully weaves the threads of faith and trust in G-d into the tapestry of her life. She prays while caring for her family, recites blessings on Kosher food, and gives *tzedakah* from her business. She weaves the three special mitzvos entrusted to Jewish women into her daily actions: She lights up her home and the world with her Shabbos candles and with every good deed. She separates challah, which encompasses all of her actions that elevate the physical world. She immerses in a *Mikvah*, sanctifying her marriage. Even her home decor is holy, with *mezuzos* on the doorposts and Torah books on the shelves!

She lives by the teaching, "בכל דרכיך דעהו — Know [G-d] in all your ways."[5] Through weaving mitzvos into her physical actions, she invites G-d into her home and brings heaven down to earth. With her thoughts, speech, and actions, she transforms her home into a dwelling place, a *dirah betachtonim* for G-d.

What is the unique role of women in creating a dwelling for G-d, and what is our ultimate goal?

As we draw closer to the times of Moshiach, the central role of women becomes clearer:

Her heart is a dwelling for G-d, guided by Torah she works from within to touch and uplift others. With her feminine and nurturing approach, she cultivates an atmosphere of peace, unity, and holiness in herself and her home, which radiates outward to the world.[6]

Just as she ushers in the light of Shabbos with her candles, a woman is at the forefront of ushering in the true and ultimate redemption, a time that the *Mishnah*[7] describes as: "The day that will be entirely Shabbos and everlasting rest."

How is the "Aishes Chayil" a metaphor for G-d and the Jewish people?

At the Giving of the Torah on Mount Sinai, G-d revealed Himself as the groom to the bride, the Jewish people.[8] In entrusting us with this sacred mission, G-d calls upon us to weave the spiritual and physical realms together, creating a dwelling place for His presence.

With this understanding of our Divine relationship, the "*Aishes Chayil*" song is relevant to everyone. G-d sings this song to each of His spiritual "brides," believing in the potential of every Jew to reveal the inner woman of valor within them.

In light of this Divine bond, readers can interpret the verses and commentaries related to marriage and women with an understanding of their connection and relationship with G-d. These teachings encompass not only the roles and virtues of women but also emphasize the bond and connection every Jew is meant to cultivate with G-d.

---

5. Mishlei 3:6
6. Sefer HaSichos, 22 Shevat 5752
7. Tamid 7:4
8. Pirkei d'Rabbi Eliezer 41; introduction to the Zohar, 8a; Talmud, Taanis 26b

Besides praising a woman, what else does "Aishes Chayil" allude to?

THE SOUL

The "*Aishes Chayil*" song praises the two souls in a person:

The "G-dly soul" descends from above into a body and is praised for revealing the hidden spirituality in the physical body and world during the week.[9]

The vital soul or the "animal soul" animates the body, through which the "G-dly soul" serves G-d.[10]

Furthermore, the soul and body are comparable to a husband and wife, respectively. The Lubavitcher Rebbe emphasized the importance of maintaining "*shalom bayis* — peace in the home" between the soul and body, the spiritual "husband and wife." This inner peace enhances the *shalom bayis* in the physical home.[11]

THE SHABBOS BRIDE-QUEEN

According to Rabbi Yeshayah HaLevi Horowitz, "*Aishes Chayil*" praises the *Shechinah*, or Divine Presence, which is associated with royalty and Shabbos is called a "bride."

The *Midrash* tells how every day of the week was created with a "mate:" Sunday with Monday, Tuesday with Wednesday, Thursday with Friday. When Shabbos was left alone, G-d paired her with the Jewish people. Therefore, we sing "*Aishes Chayil*" on Friday night, welcoming the Shabbos as both our bride and queen.[12]

THE TORAH

Aishes Chayil is a metaphor for the Torah, which was given on Shabbos. We praise the Torah, and those who study it.[13]

The word "*chayil*" חיל also has the numeric value of forty-eight, corresponding to the forty-eight ways to acquire the crown of Torah, such as listening, learning with joy, being modest, having a good heart and being precise in Torah study.[14]

How are all the above explanations really one?

Here is how all the explanations are interconnected and woven together as one:

We recognize the strengths of both souls and the Torah's guidance to transform the world into a dwelling for G-d. A woman is the *Akeres Habayis*, the "foundation of the home" and she excels at transforming her home into a mini sanctuary for G-d. This earns her praise as the Shabbos Queen enters weekly.[15]

---

9. Ma'amar Mordechai
10. Ralbag, Malbim on Mishlei 31:10
11. Based on letters of the Lubavitcher Rebbe; read more at https://asknoah.org/essay/peace-in-the-home.
12. Sefer Ziv Minhagim, page 96
13. Rashi on Mishlei 31:31
14. Pirkei Avos 6:6
15. Adapted and inspired by "Why Sing Eishet Chayil on Friday Night?" by Yehuda Shurpin for Chabad.org.

Weaving Shabbos Into the Week

Digging Deeper

Creating a home for G-d is further reflected in a commandment to our ancestors, effective upon their entry to Israel: "The land shall keep a Shabbos [rest] for G-d. Six years you shall sow your field, and six years you shall prune your vineyard and gather in its fruit."[1]

Why is "a rest for G-d" mentioned before the work?

While resting the land (*Shmitta*) only follows six years of agricultural work, the Torah first mentions a "Shabbos for G-d" as a mission statement: The purpose of all the six years of mundane work is to recognize the Creator and create a "Shabbos for G-d."

How does this apply to us today?

These verses express the mission of every Jew, and especially the Jewish woman, who is the foundation of the home — her "land." While her domain may physically resemble any other, it is distinguished by the intention she weaves into the six weekdays: All her activities are in preparation for the weekly "Shabbos for G-d."

How does Shabbos influence the week?

An *Aishes Chayil* establishes her home like an Israelite farmer, who recognizes that the purpose of entering the land is to prepare for Shabbos. The focus of an *Aishes Chayil*'s work is to bring Shabbos into her personal "land." In turn, this attitude infuses her entire week with the spirit and serenity of Shabbos. As a result she accomplishes her tasks with trust in G-d, as if all her work is complete![2]

The work begins with "sowing the field," a reference to wheat, symbolic of practicing and imparting the basics of Jewish observance. She adds by "pruning her vineyard," a reference to fruit, symbolic of beautifying Judaism.

The wheat used for the mitzvah of challah reminds

1. Vayikra 25:2-3

2. Rashi on Shemos 20:9

of the mitzvah of challah which the Jews were commanded to fulfill upon entry into the Holy Land. In addition, the mitzvah of *bikkurim* began when a farmer in Israel would find budding fruit in his field, and tie a reed around them, verbally declaring them "first fruits."

An *Aishes Chayil* infuses her home with the theme of the mitzvah of challah and *bikkurim*, gratitude and recognizing the good. In Hebrew, this is known as *hakaras hatov* (recognizing the good). The *bikkurim* ceremony teaches us how important it is to verbally acknowledge G-d, the source of our blessings, as well as His many agents.[3]

The twenty-two verses recognize and describe the various ways in which she is weaving the spirit of Shabbos into her actions all week to transform this physical world into a home for G-d. Therefore, it is fitting to praise every *Aishes Chayil* once Shabbos arrives.

May we merit the rebuilding of the third *Beis Hamikdash*, where we will fulfill all the mitzvos in G-d's everlasting home in Jerusalem speedily in our days with the ultimate Redemption — an everlasting "Shabbos for *Hashem*."[4]

Challah
IN THE TORAH

When the Jewish people first inhabited the Land of Israel, one of the many gifts they were commanded to give to the priestly tribe, (*Kohanim*) who served in the Holy Temple, was a portion of their dough — "the first and the best." G-d says to Moshe: "Speak to the Israelite people and say to them: When you enter the land to which I am taking you and you eat of the bread of the land, separate the first portion of your kneading as a dough offering... In future generations, give the first of your kneading as an elevated gift to G-d."[5]

What does "challah" mean?

This gift of dough is known as challah, from which the name of our Shabbos loaves is derived. It means "portion of dough." Today we separate a small piece of dough — about the size of an olive (1 oz) — and either burn it or dispose of it respectfully, rendering inedible the portion that G-d commanded be set aside.

Why do we separate challah today if there is no Holy Temple in Jerusalem?

Although we may not give this dough to the *Kohanim* of today, in remembrance of this gift and in anticipation of the rebuilding of the third Holy Temple, we observe the mitzvah of separating the challah portion (*hafrashas challah*).

---

3. Shemos 23:19
4. From the talks of the Lubavitcher Rebbe for Parshas Behar, 5735/1975

5. Bamidbar 15:18-21

By separating a portion of challah in accordance with G-d's will, a woman demonstrates that giving to G-d and others comes first. Through this mitzvah, an *Aishes Chayil* instills faith in her family because she acknowledges that we prepare our food with the recognition that G-d is the provider of all sustenance.

Who baked challah in the Torah?

Taking challah is one of the three mitzvos set aside specifically for women, along with lighting Shabbos candles, and observing family purity. We trace the connection between women and taking challah to the first Jewish woman, Sarah.

Our Matriarch Sarah prepared bread for the three guests. When Avraham welcomes the traveling angels[6] he prepares a large feast for them, and instructs Sarah to bake the bread: "Quick, get three *se'ah* of choice flour! Knead and make cakes!" Her dough had a special blessing, and this distinctive capability to create a dough of blessing was passed on to our Matriarch Rivkah.[7]

The *Lechem Hapanim* were the twelve loaves of specially-shaped breads, which were baked every week in the *Beis Hamikdash*. They were displayed on a special table and replaced every Friday. At the end of each week, the *Kohanim* ate this bread that miraculously remained fresh all week. To remember this miracle, we shape our challah in various combinations alluding to the number twelve.[8]

WEAVING THE CHALLAH

What is the significance of a three-strand braided challah?

The **three-strand braids** are symbolic of the commands to observe Shabbos that appear in the Ten Commandments. One strand of the braid represents the word "*Zachor*" — "Remember." A second braid strand represents the word "*Shamor*" — "Guard." The third braid strand is for "*B'Dibbur Echad*" — that these commands of "Remember" and "Guard" were said by G-d simultaneously as one unit.[9]

The three-strand braids remind us of the three meals eaten on Shabbos and the fundamental concepts connected to Shabbos:

- The Creation of the World
- The Exodus from Egypt
- The Era of Moshiach

The three-strand braids represent the three different *Amidos* (silent standing prayer) recited on Shabbos, as opposed to the weekday *Amidah* which consists of the same wording three times a day.

What is the significance of a four-strand braided challah?

The **four strands** represent our four Matriarchs: Sarah, Rivkah, Rachel and Leah, whose strengths are woven together into the fabric of our nation.

---

6. Bereishis chapter 18
7. Rashi, Bereishis 24,67
8. Rambam Hilchos Tmidin Umusafin chapter 5

9. Shmos 21, 8 Rashi

What is the significance of a six-strand braided challah?

Two *challos* together equal **twelve strands** and remind us of the twelve loaves of bread in the Holy Temple. This also represents the twelve tribes of Israel.

What is the significance of placing two challos on the Shabbos table?

When the Jews were wandering in the desert, their only source of food was the Manna that G-d sent down from heaven. Each morning a layer of dew would fall on the ground. Then the Manna, a whitish substance resembling poppy seeds, would fall, followed by a second layer of dew. The Jews would collect a portion of Manna every day. They were only permitted to take a certain amount. If they would take any more than the allotted amount, the extra Manna would rot, becoming inedible. Because they were not permitted to carry on Shabbos, they would receive a double portion on Friday.

To remember this we prepare two *challos*, called *Lechem Mishna*, for each Shabbos meal.[10]

---

10. Shmos 16,22, Talmud Shabbos page 117,b

Challah Recipe

For 2 medium challahs*
- 1 packet dry yeast
- 1 cup warm water
- 1/4 cup sugar
- 1/4 cup oil
- 1 egg
- 4 cups flour
- 1 teaspoon salt

For 10-15 challahs*
- 3 tbs yeast
- 4 cups warm water
- 1/2 cup sugar
- 1 cup oil
- 4 eggs
- 12-14 cups flour (+ more as needed)
- 1 ½ tbs salt

Pour the water into a large bowl. Sprinkle yeast and let it dissolve. Use your spoon to mix the water, sugar, and yeast for 30 seconds. Let the mixture sit undisturbed for 10 minutes. When you see bubbles and foam, you know it's ready. Make sure your bowl remains still while the yeast is activating

Add in the egg(s) and the oil and stir to combine.

Gradually add flour 1-2 cups at a time, mixing after each addition.

Pour in salt and add the rest of the flour 1 cup at a time, mixing after each addition.

Graduate to kneading as the dough thickens.

Knead for 10 minutes until smooth and elastic and no longer sticky, adding flour as needed.

Cover the bowl and leave to rise for at least 40 minutes or up to 2-3 hours. Spread some oil over the dough and cover with a cloth.

Shape into loaves and brush with beaten egg and bake 40 minutes on 350° or until golden brown. Remove from pans and cool on racks. If the quantity was enough to take challah*, remember to burn and discard the separated dough.

The requirement for fulfilling the mitzvah of separating challah is only for breads made from these five grains: wheat, barley, rye, spelt, and oats. The amount needed to take challah with a blessing is 3 lb. 11 oz., or 5 lb. according to some opinions, the majority of the liquid contents of the dough should be water. To learn more about the requirements for this mitzvah, visit Chabad.org.

Challah Meditations

MIXING

As we mix and knead the dough, we will set an intention for each ingredient and GROW. As we follow the challah recipe, remember that this is a recipe for growing each day. It is a rich spiritual experience that brings blessings into our homes and the world.

The GROW Method is woven into these meaningful meditations. GROW is an acronym for the 4 steps of prayer in the siddur: Gratitude, Recognition, Oneness, Wishes.

G — Gratitude

Yeast is alive, which symbolizes life and growth. We are grateful to be alive and to keep growing.

Water is the purity of the soul. At our essence, we are pure and perfect. The water must be warm for the yeast to rise. We need warmth and compassion to grow. We are grateful G-d restores our soul each day with compassion.

Sugar helps activate the yeast. It represents kindness and sweetness. Positive energy adds warmth to our home. We treat ourselves and others with kindness even when it is challenging. We are grateful for G-d's kindness which allows for growth.

R — Recognition

Oil stands apart and refuses to blend. Each of us is special and is recognized for our unique gifts from G-d. As we pour in the oil, acknowledge the light that shines in yourself and each member of your family.

O — Oneness

Eggs bind the various ingredients in the dough, symbolizing unity and oneness with our Creator and our community. I am one with my Creator when I fulfill mitzvos, including the mitzvah of taking challah.

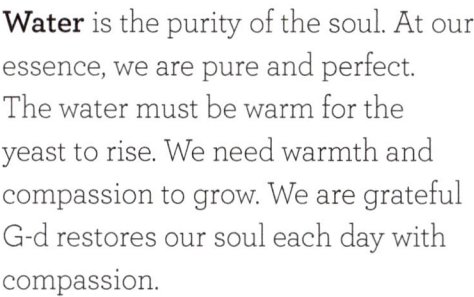

W — Wishes

Flour represents physical sustenance. We wish for a healthy body so our soul can shine. We wish for sustenance so we can serve G-d.

Salt represents preservation. We wish to preserve our Jewish legacy. We pray that our good deeds have an everlasting ripple effect on the world.

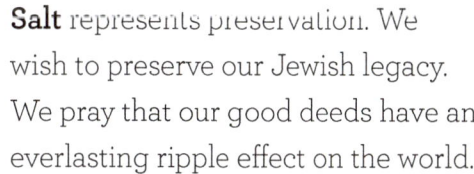

Salt brings out the sweet flavor in the dough and ensures the dough doesn't rise too much. We wish for Judaism to enhance the flavor of our lives with healthy boundaries.

KEEP GROWING AND ADDING

Begin by using a spoon to mix the dough, as you add more flour. As the dough thickens, use your hands to knead the dough thoroughly! As you knead the dough, whisper your needs to G-d.

STICK WITH IT

The dough is sticky and messy and it takes work until it is a smooth dough. Remember to keep growing and never give up despite the challenges we face.

RISE WITH THE DOUGH

As the dough rises, we GROW and rise along with it, with renewed faith and confidence in our connection to our Creator, our Core and Community.

Play some lively Jewish music while your challah rises, and dance. As your challah dough rises, envision your soul rising through song.

MEDITATION FOR SEPARATING CHALLAH

by Chana Burston

Place your hand on the dough you created with love.

Feel its soft texture, and allow your mind and body to slow down and take a peaceful pause — Shabbos is approaching. As you weave the spirit of Shabbos into the preparations, a wave of serenity enters your being and settles deep into your soul. Relax into the moment and absorb the peace around you.

G-d has gifted you with the strength to create and knead your dough, and with sight to lovingly measure the ingredients. With the ability to hear, you absorb the uplifting melodies of Shabbos and with the sense of taste you enjoy the richness of the earth's bounty. Your body and soul intertwine to infuse energy into your holy dough.

This challah will be placed in the oven in your kitchen, in your warm Jewish home, a home in which G-d resides. The sweet aroma will permeate throughout the home you created, bringing the anticipation of Shabbos to all who dwell within it.

Close your eyes and reflect on the past week. Acknowledge your accomplishments with pride, nurture yourself with compassion for the challenges that arose.

You open the gates for blessings by first giving to others — the sweet sound of coins clinking into a *tzedakah* box adds strength to your prayers.

Recognize that everything is from G-d, and so we

dedicate the first of our dough to Him. As your hands rest on the dough, feel the oneness and unity with our Creator who entrusts women with this mitzvah, fusing the spiritual and physical together. You are connecting to our Matriarch Sarah whose challah was blessed with intense holiness which stayed fresh from week to week.

As you recite the blessing on the dough, you join hands with women of valor across generations.

Recite the blessing:

> בָּרוּךְ אַתָּה ה' אֱלֹקֵינוּ מֶלֶךְ הָעוֹלָם
> אֲשֶׁר קִדְּשָׁנוּ בְּמִצְוֹתָיו וְצִוָּנוּ לְהַפְרִישׁ חַלָּה
>
> *Baruch Atah Ah-do-nai E-lo-hey-nu Melech Ha-olam*
> *A-sher Kid-shanu B'mitz-votav V'tzi-vanu L'haf-rish Challah.*
>
> **Blessed are You, L-rd our G-d, King of the Universe, who has sanctified us with His commandments and commanded us to separate challah**

Separate a piece, and proclaim "*Harei Zu Challah* — This is challah." The gates of heaven are open wide for you to ask G-d to shower you with your wishes. Whisper your personal prayers for health, livelihood, a spouse, children, *nachas*, and peace in your home and the world. We ask G-d to rebuild the 3rd Holy Temple speedily in our days.

She-yibaneh beis hamikdash bi-m'heirah v'yameinu v'sein chelkeinu b'sorah-secha.

May the Holy Temple be rebuilt speedily in our days, and grant us our portion in Your Torah.

The separate strands of dough are united into beautiful braids, connecting Jewish women and girls from diverse backgrounds, coming together as one. We weave our unique strengths into G-d's glorious tapestry and become whole and complete as a nation.

As the sun begins to set, your fresh challahs decorate your Shabbos table. Breathe in the aroma of challah. Breathe out the love. You embrace the peace of Shabbos and watch the candles flickering. You are adding spiritual and physical light into your home and to the world around you. You feel the warmth of the light and it flows through your entire being and saturates your home and your family with peace — *Shalom*, and blessing — *Bracha*. Good Shabbos!

WOMAN WARRIOR

by Tzirel Liba Greenberg

I am a woman warrior
Aishes Chayil is my name
I'm not seeking fortune
I'm not seeking fame
I am here to fight the darkness
To lift the veil of night
And my weapon, my *Neshek*
Are the Shabbos Candles' light

CHORUS
Neirot Shabbat Kodesh
The *Neshek* we all own
We illuminate the darkness
Here within our home
Neirot Shabbat Kodesh
Kindled with our holy spark
Has the far reaching power to illuminate the dark

The moment at my candles
Begin their special glow
The *Ohr Haganuz* that was hidden
Is permitted once again to flow
And in that light we bask
With that light we ask
Hashem please bring Moshiach
It feels like the time has come at last!

CHORUS

Do not despair that it has taken
So many tears
Where is the power of the *Neshek*
Throughout all these years?
For we know the light is growing
With each and every flame
And will bring the *Yom Shekulo Shabbos*
And life will never be the same

SHABBOS HAMALKA

by Tzirel Liba Greenberg

There is a day the queen of all days *Shabbos HaMalka*
She arrives royally bringing with her the key
Shabbos Ki Hi Mekor Habracha
Hayom Rishon L'Shabbos
Yom Sheini B'Shabbos
Is how we count our days

We anticipate her, eagerly await her
To bask in her glorious ways
We prepare for our Queen
All our houses will gleam
And all of us silver will shine
What else would you do
When the Queen visit you
And asks to sit with her and dine

Chorus

With braids of gold
Since days of old
Our *challos* we prepare
With the finest of wines
With her we shall dine
As befits the royal fare

Chorus
What a beautiful thing, time alone with the Queen
Of course we'll sing her praise
For we have been blessed,
With all of the best
By that glorious day of all days!

Hayom Rishon L'Shabbos, Yom Sheini B'Shabbos
Is how we count our days
We anticipate her, eagerly await her
That glorious, glorious, glorious day of all days!

Text 845-641-2313 to join the Shabbos Queen Project for daily inspirational messages, "blending Torah insights, stories, and original music" by Tzirel Liba Greenberg

AS THE SUN IS SETTING LOW
Lyrics by Chaviva Tarlow & Menucha Levin

As the sun is setting low
The Shabbos candles light a glow
I welcome in the Shabbos queen
And with it a feeling serene

Chorus:
Lighting the candles so bright
It has so much power in this dark night
Touching my soul down deep within
What a special gift G-d has given

Connecting a nation so vast
One family united at last
A bond that can never break
The power that one small candle can make

Shabbos candles' special light
I'll kindle them every Friday night
The blessing I'll thank You above
For giving this mitzvah with love.

Pearls of Wisdom

As I weave 3 strands of dough into one braid, I reflect on the **past, present and future** and how they are all one tapestry.

My actions today are a reflection of our past and build our future.

—Nechama Dina Laber

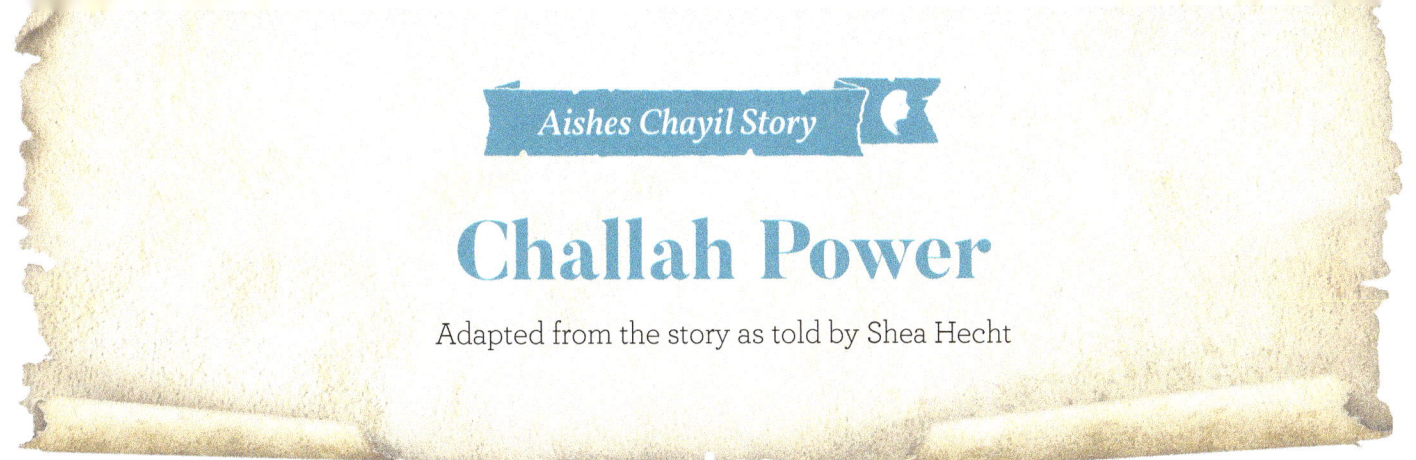

Aishes Chayil Story

Challah Power

Adapted from the story as told by Shea Hecht

We all have issues that we rally for. We all have some goal that we work for. But the spiritual power of women who get together to make a difference is a power that makes things happen.

One source of the power of women is a spiritual one. We are told that the Matriarchs prayed for their children. In particular, the Matriarch Rachel still cries for her children to this day. Our Sages tell us that not only does Rachel present the case of her children suffering to G-d: she is the one who is answered.

Two women in my very own neighborhood of Brooklyn, Yael Leibovitch and Leah Silverstein, have groups of forty or more women who weekly dedicate the merit of their mitzvah of *Hafrashas Challah* to women who don't have children.

Speaking to Yael was quite an eye-opener. Not only did I find out that there are other similar groups in the Williamsburg section of Brooklyn and many other areas all over the world, but also that since they started their program over two years ago, countless women have been helped. Women who had no children for ten years and more have given birth after their plight was kept in mind and in the merit of the women doing their special mitzvah of *Hafrashas Challah*.

My daughter is part of a group of women who do this same special thing for their classmates. Some of my daughter's classmates are not married and some don't have children. Those who are lucky enough to have both of those blessings pray for those who don't. They have witnessed the tremendous power of their prayers which have been answered when they have dedicated their mitzvah to help others.

Throughout history women prayed and accomplished for others, acting as a powerful spiritual lobby. And we can take pride in the fact that it continues even today.

> **They have witnessed the tremendous power of their prayers which have been answered when they have dedicated their mitzvah to help others.**

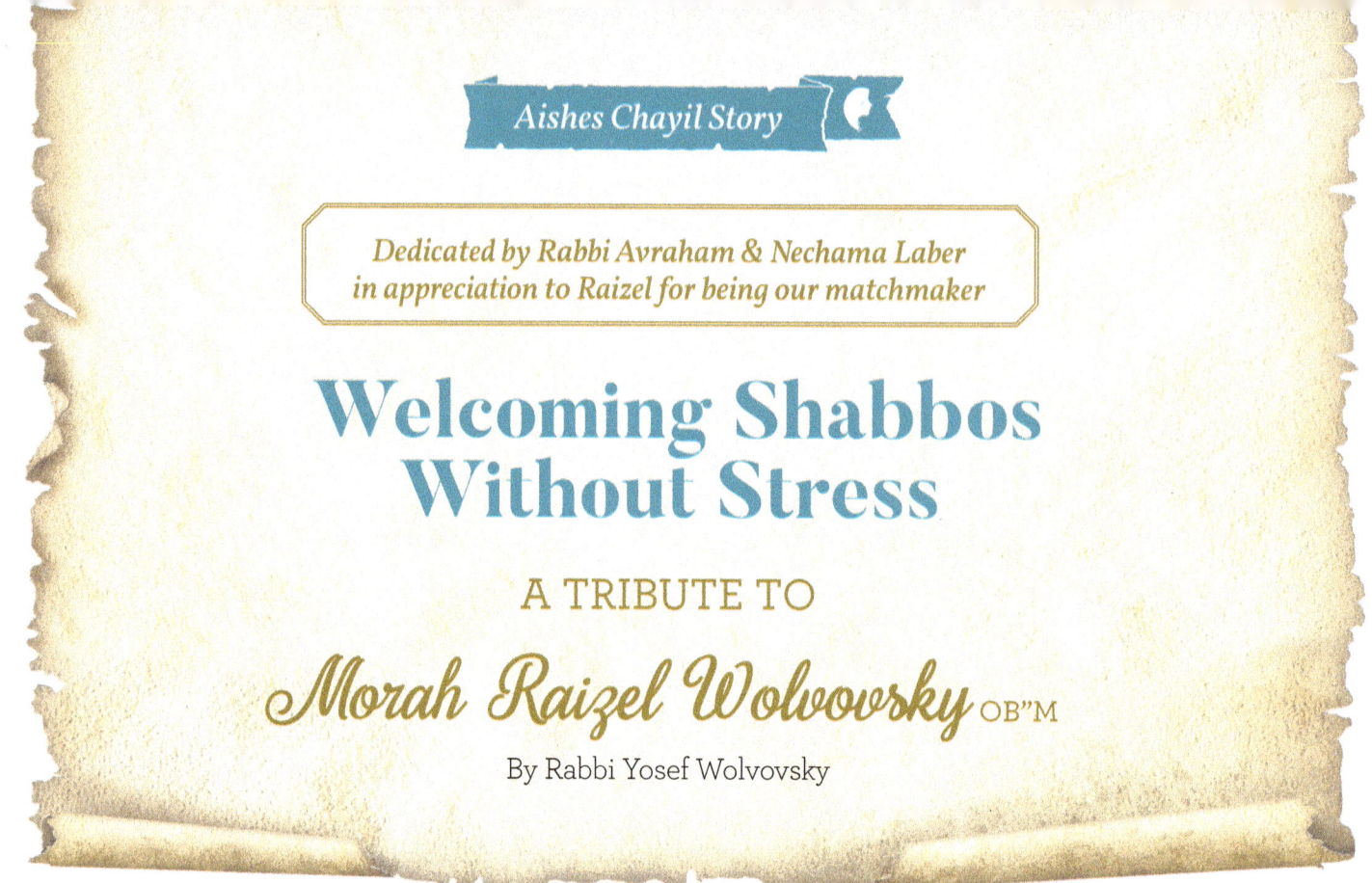

Welcoming Shabbos Without Stress

A TRIBUTE TO Morah Raizel Wolvovsky OB"M

By Rabbi Yosef Wolvovsky

Dedicated by Rabbi Avraham & Nechama Laber in appreciation to Raizel for being our matchmaker

I made an effort to call my mother every Friday afternoon. It was usually a brief "Good Shabbos" chat. But I always knew I had to call early. If it was too close to Shabbos, her phone would be turned off.

Every Friday evening, 18 minutes before sunset, Jewish women and girls throughout the world light Shabbos candles. While this ritual may be inspiring, the time leading up to candle lighting is quite stressful in many Jewish homes. Countless last-minute tasks must get done before Shabbos.

In my parents' home, my mother's Shabbos preparations were quite hectic. Most Friday evenings she would host dozens of people at her table, including family and friends, both old and new. There was so much to do, and the clock was ticking.

Thirty minutes before sunset (approximately 10 minutes early), amidst all the frenetic activity, everything changed. My mother's demeanor would become decidedly calm. She made sure to dress in her festive finest, fully focused on bringing in the light of Shabbos. She was prepared to light the candles and usher in the peace that comes with them. At this lofty time of the week, my mother infused our home with serene energy.

How did this all start? What inspired her to be so intentional about her pre-Shabbos moments?

As my parents were raising a growing family of young children, they were both working full-time. In addition to her many responsibilities at home, my mother was a fully invested preschool teacher, community leader, and mentor to many. There was so much going on. She was finding it difficult to balance her many obligations.

> *By making this mitzvah her top priority, despite everything else going on, she would find it within her to juggle her many responsibilities.*

Feeling overwhelmed, my mother turned to the Lubavitcher Rebbe. She asked the Rebbe for his blessing and advice on how to manage her many obligations. The Rebbe's response was simple yet profound: "Light the candles without stress."

It seems the Rebbe was telling her that by being focused and present during this special (and otherwise chaotic) time, many blessings would be unlocked for her. By making this mitzvah her top priority, despite everything else going on, she would find it within her to juggle her many responsibilities. My mother took the Rebbe's words to heart. Indeed, this approach brought her much peace and many blessings.

I wish I could pick up the phone and call my mother. Just a quick chat. I want to say, "Good Shabbos, Mommy" again. Early, of course. For now, I will try to live a bit more like her, without stress.

We learn from Raizel that we, too, can weave the serenity of Shabbos into our Shabbos preparations and welcome in the Shabbos queen without stress.

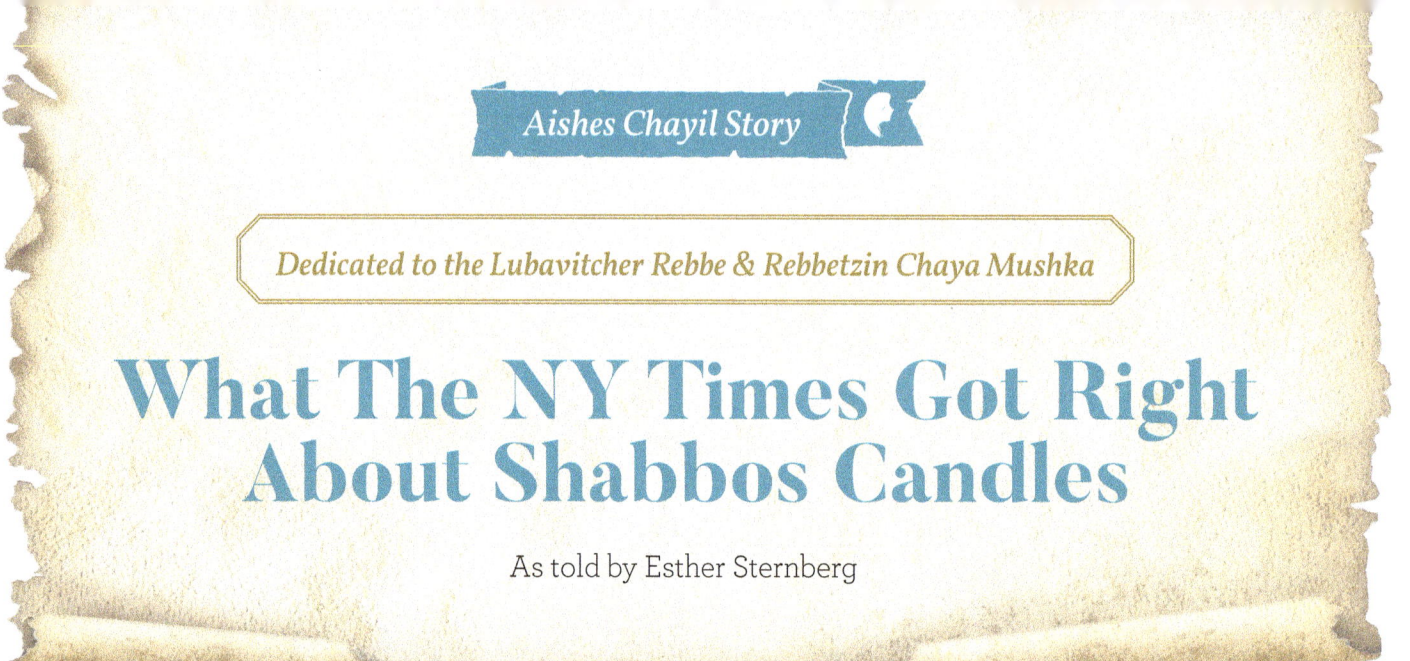

Aishes Chayil Story

Dedicated to the Lubavitcher Rebbe & Rebbetzin Chaya Mushka

What The NY Times Got Right About Shabbos Candles

As told by Esther Sternberg

The Lubavitcher Rebbe was deeply committed to the Shabbos Candle Lighting Campaign, which he started in 1974, with the aim of encouraging all Jewish women, including young girls, to light Shabbos candles to illuminate the world.

When his wife, *Rebbetzin* Chaya Mushka, passed away in 1988, Mrs. Sternberg, director of the Candle Lighting Campaign, decided to dedicate the fundraising event in her memory and established a special fund in her merit to further promote the campaign.

After the *shivah* period, Mrs. Sternberg and her father, Rabbi Shneur Zalman Gurary, were called to the Rebbe's home, where they went trembling with emotion. They were welcomed into the Rebbe's personal study. During their meeting, the Rebbe contributed $470 to the fund they created in honor of his wife. This amount was the numerical equivalent of the Rebbetzin's name, and the Rebbe also added one dollar as his personal contribution to their success. The Rebbe said that good fortune should smile upon the people involved in the campaign and it should brighten the lives of all those who are trying to influence others to light Shabbat candles and all those who are moved to fulfill this mitzvah as a result.

Mrs. Sternberg reported this to their publicity manager, Mr. J.J. Gross, who suggested using the Rebbe's contribution to buy a spot on the bottom of the front page of the New York Times to promote candle-lighting. He said, "Let's call this Project 470."

The ad read, "JEWISH WOMEN/GIRLS LIGHT SHABBAT candles by 5:15 PM. Info 718-774-2060"

The ad received a tremendous response. The campaign continued to run the ad every week for ten years, and

They gave considerable thought to what could possibly be the news a hundred years from now. One thing they knew for sure was that Jewish women and girls would still be lighting Shabbos candles.

they also set up an automated number that allowed callers to enter their zip code to hear the proper candle-lighting time for their area. They only stopped buying the ad when the cost became too exorbitant.

On the day that the new millennium rolled around, the year 2000, the ad suddenly reappeared in a most mysterious way. The New York Times created a fake front page anticipating the news in the year 2100, and on the bottom of the page where they usually printed the candle-lighting times, it read,

"JEWISH WOMEN/GIRLS LIGHT SHABBAT candles today 18 minutes before sunset. In New York 4:39 PM. Elsewhere touch for local times and for information."

Intrigued, Mr. Gross reached out to The New York Times to inquire about this unexpected inclusion. They explained that they gave considerable thought to what could possibly be the news a hundred years from now. One thing they knew for sure was that Jewish women and girls would still be lighting Shabbat candles.

This occurrence highlights the eternal resilience of the Jewish people and the power of Shabbos candles. While the future remains unknown, there is one undeniable truth: in the year 2100, Jewish women and girls will faithfully light Shabbos candles, preserving the flame of Judaism for generations to come.

Thanks to Project 470, initiated with the Rebbe's contribution in honor of his wife, millions of people viewed the unexpected ad and discovered the significance of Jewish women lighting Shabbos candles.

Mrs. Esther Sternberg, director of the Shabbos Candle Campaign, was interviewed by JEM for Here's My Story. This is a shortened version of her interview.

For more inspiration about Shabbos candles, order your copy of the JGU Press book, One More Light, an anthology on candle lighting by Jewish girls.

GROW as an *Aishes Chayil*

Gratitude: **Express gratitude for a woman of valor whom you admire. Express gratitude for your skills and talents.**

_____
_____
_____
_____

Recognition: **Recognize the skills and talents which you or a woman of valor are weaving into beautifying G-d's world.**

_____
_____
_____
_____

Design a card praising a woman of valor with traits that begin with each letter of the alphabet. Then, do the same for yourself!

Oneness: **How can you weave the spirit of Shabbos into your weekday activities? What are your action steps?**

_____
_____
_____
_____

Wish: **What is your wish from G-d?**

_____
_____
_____
_____

א
A Thread of Self Discovery

"A Woman of Valor, who can find?"

Digging Deeper

Why does King Shlomo begin his eloquent tribute to "Aishes Chayil — A Woman of Valor" with this question?

1. The *Aishes Chayil*'s uniqueness makes her hard to find.[1]

At first glance, women in the Torah appear to play only a supportive role in a story dominated by men. Once we delve deeper, as in the following chapters, we find women who shaped history and nurtured great leaders.

Like divers who explore beautiful underwater life, we will dive into the waters of Torah to explore the lives of women of valor and discover pearls of wisdom. These lessons offer us the strength to accomplish our mission today.

2. "Who can find [her]?" teaches us that when we are open to searching, we will discover the traits of the *Aishes Chayil* within ourselves and others. Let us consider how we can reveal this hidden potential as we learn the meaning of the beautiful song, "*Aishes Chayil*."

The great Chassidic master, Reb Zushe of Anipoli, once said: "When I come to the Next World and stand before the Heavenly Court, I won't be asked, 'Why weren't you like Avraham *Avinu* or Moshe *Rabbeinu*?' I was not equipped to be Avraham or Moshe. But I tremble for the day when I will be asked, 'Why weren't you like Zushe?'"

1. Metzudas Tzion

Your mission is not to be an Avraham or Moshe but the best version of yourself. The *Aishes Chayil* within you is waiting to be revealed. You are ready to weave your individual tapestry and GROW as an *Aishes Chayil*!

WOMEN IN THE TORAH
Sarah

The Midrash Shachar Tov on Mishlei explains how the twenty-two verses of "Aishes Chayil" correspond to nineteen great Jewish women. The order of women begins with our first mother, Sarah, whose life epitomizes the entire "Aishes Chayil."

The Sages explain that the verse, "In old age they still produce fruit"[2] refers to Sarah and Avraham, who were equal in their charity and acts of kindness and they were a good sign for the world.[3]

They were Divinely suited to each other for a shared life-mission. They had a harmonious marriage and active partnership throughout their lives. They jointly hosted many guests and Sarah taught the women about G-d while Avraham taught the men.

As his wife, she possessed all the qualities of a Woman of Valor; Avraham composed the "*Aishes Chayil*" song in Sarah's memory. Her birth name was Yiscah, which

2. Tehillim 92:15
3. Midrash Shachar Tov

literally means "to see."[4] She was born with vision, with prophecy. Later, she was called "Sarai — my princess."[5] She was the princess of her home. Before their son Yitzchok's birth, "G-d said to Avraham, 'Your wife... you shall not call her name Sarai, for Sarah is her name' — a "princess for the entire world."[6] Indeed, in all aspects of her life, the first matriarch of the Jewish people was the essence of royalty.

Journey to Self-Discovery

Avraham and Sarah embarked on a journey out of their homeland, never to see their family again, when they were respectively seventy-five and sixty-five years old.

G-d appeared to Avraham — then known as Avram — and told him: "*Lech Lecha* — Go to yourself, from your land, and from your birthplace, and from your father's house, to the land that I will show you."[7] In order to grow into their full Divine potential, they needed to depart from their ordinary habits and ways of thinking.[8]

Upon following G-d's command to settle in the promised land of Canaan, the couple faced another challenge. A famine took hold and they were forced to seek refuge and food in Egypt. Then, when they arrived in Egypt, the Egyptians were struck by Sarah's exceptional beauty to such an extent that Avram feared for his life. To protect himself, they claimed to be brother and sister. However, Sarah was eventually taken by force and brought to the king.

What is the message for us?

On our own spiritual journey, we may face obstacles, but they challenge us to push our natural limits, habits, or mindsets and search our soul more deeply. When our difficulties motivate us to find new strengths to persevere and succeed, we discover more about ourselves, G-d, and how both of us are truly One.

"*Areka* — I will show you," also means that when one follows G-d's directions, He says "I will reveal YOU," your true self, in all your greatness.[9]

4. Bereishis 11:26
5. Bereishis 11:29, Malbim
6. Bereishis 17:15, Rashi
7. Bereishis 12:1
8. Sefer Hamamarim 5666 Parshas Lech Lcha

9. Alshich, Ohr HaTorah

Meaningful Melody

I AM A JEWISH GIRL, AN AISHES CHAYIL
by JGR Staff

Every Jewish woman has
Something deep inside that can
Illuminate her beauty, her talents and her pride
She's different — she's special!
She is the cornerstone who creates a loving family
A warm and Jewish home

Chorus:
I am a Jewish girl
An *Aishes Chayil*
I can determine my future at will
Uncover to discover, that no goal is too far
With joy in every step, expressing who we are

Each and every girl is one of a kind
So do what you can
Search and you will find
The further you go, the more you will see
We each are unique yet
We can join in unity
In (JGU) we are, one family!

Who we are and what we can do
Is greater in unity, so see right through
Sheker Hachein, what's beautiful is deep within
Bring it to the fore
United from our core
In JGU we are, one family!

Meaningful Melody

AISHES CHAYIL
By Chaya-Bracha Rubin

Aishes Chayil, Aishes Chayil
Your mother sang to you as a child
You'll be an *Aishes Chayil* 2x

For saying the *Shema* without being told
Washing *negel vasser* though the water's cold
And lighting Shabbos candles at three years old
You heard "*kol ha'kavod!*"

Aishes Chayil, Aishes Chayil
Your mother sang to you as a child
You'll be an *Aishes Chayil* 2x

For taking on new mitzvos every day
Blessing *Hashem* in all your ways
And helping out your family come what may
You heard your Tatty say...

Aishes Chayil, Aishes Chayil
You're growing all the while
Into an *Aishes Chayil* 2x

She opens her mouth with wisdom
The teaching of kindness is on her tongue
And smiles towards the future although she's young
A G-d fearing woman is this one

Aishes Chayil, Aishes Chayil
You're no longer a child
You're an *Aishes Chayil*

Pearls of Wisdom

*Where I am is up to G-d;
who I grow to become*
IS UP TO ME!

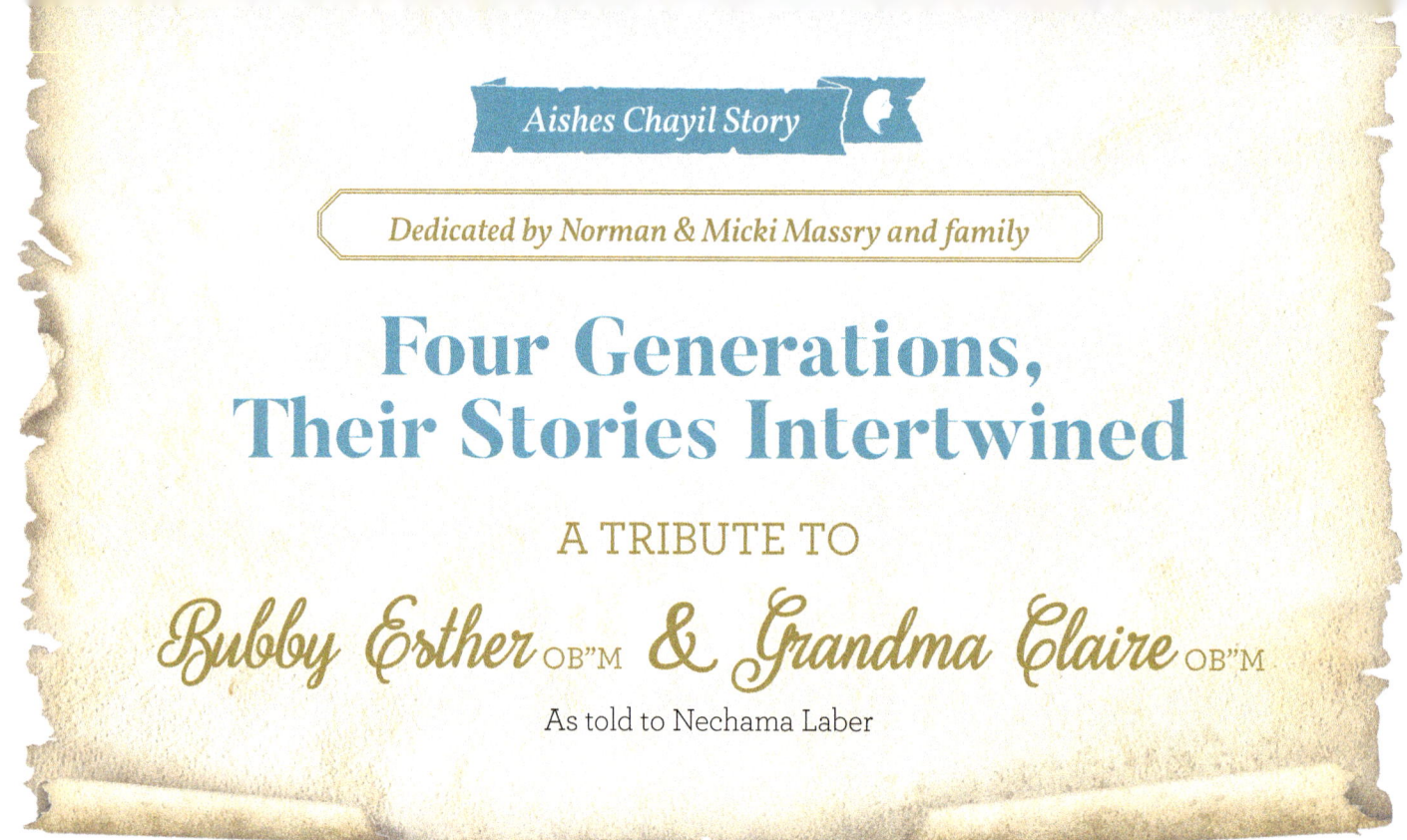

Aishes Chayil Story

Dedicated by Norman & Micki Massry and family

Four Generations, Their Stories Intertwined

A TRIBUTE TO

Bubby Esther OB"M & Grandma Claire OB"M

As told to Nechama Laber

"I was cleaning my shelves," reflects Micki Massry, "because I always love to clean. I took down my grandmother Bubby Esther's candlesticks that she had brought with her from Czechoslovakia, those priceless candlesticks from the Old Country. They are gorgeous, and I remember my grandmother lighting them, but I never did, as I lit my own. They are so magnificent. They were standing on the countertop when my husband, Norman, began polishing them. 'This light means something to you,' he said softly. 'Micki, I think you need to be the one to do this.'"

Micki's maternal grandparents, Esther and Eugene Fuchs, met in Prague, Czechoslovakia, where he served as head cantor at the famed *Altneuschul*, or Old-New Synagogue. They were married on February 7, 1933 in Prague. Their two children, Claire and Harry, were born into the happiest of worlds, but soon after, WWII's ominous clouds began looming over Europe. Eugene heard about the Kindertransport, an organized effort between 1938 and 1940 to rescue children from Nazi-occupied territories and bring them to Great Britain. The Agudas Israel World Organization invited Eugene to London to appeal for support and discuss foster homes with the local authorities in December 1938. He temporarily returned to Prague and then back to London in March 1939 when the Germans occupied his home city. Eugene's bold intervention ultimately saved hundreds of precious lives.

siblings. Esther's mother died at Nazi hands, but her father, Mendel Braun, survived since he was on business in Sweden when the Nazis seized Prague. Esther and Claire visited him in Sweden after the war, where he remained until the end of his life. Moshe had miraculously escaped to Israel, where he met and married Helen and raised two children.

When Bubby Esther and her husband struggled to take care of Claire in London, she was compelled to send her to an orphanage, although she kept two-year-old Harry with her. Claire was fostered by the Sampsons, a wealthy, childless Jewish couple, and attended a British private school for two years. Eventually, the Fuchs family of four reunited. However, the war delayed their immigration plans. Finally, after difficult years in London, on September 8, 1948, Eugene was the first to leave on the S.S. America. The others soon followed, arriving in the U.S. on September 21, 1948, on the R.M.S. Queen Elizabeth. At the time, Claire was fourteen and Harry was eleven.

Meanwhile in Prague, Esther sheltered the children from what was happening around them. Claire, who was then five years old, recalled: "I remember looking out of the apartment window and seeing troops marching." Jews were constantly arrested, taken away in trucks and never heard from again. A few months later in July 1939, Esther escaped by train in the middle of the night with her children. She obtained forged passports enabling them to travel to London and reunite with their husband and father. Of course, her cherished candlesticks made the journey with them.

Tragically, Bubby Esther's own siblings were largely decimated in the Holocaust; she and her widowed brother Moshe were the sole survivors of eleven

A few months later in July 1939, Esther escaped by train in the middle of the night with her children.

Bubby Esther's fortitude accompanied the family along their frequent moves to rebuild a new life, starting in Charlotte, North Carolina, where the children entered school. However, November of 1948 found them staying with their Floridian cousins while their parents sought out employment and a home in Baltimore, Maryland. Unable to teach children cantorial skills due to his limited English, Eugene established a leather-goods factory, having run a successful business in London. Unfortunately, this time it failed, leaving the family

Bubby Esther

Grandma Claire

penniless. Esther found work as a cook and Harry's yeshiva dismissed him since his parents could not afford the tuition. The Fuchs family never dreamed they would struggle so much in America. In the spring of 1950, they finally settled in Atlantic City, New Jersey.

It was here, in 1951, that Bubby Esther, a multitalented homemaker, founded and operated her own business: a guest house. They were always sold out for Jewish holidays and during the summer months, especially due to Esther's excellent hospitality and famous home-cooking. Even a plain chicken became a delicacy in her hands, and people still recall her authentic latkes, knishes, kugels, holishkes, blintzes, and babkas that her grandchildren crave. After a fire damaged the building around 1954, the family bought a house where they rented out rooms in the summertime. Esther also managed a hotel, while her husband served as a cantor

It was here, in 1951, that Bubby Esther, a multitalented homemaker, founded and operated her own business.

and supervised a kosher kitchen at another nearby hotel. When Eugene passed away at sixty-one years old from heart failure in 1964, Bubby Esther continued to support herself and her family. Before his passing, Eugene asked Claire to take care of Esther, and she was very devoted to her elderly mother.

Bubby Esther lived a long life, bonding with her great-grandchildren before her passing at the age of ninety in 1999. She was extroverted, commanding, and multilingual with a heavy accent. Esther's daughter, Grandma Claire, as her family called her, was more reserved; and though she spoke Yiddish, she strove to erase her accent. However, she did inherit her mother's striking resilience, resourcefulness, and regality, which manifested throughout her life, as she refused to surrender to the many difficulties she experienced.

Claire raised three beautiful daughters with her husband, Buddy Kosden: Sheryl K. Schiraldi, Micki K. Massry, and Ava K. Lubert. Unfortunately, Buddy passed away at the untimely age of forty-seven on November 18, 1977. At the time, Claire was forty-two, and Micki had just been newly wed to Norman. Nevertheless, Claire persevered and obtained a real estate license, worked in hotels, and managed a jewelry store to support her family. She adroitly maintained her home and finances alone, and with her thrifty ability to save for the future, she fully supported herself in her later years. She traveled independently, drove interstate to visit her children, and even flew to London to retrieve her granddaughter Julie, who was arriving from Israel amid the turbulence of an intifada. Until her passing, Claire fought for life every day, even as illness severely weakened her body, with the same indomitable class with which she always lived.

Grandma Claire also authored *The Forsaken Suitcase*. It retells the story found inside an old, dilapidated leather suitcase containing her father's letters to his American relative, Katie Finkelstein, seeking help with his family's emigration from London. Grandma Claire's story would be largely unknown if not for Josh Wilks, the historic preservationist who discovered the suitcase in 2009 on a Florida curbside in a pile of discarded items.

"A Woman of Valor, who can find?"

Esther Fuchs and Claire Kosden exemplify the traits of true women of valor, balancing multiple roles and taking initiative to endow their families and the future. Micki's daughter Julie cherishes her memories with both her grandmother and great-grandmother. "I learned from my grandmothers to work hard and to stand up for myself," she expresses. "They show me that I can manage to balance my family and work-life successfully. I remember how they always lit Shabbos candles and celebrated the Jewish holidays, and they inspire me to carry on our traditions with my children."

Micki confides, "I regret that my mother, of blessed memory, never really spoke about the Holocaust or told the family's stories. I did not tell them to my children and did not teach them enough about where they come from, but I know it is not too late. I regret that I did not give my kids Shabbos, because growing up, we did not observe it in my home. Judaism was not infused in me, and my father was not religious, but I want my children to know their Judaism. I thought if I sent them to a Jewish school, they would get what I did not have, but now I realize that Judaism must be passed on from the home. I want my kids to do Shabbos... I want us to be together for Shabbos. So, I hope that by telling this story, my children will realize the precious legacy that is theirs to treasure and pass on to the next generation."

> *"I hope that by telling this story, my children will realize the precious legacy that is theirs to treasure and pass on to the next generation."*

Since the memorable day of rediscovering Bubby Esther's candlesticks, Micki uses them to usher in the holy Shabbos. Now, her children also light the candles and savor the challah. Each Friday night, when she kindles the flames, Micki feels her grandmother's warmth and love. She is inspired by Bubby Esther's resolve to imbue her family with the joy of Judaism and the light of Shabbos. She prays for her children to cherish their heritage, to know the sacrifices their forebears made, and to freely live and practice as Jews. She prays for the good health and peace of her family, and the world. And in her heart, Micki knows that she is keeping her grandmother's and mother's flames alive.

GROW as an Aishes Chayil

Gratitude: **Identify a Woman of Valor whom you are grateful for past or present.**

___

Oneness: **How have you grown from her example and what steps are you taking to reveal those attributes within yourself?**

___

Recognition: **Recognize why you admire her, and which of her qualities you want to emulate?**

___

Wish: **What do you wish from G-d for your future?**

___

וְרָחֹק מִפְּנִינִים מִכְרָהּ.

א
A Thread of Pearls of Wisdom

"She is more precious than pearls."

Digging Deeper

The song "*Aishes Chayil*" opens with "A Woman of Valor, who can find?" then states, "Her worth is far beyond pearls."

Why compare a woman's value to that of pearls?

This verse poetically describes her incomparable value, which far exceeds the worth of all gems or pearls.

In Hebrew, the word for "inside," *penima*, is similar to the word for "pearl," *penina*. A pearl can only be formed inside an oyster.

Let us first understand how pearls are formed.

Natural pearls form when an irritating substance, such as a grain of sand, works its way into an oyster. As a defense mechanism, the oyster coats it with a milky substance called "mother of pearl." The oyster deposits layer upon layer of this coating until a dazzling pearl is formed.

With difficulty, divers excavate the pearls from within the mouths of oysters hidden in the depths of the sea. They plunge forty-eight to one hundred twenty feet deep to access the beds of pearl oysters. They carry a net to capture them and place them in boats. The shells are unloaded on the sand and allowed to remain there until the oysters inside the shells have decayed. Finally, the shells are washed in seawater and opened in search of pearls.

What is the lesson for our lives?

Irritants are cumbersome, often painful, yet they can also be catalysts for great transformation.

Similarly, the *Aishes Chayil* faces many challenges and responsibilities in the home, community and workplace. However, through all the difficulties of life, she recognizes each one as an opportunity to reveal the hidden G-dliness and goodness in the world.

The beautiful words in "*Aishes Chayil*" beckon the potential within, awaiting the revelation of new strengths in every woman. Through layer upon layer of courage, persistence, and wisdom, she transforms the irritations — and herself — into a pearl shining with her unique light.

Once she creates her pearls, she shares them with others. These are her pearls of wisdom, insights and lessons learned through her process of transformation.

WOMEN IN THE TORAH
Sarah

Our first matriarch Sarah faced many challenges in her lifetime. Among them, she was seized by two kings and Avraham fought a dangerous war to rescue his nephew Lot. She was childless for many years. At one point, she decided to offer her maidservant Hagar to her husband as a wife.

At the age of ninety, she finally gave birth to a son, named Yitzchok. Even at this joyous occasion, she faced embarrassment: Guests at the celebratory banquet gossiped about whether he was truly her son or an adopted baby from the market. G-d miraculously made Yitzchok closely resemble Avraham, and Sarah nursed everyone's babies, as well[1].

Later, she had to send away her maidservant Hagar and her son, Yishmael, whose behavior posed a negative influence that threatened to corrupt Yitzchok. At the age of one hundred twenty-seven, Sarah passed away suddenly from shocking news, and did not live to celebrate Yitzchok's marriage to Rivkah.

When the Torah sums up Sarah's life, Rashi explains the wording to mean, "all her years were equally good."[2]

Despite these difficulties, Sarah's unwavering faith in G-d and her devotion to her Divine mission inspires future generations. Open on all four sides as a prominent sign of welcome, her dwelling bustled with guests, who were provided with the finest food, drink and lodging. She sewed clothes and baked bread for the poor. Avraham taught the men and Sarah taught the women to believe in One G-d and to reject idol worship.[3] As a result, "all her years were equally good."

What does Sarah teach us today?

From Sarah, we learn to stay focused on our mission, transform irritations into pearls and illuminate the world with goodness and kindness.

G-d blessed her tent with three miracles:

1. Her Shabbos candles stayed lit from week to week.

2. Her challah stayed fresh from week to week.

3. The cloud of G-d constantly hovered over her tent as a reward for her observance of Family Purity.[4]

We, too, can spiritually recreate these miracles in our homes today with our dedication to the three special mitzvos entrusted to Jewish women: lighting Shabbos candles, baking challah and observing the laws of Jewish marriage.

Every Jewish girl and woman is a strong link in the chain connecting to the legacy of our matriarch Sarah, the original subject of the song *"Aishes Chayil."* Sarah's candles influenced the entire week and an *Aishes Chayil* keeps the glow of Shabbos shining all week.

1. Rashi Bereishis 21,7, based on Talmud Baba Metzia 87,a
2. Bereishis 23:1
3. Rashi, Bereishis 12:5
4. Midrash, Rashi, Bereishis 24:67

WOMEN OF THE FUTURE

by Mali New, JGR Staff

Here I stand today
Paving my own way
Just like Sara, I will too
Touch the soul of every Jew

Leah changed the norm
Went out to transform
How, *Hashem*, can I be like them?

There's more there than it seems
Take Esther, who was queen
Devorah judged beneath a tree
Left her home so modestly

I'll run that extra mile
Show the world my style
I yearn to be a true *Aishes Chayil*

Time and time again
The power of us women
We can shine our inner light

It's in our hands today
Spread forth the holy way
How can I be a *Shlucha*?

Chorus
Women of the future
Now is your chance to
See your greater strength unfurl
Shove away the darkness
You have the power to
Bring day to the world

Pearls of Wisdom

Just as G-d transforms irritants into pearls in the depths of the sea, I CAN TRANSFORM LIFE'S IRRITATIONS *into pearls sparkling on a thread of simple faith.*

–Nechama Dina Laber

Aishes Chayil Story

Diving into a Sea of Pearls in the Hospital

by Nechama Dina Laber

As I sit in the hospital with my son Yosef Chaim on Thanksgiving 2018, I have many thoughts. I have two options: to feel sorry for myself or to find the pearl in life's irritations. I could be upset that I missed my daughter's birthday celebration and that I'm not home with my children during their vacation. Instead, I choose to reflect, express gratitude, and recognize the good.

It's easy to take our health for granted, but when we have it, we have the strength to take action. Walking through the hospital hallways, I see how many people have bigger challenges. I met a mother of a child who needs a feeding tube and is also deaf and blind. Her unconditional love for her child inspires me to be even more grateful for the love and support I receive from my husband, family, and friends. I am also grateful for the nourishing food they bring me.

This is my Thanksgiving.

I meet many caring nurses. One nurse shares that she would love to be at her family's Thanksgiving dinner. She's grateful she has a job and can help Yosef Chaim get better. I tell her that she is a pearl. "What do you mean?" she asks. I share with her that King Solomon compares a woman to pearls in his opening verse of *Aishes Chayil*. One reason for the comparison is that

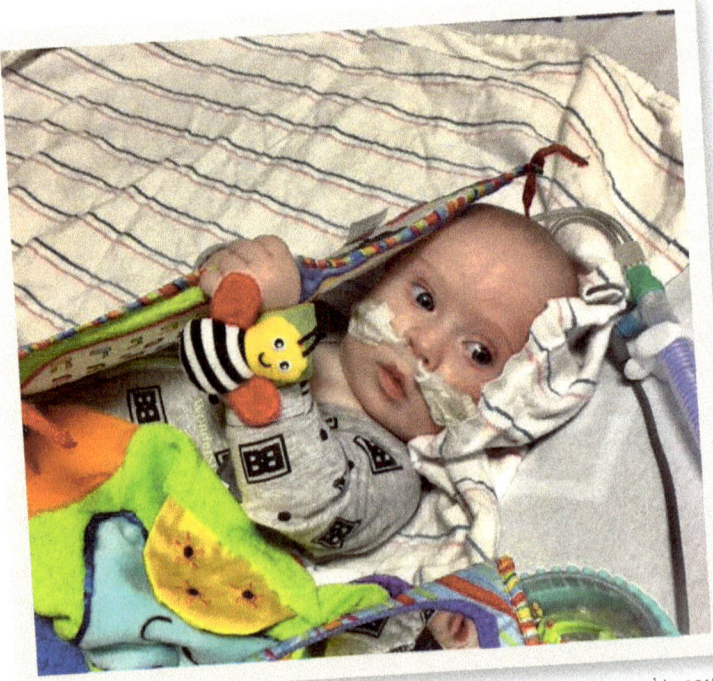

Little Yosef Chaim in the hospital in 2018

just as an oyster transforms an irritating grain into a lustrous pearl, a woman transforms life's irritations into pearls. She smiles and says, "Thank you for your inspiration." We both see the pearl while spending time in the hospital, and I am grateful for the kind hospital staff.

This is my Thanksgiving.

> *"Sometimes, the good is hidden, but we will never stop searching for the beautiful pearls."*

My dear children pile in to visit us. Yehudah sees his precious brother with a blue tube providing "high flow" attached to him. He says, "It looks like he is a scuba diver in the sea." I hug him and respond, "Yes, Yosef Chaim is a deep sea diver helping us to find the pearls in life. Sometimes, the good is hidden, but we will never stop searching for the beautiful pearls." I embrace each of my children and they hug me like never before. I am grateful for their love that fills my heart.

This is my Thanksgiving.

Dear Yosef Chaim,

This experience has taught me to appreciate every breath of life. And that every day is Thanksgiving. Every morning, we say *"Modeh Ani"* together, and you smile back at me. We thank *Hashem* for restoring our soul and say, "Thank you, *Hashem*, for our little *Chayil*'s (soldier) complete recovery from RSV, a respiratory virus!" We are so grateful for our precious baby boy!

This is my Thanksgiving!

I weave the strengths of women of valor throughout history into the tapestry of my life. Our first mother, Sarah, inspires me to transform irritations into pearls. Additionally, I am grateful for the role models in my family who have paved a path for me. I especially recognize my beloved grandmothers and my mother, Mrs. Daniella Katzenberg (may she live a long and healthy life). Despite losing her first husband, my father, at the young age of 37, she persevered and raised my three brothers and me on a solid foundation of Torah and mitzvos.

This is my Thanksgiving!

Nechama Laber and Yosef Chaim in 2023

GROW as an *Aishes Chayil*

Gratitude: **What or who are you grateful for?**

_____
_____
_____

Recognition: **Recognize how a Jewish woman is likened to pearls. Recognize an irritation or challenge in your life.**

_____
_____
_____

Oneness: **How can you transform an irritation or challenge into a "pearl"? What action can you take?**

_____
_____
_____

Share your pearls of wisdom — new insights and life lessons — gained from the irritating experience.

_____
_____
_____
_____

Wish: **What is your wish from G-d?**

_____
_____
_____

בָּטַח בָּהּ לֵב בַּעְלָהּ וְשָׁלָל לֹא יֶחְסָר.

ב

A Thread of Trust

"Her husband trusts in her and he shall lack no fortune."

Digging Deeper

What is the literal meaning of this verse?

When a woman's husband is out of town, he trusts that she will guard everything in the house.[1] He does not lack goodness in life, thanks to his wife.[2]

What is trust?

The foundation of any good relationship is trust. In Hebrew *botach* בטח, means trust, security and reliance. It is also a derivative of the word *tach* טח meaning plaster in Hebrew. Plaster is a bonding agent. The greater the connection, the greater the trust.

Building trust in a relationship requires honesty, commitment, compassion, respect and keeping an open line of communication. Another way to build trust is to be consistent, reliable and dependable.

Trust between a husband and wife creates harmony in the home. Peace is the vessel for blessings, as the verse says, "he shall lack no fortune." Rabbi Shimon ben Halafta said: "The Holy One, Blessed be He, found no vessel that could contain blessing for Israel save that of peace, as it is written: 'The Lord will give strength unto his people; the Lord will bless his people with peace'.[3,4]

The Aishes Chayil refers to the Jewish people and G-d is the husband. How does G-d, our Husband, trust us?

G-d trusts us to acquire Torah and mitzvos, the greatest treasures in this world, and the means to fulfill them. We trust that He equips us with the strength to accomplish our mission. When it may seem that a challenge is too difficult, remember: "G-d doesn't give us anything we can't handle; along with the challenge we are given the strength."[5]

Every morning, we wake up with the mindset, "G-d, You trust in me and I trust in You," and reaffirm it by reciting:

מוֹדֶה אֲנִי לְפָנֶיךָ מֶלֶךְ חַי וְקַיָּם, שֶׁהֶחֱזַרְתָּ בִּי נִשְׁמָתִי בְּחֶמְלָה. רַבָּה אֱמוּנָתֶךָ

"I offer thanks to You, living and eternal King, for You have mercifully restored my soul within me; Your faithfulness is great."

How can we develop genuine trust in G-d?

We can cultivate trust in G-d by tapping into our Divine soul, which is inherently connected to G-d. However, achieving genuine trust, or *bitachon*, is a lifelong process, and we may encounter internal and external conflicts along the way. The Alter Rebbe teaches that our animal soul and G-dly soul are in a constant state of "conflict."[6] Nevertheless, through cultivating a personal connection with G-d, we can transform difficulties into new realities. By placing trust in G-d, we open ourselves up to receiving overflowing blessings, like the "*shalal*" or spoils one wins in a war.

---

1. Metzudas Dovid
2. Rashi
3. Psalms 29:11
4. Mishna Oktzin, end of chapter 3

5. Talmud, Avodah Zarah 3a
6. Tanya

WOMEN IN THE TORAH
Sarah

Avraham grew rich because of Sarah [and did not lack fortune], as it says[7], "And Pharaoh gave wealth to Avraham for her sake."[8]

Avraham and Sarah roamed the wilderness until famine struck Canaan. Although they had just arrived, they trusted in G-d's plan and descended to Egypt for food. Recognizing Sarah's beauty, Avraham feared that the immoral Egyptians would kill him to marry her. Avram says to Sarai, "I know what a beautiful woman you are. If the Egyptians see you, and think, 'She is his wife,' they will kill me and let you live. Please say that you are my sister, that it may go well for me because of you, and I will remain alive thanks to you."[9]

At the border, officers forced open the trunk and were stunned by the radiant Sarah. Even as they swept her away to become Pharaoh's queen, she trusted G-d would protect her, and Avraham trusted her to uphold their values in the palace. Sarah rejected the royal glamor and yearned to return to her husband, praying to G-d all night for salvation.

G-d sent an angel to punish Pharaoh, forcing him to release Sarah to Avraham unharmed, along with royal gifts and his own daughter, Hagar, as a maidservant[10]. Avraham became wealthy in Sarah's merit but perhaps the even greater gift was that she had his trust. Avraham knew he could count on Sarah to stay loyal to him and their values even in such a difficult situation.

How could Avraham risk Sarah's life so that he would acquire material benefit?

Avraham trusted that her spiritual merit as a great prophetess would protect her from harm. The Lubavitcher Rebbe explains, based on the *Zohar*, "He was not afraid to say, 'She is my sister,' since Avraham saw that Sarah was protected by an accompanying angel. Therefore, he was certain the Egyptians would not be able to harm her."

10 Bereishis 12:10-20; Rashi

7 Bereishis 12:16
8 Midrash Shachar Tov
9 Genesis 12:12-13

Avraham searched for the Divine Providence in this dangerous situation. He realized that it was in order to receive G-d's blessing of wealth that would come through the disguised vessel of Pharaoh in the merit of Sarah's holiness. As it says,[11] "The heart of her husband relies on her and he lacks no treasure."[12]

How does Sarah give strength to her children today?

Sarah paved the path and provided spiritual strength to her descendants, the Jewish girls and women, who lived in Egypt and in all future exiles. Sarah was not swayed by the temptations in Egypt and kept her holiness. She gives strength to Jewish women today to remain committed to our Torah values.

SHINE YOUR INNER LIGHT

by Rivka Leah Popack

In those times
When you find
That each door that you try
Is locked, yet again, and it won't let you by,
In your heart lies the key
Look inside and you'll see
Believe
Just Believe

In those days, in the haze
When all you see is true
Seems to fall far behind
And you're lost within you
And you try to be strong
But it's hard to hold on
For so long

Trust your inner light (clap clap)
Shadows fall away (clap clap)
Hold your candle high (clap clap)
Night will turn to day (clap clap)

Moments when you're feeling small
No reason to give in
Don't you know in the greatest darkness
Light will always win

So be the miracle I believe in
Be the candle burning bright
You can be the flame we're reaching for
Light up, light up the night

Chorus

Don't you know, this place in time
Is waiting just for you
To learn, to give, to love, to live
There's so much you can do

So be the miracle we believe in
Be the candle burning bright
You can be the flame we're reaching for
Light up, light up the night

Chorus

---

11 ibid 31:11
12. Likutei Sichos Vol. 20, page 37-40

Pearls of Wisdom

BLESSED
is the one who
TRUSTS IN G-D

-Tehillim Chapter 40

Aishes Chayil Story

Dedicated by Norman & Micki Massry and family

A Beautiful Partnership

A TRIBUTE TO

Esther Massry OB"M

Esther was born in Brooklyn on December 9, 1930, to Morris and Mollie Franco. In 1949, Esther met and married the love of her life, Morris (Murray) Massry. They soon began their journey together in Saratoga Springs, NY and opened what, at the time, was a modest retail store. This laid the groundwork for their next move to Troy, NY where they opened the Janie Shop, a children's clothing store.

"Her husband trusts in her and he shall lack no fortune." Morris and Esther were a team, building the retail business while raising a family of six kids. Esther can be remembered running the cash register, making trips to New York City with Morris to shop for the store, and in many cases, loading up the station wagon with merchandise. In the mid-1960's, their business transitioned from retail to real estate, which enabled Esther to devote her full attention to raising her five daughters and one son.

Always full of people, her home was the hub of neighborhood gatherings and home-cooked food including Sephardic delicacies. As spouses, grandchildren, and great-grandchildren joined the family, the Jewish holidays became the center of extended family gatherings. This laid the foundation for each generation to follow and emulate with their own families.

Esther's daughters Jane, Marilyn, Linda, Sheila and Lisa and daughter-in-law Micki learned many Sephardic recipes from Esther. They continue to share the holiday dishes with their daughters and families, keeping the family traditions alive.

Esther and Morris traveled the world together. Destinations such as Rome and Paris were semi-annual visits. As the family grew, Esther looked forward to annual family cruises — an event that continued for twenty years with more than thirty family members each time.

In addition to Esther's devotion to her family, she had an amazing way with everyone she met. She touched each person with her beautiful smile that lit up the room. Her grace, elegance, and soft-spoken manner always made everyone feel loved and special. It was a quality that defined her and is now her legacy.

Esther and Morris were generous philanthropists and actively supported both the Jewish community and the broader Capital District population in countless

> *Her grace, elegance, and soft-spoken manner always made everyone feel loved and special.*

ways. This includes Synagogues, the United Jewish Federation, Daughters of Sarah Massry Residence, the University of Albany, Massry Family Children's Emergency Center, Samaritan Hospital, Chabad Centers and so many more.

Their legacy of kindness and generosity is alive today, as the next generation follows their example and perpetuates the same values. They continue in their philanthropic ways and Norman and Micki Massry are founding benefactors of the JGU GROW Connection Network.

Her granddaughter Julie says, "I have a deep admiration and closeness for my grandmother that is unlike any other relationships I have. I have fond memories of spending time with her on the weekends, cooking together and learning from her how to live a full and meaningful life. She was a source of endless love and support. I wouldn't be the person I am today without her and the wisdom she has shared with me over the years. She is an incredible role model, and I look up to her with admiration and love."

GROW as an Aishes Chayil

Gratitude: **In the morning, we express our gratitude with Modeh Ani and conclude with "Rabba emunasecha — great is Your faith [in us]." How does G-d trust in you? How do you trust in G-d?**

_____

_____

_____

_____

Recognition: **"Happy is the one who trusts in G-d.¹" How has trusting in G-d given you strength in life?**

_____

_____

_____

_____

Oneness: **What are ways to build trust in your relationships with family and friends?**

_____

_____

_____

_____

_____

_____

Wish: **What is your wish in connection with this verse?**

_____

_____

_____

_____

1. Mishlei 16:20

ג

A Thread of
Loyalty

"She repays him with good and not evil all the days of her life."

Digging Deeper

What does this verse mean?

The *Aishes Chayil* is loyal to her husband and repays him for all the good he does but not for any bad.[1]

She responds with loyalty, goodness, and kindness, even in the face of negativity or adversity in life. She recognizes that everything comes from G-d and looks beyond what meets the eye.

An *Aishes Chayil* uncovers her inner strength to reveal the good in situations that may initially appear to be the opposite of good.

How do we respond with goodness in challenging times?

We recognize that painful situations help us grow, just as thorns protect a rose so that it can blossom. In the midst of a challenge, we can remind ourselves that it is an "OFG" — **O**pportunity **F**or **G**rowth! We can purify our thoughts, words, and actions, strengthen our trust in G-d, and formulate creative solutions. Although we may feel the thorns at times, our *neshama* still shines with goodness, like the beauty of a rose.

WOMEN IN THE TORAH
Rivkah

Rivkah, our second matriarch, bestowed good upon Yitzchok when his mother, Sarah, passed away. She comforted him because she followed in his mother's footsteps with her commitment to Sarah's values and ideals.[2]

How does this verse relate to Rivkah's actions as a young girl, wife, and mother?

As a young girl: Rivkah disapproved of the wicked ways of her father Besuel, brother Lavan, and environment in the city of Charan. Whenever she went out and saw the people quarreling and cursing one another, she would want to leave. Instead of being influenced by it all, she made every effort to rise above the negativity. She fed all the poor who came to her house and they praised her good deeds and said of her, "She is like a rose among thorns." She disliked the conduct of the maids, so she would perform the household chores all by herself—cooking, baking, and even drawing water. One day, while she was drawing water at the well, she met Eliezer.[3]

What gifts did Eliezer give Rivkah at the well?

Eliezer, Avraham's trusted servant and Rivkah's matchmaker, was sent to Charan with the specific

---

1. Metzudas Dovid
2. Midrash Shachar Tov
3. From Our Torah Treasury, Aggadot

mission of finding a wife for Yitzchok who possessed the trait of kindness. When he arrived, Rivkah exemplified this quality by generously offering water to him and his camels. Eliezer knew he had found the perfect match. He gave Rivkah a nose ring and two bracelets,[4] each of which symbolize her commitment to living a life based on Torah principles.

What is the life lesson from the nose ring?

The nose ring weighed a half-shekel, symbolizing the annual half-shekel donation made by every Jew for the *Beis Hamikdash*. Even today, this amount is customarily given to charity before Purim. This ring serves as a reminder that a Jewish home is built on the foundation of giving and acts of kindness.

Furthermore, the half-shekel weight symbolizes the idea that every individual soul is incomplete on its own and needs to connect with its source of life, the Creator. The *Zohar* explains[5] a soul is divided into two bodies at birth, one in a man and one in a woman. It is through a marriage grounded in Torah values that these two halves are reunited.

What is the life lesson from the two bracelets?

The two bracelets, each weighing five *shekalim*, symbolize the Ten Commandments (2 x 5 = 10) that were engraved on the stone tablets. Engraved letters are one with the stone itself. Similarly, in a home committed to Torah, each person internalizes G-d's commandments; they are one. Torah values are ingrained into their daily actions. Along with accepting the precious gifts, Rivkah was committing to follow the above principles for a Jewish home that is permeated with goodness, G-dliness, and Torah.[6]

As a wife: Rivkah comforted Yitzchok after his mother's passing. Rashi tells us that when Sarah was alive, there were three clear signs of G-d's presence in her tent. When Sarah *Imeinu* died, these three miracles disappeared, but were restored when Rivkah married Yitzchok and carried on her legacy.

- Her candles stayed lit from one Friday to the next.
- Her dough was blessed.
- A cloud hovered over her tent.

Despite Yitzchok's old age and blindness, Rivkah remained loyal and treated him with unwavering goodness.

As a mother: Rivkah was aware of Yitzchok's intention to give their elder son Eisav the firstborn's blessing. However, she discerned Eisav's wicked ways due to her own upbringing surrounded by evil. Despite disagreeing with her husband, Rivkah chose to avoid conflict and devised a plan with her righteous son, Yaakov, for him to receive the blessing instead. Rivkah was prepared to endure suffering for the sake of her children. She told Yaakov, "If Yitzchok shall curse you for taking the firstborn's blessing from Eisav, the curse shall come upon me."

What can we learn from Rivkah?

Rivkah exemplifies the lesson that even in challenging situations, we can remain loyal to G-d, uphold our Torah values, and act with goodness and kindness like 'a rose among thorns.'

---

4. Rashi, Bereishis 24:14
5. Zohar III, p. 7b, 119b, 296a

6. Likkutei Sichot, Vol. 1, Parshas Chayei Sarah

Meaningful Melody

GLOW

by Chavie Sobel

Let's get glowing
Let's illuminate the night
Light a spark that always stays
Warm and lit and bright

Today let's light a flame
With actions that carry on
Legacies left behind
Outlines that were drawn

Chorus:
[NAME] it's in our hands
Together, as one we stand
Learning Torah, sharing what we know
Flames that they have lit
We have the power to transmit
For eternity they will glow

Though the night is cold and dark
In our soul, there lies a spark
Girls Light up Our World!
Let's get glowing now!

Dedicated in honor of our mother and grandmother,

Ophra Weisberg

who is truly selfless, and who sees the best in everyone.

She is modest, kind and thoughtful, loved and admired by her family and friends, and a devoted teacher who has inspired generations of children through Jewish education.

Pearls of Wisdom

Moshiach is ready to come now; it is our part to do something additional in the realm of

GOODNESS & KINDNESS

—The Lubavitcher Rebbe to a CNN Reporter

Bubby Dina & Roza's Devotion

A TRIBUTE TO

Bubby Dina Levin OB"M

As told to Nechama Laber

Bubby Dina Levin was born on July 5, 1915 in the city of Pabyanitzye in Poland. The city's main industry was manufacturing various fabrics, which were crafted into linens and clothing. Dina was the oldest of five children, three girls and two boys. Her mother Sarah would stay at home with the children, preparing meals and cleaning. Her father Moshe worked as a tailor and toiled arduously to support his family, sewing one suit each week. At the young age of 42, he tragically passed away due to a severe case of pneumonia. Dina was merely a young girl of 13 when this tragedy occurred, and the youngest child in the family was the tender age of two. The task of supporting the family now fell on the mother, so she went to work as a peddler and delivered items to homes upon request.

Though Sarah worked tirelessly to provide for her family, her earnings were meager. As a result, the children were forced to help and go to work. Dina and her sister Roza would attend school for half the day and would work afterwards. Dina would sew curtains and sell them in the marketplace while her eleven-year-old sister Roza worked as a sales lady in a coat store. Dina got married at the age of 19 to a wonderful man named Chaim. He was a tailor and he made Dina's first coat. Until then, she wore a wool cape because she was too poor to buy a coat.

The relationship between Jews and Gentiles was quite favorable; many Gentiles were employed by Jews. They would often bring eggs to their Gentile neighbors. Unfortunately, the peaceful times came to an end.

Roza on the left, and Bubby Dina on the right

Suddenly the Gentiles' attitude towards their Jewish friends changed drastically. They would barge into Jewish homes and steal. The Jews were left helpless in the face of their former Gentile friends. Feelings of anti-Semitism kept growing stronger, and the number of new decrees passed against the Jews constantly increased. All Jews were required to wear the yellow star, which made them targets for anti-Semitic attacks. Dina had one baby girl with her husband in 1937. This wonderful chapter of her life abruptly ended in 1939. It happened on an ordinary morning when the Nazis came to their town and gathered all the children. These children were never heard from again. Bubby Dina's daughter was two years old when she last saw her.

Dina and her family remained in the Lodz Ghetto

> *Soon they heard the sounds of horses drawing near. The American soldiers had arrived to liberate them.*

for two and a half years, and from there they were deported to Auschwitz. When they arrived, the young men, women, and elderly were divided into different lines. Dina and her sisters were separated from their husbands and mother. Dina was ordered to stand in a line with her younger sister. Her sister Roza was sent to another line. At that moment, she did not realize it would be the last time she would see several members of her dear family.

After enduring two miserable weeks in Auschwitz, Dina and her sister were transported to Bergen-Belsen, and from there to an ammunition factory where they were tasked with making bullet chambers for guns. They worked until the wee hours of the morning and were given coffee to keep them awake. Dina recalled that they were always starving during those five years.

They wondered if they would ever live to see the end of their bitter plight. They could not believe the news when they heard that the war had drawn to a close and that the Germans had been defeated by the Allies. Soon they heard the sounds of horses drawing near. The American soldiers had arrived to liberate them. They were filled with relief and excitement. The soldiers took them to a home to recuperate for two months, where they slept and ate properly.

After two months, Dina and her sister decided to return to their hometown to seek out any living relatives. Upon arrival, they found an old friend and asked him if anyone from their hometown had survived the war. He smiled and said, "Your sister Roza is alive. She has even remarried." They were both shocked and thrilled. They had a joyous reunion and thanked G-d that they

> *In her senior years, Dina exclaimed, "I was truly happy. Today I'm so grateful for my son Moshe, his eight wonderful children, and grandchildren."*

were together once again. Roza had lost her husband and two children in the war. After remarrying, she had three children.

Dina discovered what had happened to her own husband Chaim: he was transported from Auschwitz to Czechoslovakia to work. Sadly, he died of illness just one week before the war ended. Dina remarried Refoel Levin from Pinsk, Lithuania, who was the only survivor of a family of sixteen children.

The German Council granted visas to Roza, her husband and sister to emigrate to Canada. Dina and her husband were refused a visa because the German Council claimed that her husband was an enemy since he had fought in the Russian army during the war. After Dina and Refoel had waited for two years to immigrate, her sisters arranged for a wealthy friend of theirs living in Canada to pose as their guarantor. He put a large bank account in their name. Dina and her husband emigrated to Canada in 1948. She was pregnant at the time, and her son Moshe was born in 1949. Dina and her husband worked in their guarantors' clothes factory for 20 years. They adapted to their new life in Canada, and in her senior years, Dina exclaimed, "I was truly happy. Today I'm so grateful for my son Moshe, his eight wonderful children, and grandchildren."

Bubby Dina and Roza lived through many hardships, yet they responded with goodness and rebuilt their lives in a new country. Their devotion to their family and faith built generations who are continuing their legacy today. They both lived until the ripe old age of 96 years old.

Aishes Chayil Story

A Mother's Lesson

Author Unknown

A young woman went to her mother and told her about her life and how things were so hard for her. She did not know how she was going to make it and wanted to give up. She was tired of fighting and struggling. It seemed that as one problem was solved, a new one arose.

Her mother took her to the kitchen, where she filled three pots with water and placed each on a high fire. Soon, the water came to a boil. In the first pot, the mother placed carrots; in the second, she placed eggs; and in the last, she placed ground coffee beans. She let them sit and boil without saying a word.

After twenty minutes, she turned off the burners. She fished the carrots and eggs out and placed them in separate bowls. Then she ladled the coffee out and placed it in a bowl.

Turning to her daughter, she asked, "Tell me, what do you see?"

"Carrots, eggs, and coffee," the daughter replied.

Her mother brought her closer and asked her to feel the carrots. She did, noting that they were soft. The mother then asked the daughter to take an egg and break it. After pulling off the shell, she observed the hard boiled egg. Finally, the mother asked the daughter to sip the coffee. The daughter smiled as she inhaled its rich aroma.

The daughter then asked, "What does it mean, Mother?"

She explained that each of these foods had endured the same boiling water, yet each reacted differently. After subjection to boiling water, the tough carrot grew soft and weak. The fragile egg with a liquid interior grew stiff, like a person's heart hardened by loss, disappointment or other trials. The ground coffee was unique, however; it had rather changed the water, releasing flavor and fragrance through its heated experience.

"Which are you?" the mother asked. "When adversity knocks on your door, how do you respond? Are you a carrot, an egg, or a coffee bean?"

> *"When adversity knocks on your door, how do you respond? Are you a carrot, an egg, or a coffee bean?"*

If you are like the bean, then when things are at their worst, you grow and transform your situation. When the hour is the darkest and trials are their greatest, you elevate yourself to a higher level. The beauty of life is that we can consciously choose to live this way, even if one may have begun as a carrot or an egg. The woman of valor gives us the strength to be loyal and respond with goodness in times of adversity.

GROW as an Aishes Chayil

Gratitude: **Express gratitude for a relationship that was strengthened through shared joy or pain.**

_____
_____
_____

Recognition: **How are Jews a "rose among thorns" like Rivkah? Have you ever felt like a rose among thorns?**

_____
_____
_____

Oneness: **How can you offer support as a loyal friend or family member in both good and difficult times?**

_____
_____
_____
_____
_____

Wish: **What is your wish from G-d?**

_____
_____
_____
_____

ל

A Thread of Leadership

"She seeks out wool and linen, and her hands work willingly."

Digging Deeper

What does this verse mean? Why does it say "she seeks"?

The *Aishes Chayil* is a leader who demonstrates initiative as she seeks out the raw materials for her projects rather than wait for someone to bring them to her.

After purchasing the best quality, color and price of wool and linen, she completes her task of spinning them into cloth "*b'cheifetz* — willingly."

When one does something with great speed, it shows how willing and happy one is to fulfill the task.[1]

1. Metzudas Dovid

WOMEN IN THE TORAH
Leah

Leah greeted her husband Yaakov with a pleasant countenance, as it is written, "And Yaakov came from the field in the evening, and Leah went out to meet him."[2]

How did Leah show leadership by "seeking out" the best before and after her marriage to Yaakov?

Throughout her life, Leah did not passively wait for things to fall into her lap. She sought the good by taking initiative and pursuing ways to improve her situation.

Leah seeks a better future through prayer.

Rivkah had two sons and her brother, Lavan, had two daughters. Therefore, the townspeople often said the elder son, Eisav, would marry the elder daughter, Leah, while the younger son, Yaakov, would marry the younger daughter, Rachel.

Leah's eyes became red and tender as she cried to G-d, beseeching Him to change her fate: "Please, let my lot not fall with the evil Eisav."[3] Leah did not accept her fate and prayed for a husband who would share her vision and values. Her "tender eyes" were the physical expression of her longing to build the Jewish nation.

Through her tearful prayers, Leah changed her destiny and became the first of the two sisters to marry Yaakov, and she mothered six of the twelve tribes.

2. Bereishis 30:16
3. Rashi on Bereishis 29:17

Leah seeks a better relationship with Yaakov.

When "Yaakov loved Rachel" more than Leah, again she refused to settle. G-d had compassion and blessed her swiftly with four sons, and through each of their names, she expressed her desire for love and connection with Yaakov.

Leah named her first two sons Reuvain and Shimon, "see" and "hear," for G-d saw her pain and heard she was unloved. When she birthed Levi, meaning "attach," she hoped that Yaakov would feel more attached to her. Yehudah means "thankful praise" and his birth raised Leah to a new level in her relationship with Yaakov, as you will read below.[4]

Leah seeks a grateful relationship with G-d.

Leah did not take G-d's kindness for granted. After the birth of her fourth son, whom she called Yehudah, she expressed her gratitude: "*Hapa'am odeh es Hashem* — This time, I will thank G-d."[5]

Reb Yochanan said in the name of Rabbi Shimon bar Yochai: "From the day that G-d created His world, there was no one who ever thanked G-d the way Leah did."[6]

Why was Leah's gratitude unique if others before her thanked G-d?

Leah's gratitude serves as a valuable example for us as Jews, inspiring us to appreciate everything we have in life as an unexpected gift. According to Divine spirit, the Matriarchs knew that Yaakov's four wives would give birth to twelve tribes. The division of the twelve sons among four wives meant that each wife would have three sons. When Leah gave birth to her fourth son, she said, "I have received more than my fair share. Now I give special thanks to G-d."[7] Leah named her son Yehudah, which means gratitude. Since Yehudah was an unexpected gift, her appreciation was deeper and more heartfelt.

Leah seeks her husband and greets him.

Although it took many years for Yaakov to appreciate Leah, she worked steadily to improve their relationship. She went out into the field and cheerfully greeted Yaakov to invite him to her tent. Her desire to be close with him stemmed from her deepest wish to build the Jewish people. She demonstrated her eagerness to bring righteous children into the world. Therefore, she merited to have kings and prophets descend from her.[8]

How does Leah empower us to be leaders?

Leah took initiative to accomplish what seemed impossible, playing a crucial role in weaving the tapestry of our nation alongside her righteous husband and sister. Leah's example teaches us the importance of personal effort and genuine prayer. By taking the lead in our own lives, we have the ability to influence our present and future generations.

---

4. Rashi, Midrash
5. Bereishis 29:35
6. Mishnah Berachos 7b

7. Breishis 29, 34 Rashi
8. Midrash Shachar Tov

Why do you think that happens, that unraveling in life? Why do we struggle to find the parts of us that are scattered in the wind—and then tie them together in ways that we can gift to the world? Do you think it is for the best?

I find the answer in a song I have written—a song, like all deep melodies, that has come from a world beyond my understanding.

The unraveling, the apparent disarray, the unrest in our world, is all the very essence of life. G-d could have woven our lives to look picture-perfect, but instead He chooses to unravel the strings and leave them for us to tie up.

I believe it is because He wants a real relationship with us. Although He is whole, complete and perfect, He says, "I want something else: I want a connection with you. I want you to find Me and choose Me on your own."

So, instead of handing us life on a silver platter and making His existence blindingly apparent, He hides. And He clips our wings so we can grow our own, enabling us to become partners with Him. Then life becomes a rich and meaningful relationship between man and Creator.

Yes, the unraveling is for the best. G-d wants us to appreciate our lives in the deepest and sweetest of ways—something we can experience only by taking our own steps in this cosmic dance.

But this answer isn't mine. It's the answer I was taught the heavens give when a soul in turmoil asks, "Why?"[9]

9. Copyright and reprinted with permission of Chabad.org and Sara Hecht

Meaningful Melody

UNRAVELED

by Sara Hecht from the debut album Pieces

Clipped my wings, so I could GROW my own
You sent me away, to find a new path home
You turned out the lights, so I would look inside
And I thought, "How do I dance when the music's died?"

Chorus:
Oh, dance you will
But those steps won't be mine
I can't promise it's easy
But I promise you'll shine
And when you feel me deep inside
Then you'll know I no longer hide

Unraveled the strings
I will tie them back up
You rain me down with your blessings
Don't ever stop
Unthreaded your dream
Because you knew I could weave
Now, together we'll both make it different
Now, together we'll both make it ours

You pushed me gently through an unknown door
You said, "Walk where nobody's walked before"
You turned out the lights, so I would look inside
And I thought, "How do I dance when the music's died?"

Chorus

Pearls of Wisdom

A needle is for connecting fabric. G-d asks us to create a small opening to receive His blessings by connecting with Him.

"Open for Me an opening the size of an eye of a needle and I will open for you an opening the size of a hall."

-Midrash Shir Hashirim Rabbah

Aishes Chayil Story

A Mother's Prayer

Author Unknown

The daughter of the *Chafetz Chaim*, Rabbi Yisroel Meir Kagan of righteous memory (1838-1933), related the following story about her grandmother:

My grandmother was not a miracle worker, so towards the end of her life, after my father became the renowned *Chafetz Chaim*, close friends asked her: "How did you merit to have a son that illuminated the eyes of the world?"

One thing came to mind: Before her wedding, her mother gifted her a *Siddur* with *Tehillim* and said: "My daughter, we are commanded to raise our sons to study Torah and fear Heaven. Therefore, I ask of you in every free moment you have to take your *Siddur* in hand and pray to *Hashem* to merit raising your children as G-d-fearing, observant Jews who devote themselves to Torah study. Do not forget to shed tears when you pray."

"That is all I did," my grandmother continued. "In any free moment, I would take out the *Siddur* and recite *Tehillim*, crying from my heart to *Hashem* that my Yisroel'ke develop into a G-d-fearing Torah scholar."

When my father held his mother's old, tattered prayerbook, he was visibly moved and asked, "Do you have any idea how many tears my mother shed over this *Tehillim* as she entreated *Hashem* to fulfill her wish for her son to be a proper Jew?"

> "Do you have any idea how many tears my mother shed over this Tehillim as she entreated Hashem to fulfill her wish for her son to be a proper Jew?"

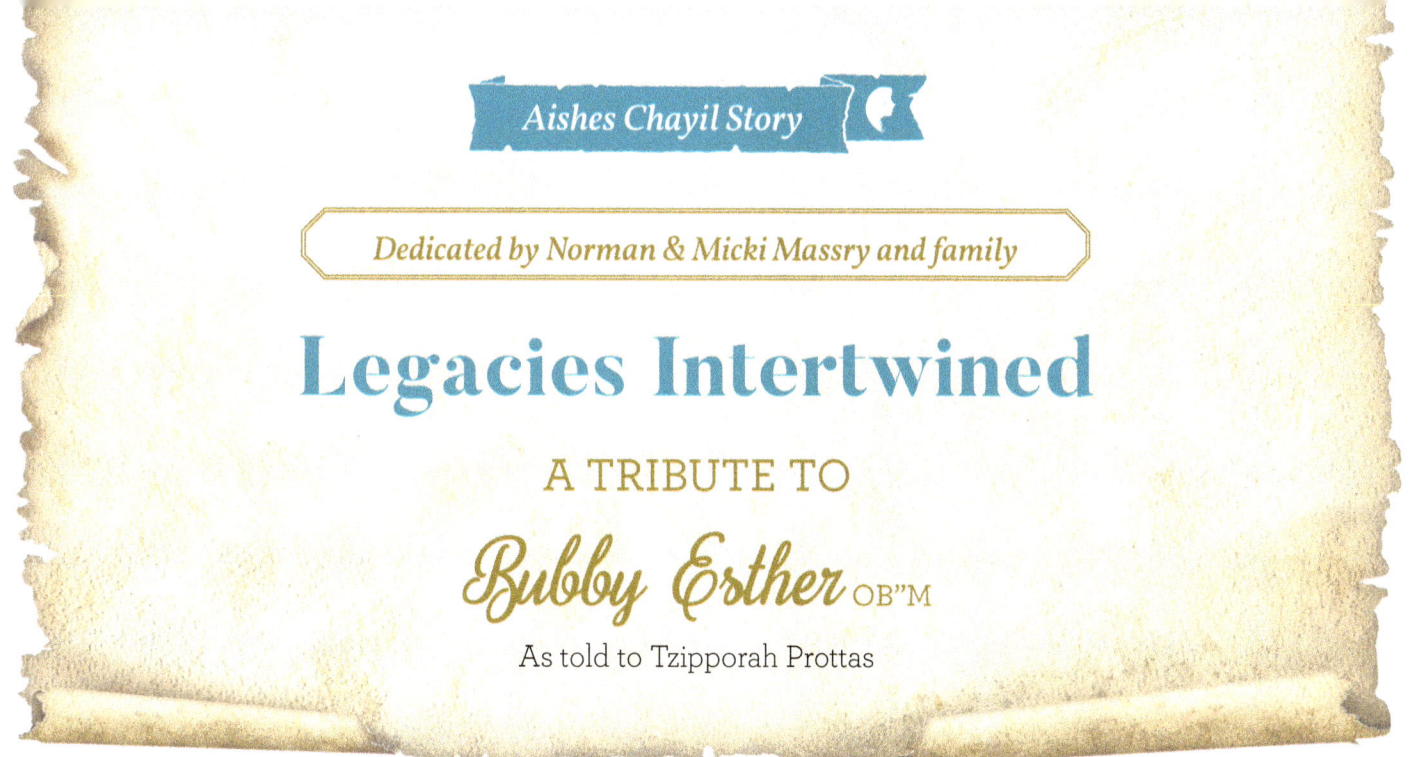

Aishes Chayil Story

Dedicated by Norman & Micki Massry and family

Legacies Intertwined

A TRIBUTE TO

Bubby Esther OB"M

As told to Tzipporah Prottas

One day, during a visit, Micki Massry and her friend Nechama Laber recalled Micki's grandmother, Bubby Esther. Micki retrieved two garments that Bubby Esther had lovingly made for her family and, presenting them to Nechama, she made a request.

Nechama brought Micki's request to her mother-in-law, Gittel Laber, also known as Bubby Laber, to her grandchildren and their friends.

Gittel recounts, "My daughter-in-law, Nechama Dina, called one day, asking if I could take on a special project," "Her friend, Micki, had handmade garments from her grandmother and was wondering if someone could repurpose the yarn for a gift for her expected new grandson. Nechama thought I could figure out what to do, although I was unsure of what to expect...

I realized my hands were touching the same yarn that Micki's grandmother, Bubby Esther, a Holocaust survivor, had touched over half a century ago.

As I began to unravel two crocheted, pale blue-and-white children's vests, a sense of awe overwhelmed me: I realized my hands were touching the same yarn that Micki's grandmother, Bubby Esther, a Holocaust survivor, had touched over half a century ago. How amazing it would be to be a part of continuing her legacy.

Micki's grandson enjoying his blanket

Fortunately, I salvaged plenty of yarn to knit into a beautiful baby blanket. It was emotional for me to deliver it to Micki shortly before her grandmother's birthday on March 15, and to learn more about her. I was struck by the fact that it was my grandmother, Sara Reitman, who introduced me to the art of knitting. She used to sew and knit clothing for her grandchildren, and on Chanukah, she would gift her family with aprons that she made from extra material.

By reweaving those threads into a new blanket, I experienced a deep joy and appreciation for this G-d given talent that has been bestowed upon me to share with others.

Another Divinely-coordinated event unfolded about one month later when Nechama Dina dropped by Micki's to deliver freshly-baked babka. As Bubby Esther was renowned for this confection, Nechama Dina warmly remarked, "We're kindling Bubby Esther's flame!"

Unbeknownst to her, the visit coincided with an auspicious time. Micki revealed, "I am lighting a candle tonight for Bubby Esther's *yahrzeit*... Bubby Esther is with you!"

"She is with all of us," responded a moved Nechama Dina.

Today, Micki lights her Shabbos candles with Bubby Esther's inherited candlesticks. (See full story on page 58.) As she holds the blanket woven by Bubby Esther's hands, she feels the warmth and love it carries. Micki is imbued with her grandmother's resolve to clothe her family with the joy of Judaism and the light of Shabbos.

A woman of valor "seeks out wool and linen, and her hands work willingly." From Bubby Esther to Bubby Laber, their goods deeds are intertwined threads, weaving the tapestry of our legacies from generation to generation.

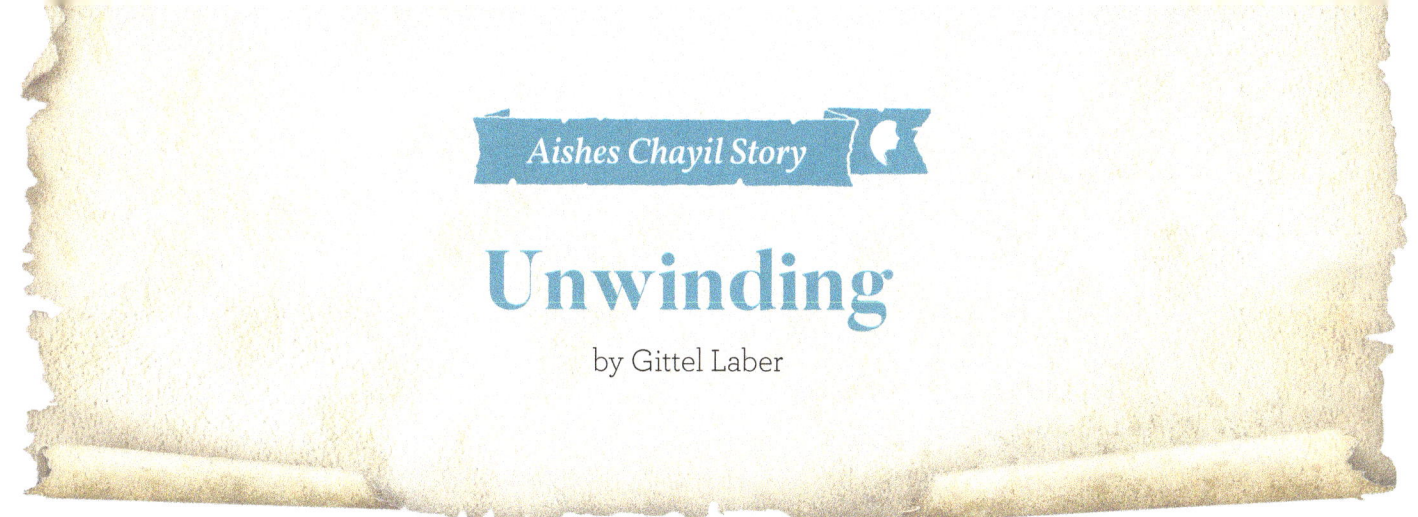

Aishes Chayil Story

Unwinding

by Gittel Laber

I remember an icebreaker exercise at a women's retreat where we used a ball of yarn to connect with each other and express gratitude and praise. We took a ball of yarn and used it to connect to others as we expressed gratitude and praise for each other. The strands of yarn became intertwined, criss-crossing over and under, and at the end of the exercise, the yarn was dropped. I took all the scrambled yarn and stuffed it into a bag.

> *It went smoothly for a while and it was easy to rewind, until I ran into a snag again. So too is life!*

A day later, I decided to rewind the scrambled yarn into a ball. Initially, my efforts went smoothly without any snags or knots. However, all of a sudden, my progress came to a stop as the yarn became a tangled mess. I had to take the time to untangle the strands, unraveling the knots and freeing up enough yarn to continue winding it. It went smoothly for a while, and rewinding was easy, until I encountered another snag. So too is life!

We go through life and things go smoothly, with *Hashem*'s guidance. At times our life unravels and we strive to rewind. Then we find a knot or a tangled mess and we spend time freeing things up. We seek guidance from others and take time to listen and hear others' viewpoints. We also may choose to change direction. We are grateful when life goes smoothly again.

GROW as an *Aishes Chayil*

Gratitude: Who is a leader? What are her leadership qualities which you are grateful for?

_____
_____
_____
_____

Recognition: Recognize the leadership qualities you are expressing in your life. Recognize where and when you are needed to take the lead.

_____
_____
_____
_____

Oneness: What is one positive action you can take as a leader in your home or community?

_____
_____
_____
_____

Wish: What is your wish from G-d?

_____
_____
_____
_____

ה

A Thread of Empathy

"She is like the merchant's ships bringing her bread from afar."

Digging Deeper

What does this verse mean?

She imports food from far away to nourish her household. An *Aishes Chayil* "bringing her bread from afar" means that she goes out of her way to nourish her family physically, emotionally, and spiritually. Her empathy, or ability to understand and share the feelings of others, allows her to tune into and provide their various needs.

What is the deeper meaning of "lechem — bread"?

Lechem (לחם) shares a Hebrew root with *milchama* (מלחמה) meaning "fight." The connection between struggle and bread, the most basic sustenance, appears in the Torah when G-d banished Adam and Chava from Gan Eden, saying, "With the sweat of your brow, you shall eat bread."[1]

1. Bereishis 3:19

In Hebrew, *Lechem* לחם shares the same letters with "*melach* — salt". Before we eat bread, symbolizing Divine kindness, we dip it in bitter salt, symbolizing Divine severity, so that G-d's kindness should prevail in our efforts to sustain ourselves.[2]

Even in times of struggle (מלחמה), an *Aishes Chayil* goes far to provide all of her family's needs with empathy and kindness (לחם), overcoming life's bitterness (מלח).

WOMEN IN THE TORAH
Rachel

Fighting humiliation daily while awaiting a child, Rachel yearned to fulfill her basic need to become a mother just as one waits for a ship from afar to arrive with food. Therefore, she merited her son Yosef, who brought an abundance of goodness to the world like a fully loaded ship. As the viceroy of Egypt, he supported the people during the years of famine, and the world was sustained in his merit.[3]

How was Rachel like a "merchant's ships bringing her bread from afar" as a sister?

Just as a ship embarks on a long journey to transport goods, Rachel went far beyond her obligation on her wedding day to preserve her sister Leah's dignity. When Rachel discovered that her deceitful father, Lavan, was tricking Yaakov into marrying Leah, Yaakov

2. Arizal, Shaar Hamitzvos, Parshas Eikev
3. Midrash Shachar Tov

devised secret signs to identify Rachel under the veil. Understanding Leah's pain, Rachel selflessly gave her sister the signs to spare her from humiliation before the crowd.[4]

In later events, Rachel was rewarded for sacrificing her own chance to marry her beloved first. G-d responded by promising to return her children from exile to the Land of Israel.

How was Rachel like a "ship bringing her bread from afar" as a mother?

Through heartfelt prayers, sisterly love and empathy, she birthed two of the tribes: Yosef and Binyamin, who followed in her ways.

After seven painful, childless years, Rachel's "ship" arrived with the birth of Yosef, whose name means "He will add." His name expressed her dream: "*Yosef Hashem li ben achair* — May G-d add on another son for me."[5]

Leah prayed for Rachel to bear a second son instead of giving birth to a seventh son herself, sparing Rachel the shame of mothering fewer tribes than the maidservants, Bilhah and Zilpa, who each had two sons. After eight years of prayer, Rachel gave birth to Binyamin but sadly died in childbirth on *Cheshvan* 11 at the age of thirty-six. As her soul departed, she named him "*Ben Oni* — son of my mourning."

She passed on the traits of self-sacrifice and empathy to Yosef, who, like a ship bringing food from afar, saved the world from famine. Although he dwelled amid a foreign culture far away, Yosef sustained his soul with Torah taught by his father and the love and sensitivity modeled by his mother.[6]

How did Rachel continue to sustain her children "from afar," beyond her physical life?

Rachel, buried alone on the road in Bais Lechem, resembles a ship sailing far away. At the end of his life, Yaakov *Avinu* told Yosef, "I buried your mother on the road because I was commanded by G-d, so that she would be of assistance to her children. When Nebuzaradan exiles them and they pass by there, Rachel will emerge from her grave and weep and beg mercy for them."[7]

When the Jews were exiled to Babylonia, Avraham, Yitzchok, Yaakov, and Moshe all prayed for their return to the Land of Israel, but none of them aroused G-d.

Rachel *Imeinu* then cried to G-d: "Do You remember when I spared my sister embarrassment and let her marry my beloved Yaakov? I was not jealous. Then why should You be so zealous in punishing Your children for bringing idols into Your Temple? Please, return my children to their Land!"

His mercy aroused by Rachel's self-sacrifice and sensitivity, G-d accepted her plea and promised that the Jewish people would be redeemed in her merit: "Refrain your voice from weeping and your eyes from tears, for there is a reward for your efforts...and the children shall return to their own border."[8]

How does Rachel empower us today?

Although Rachel's dream to become a mother seemed distant, like a "merchant's ship bringing her bread from

---

4. Bereishis 29:22-25; Rashi; Talmud, Bava Basra 123a
5. Bereishis 30:24
6. Based on Rashi on Shemos 1:5; based on Likkutei Sichos: vol. 6 — Bereishis, for Parshas Vayigash
7. Bereishis 48:7; Rashi
8. Yirmiyahu 31:14-16; Midrash Eicha Rabbah

afar," she became the ultimate mother of our people. She continues to pray for us from afar, as she empathizes with our pain.

Today, as we sail through the stormy seas of exile, Rachel's example empowers us to love unconditionally and go any distance to help others. Through these efforts, we will rebuild the *Beis Hamikdash*, which was destroyed due to baseless hatred among Jews.[9] We will make her dream a reality by sustaining the world with our Torah and mitzvos. Together with Rachel, we will beseech G-d to fulfill our ultimate dream to return us to our Holy Land with Moshiach.

MAMA ROCHEL

By Abie Rotenberg

With the rising sun, on her wedding day
She raised her eyes to the heavens
And she thanked *Hashem*, for the man of truth
With whom she would build a nation.

But with nightfall came, destiny betrayed
The veil concealing another
Yet a sister's shame, not her shattered dreams
Took hold of her heart and her senses

Chorus:
Mama Rochel cry for us again
Won't you shed a tear for your dear children
If you raise your sweet voice now as then

The day will come
Mama Rochel cry for us again
Won't you shed a tear for your dear children
Bi'zechutaich v'shavu vonim lig'vulom

In a roadside grave, she was laid to rest
In solitude forever
But her voice gave hope to the broken hearts
Of her daughters and sons — bound for exile

When her plaintive cry gained Divine consent
A challenge to her Maker
Can the mercy of mere flesh and blood
Run deeper than Yours — our Creator!?

Chorus

Now your voice is still as you heed the call
Of *m'ni kolaich mi'bechi*
It's our Father's will, He who made us all
Dare we ask of you — to defy Him?

Yet a frightened child,
Numb from pain and grief
Remains forlorn and uncertain
Clinging to the faith, that it can be heard
As it cries out to its mother
Mama mama vain nochamol
Trerren zolttz du gissen un a tzohl
Beten fun bashefer in himmel, b'kol rom
Mama mama vain nochamol
Trerren zoltz du gissen un a tzohl
Bi'zechusaich v'shovu vonim lig'vulom

---

9. Talmud, Yoma 9b

Pearls of Wisdom

It is better to jump into a BURNING FURNACE than to EMBARRASS ANOTHER PERSON.

—Rabbi Shimon Bar Yochai

Aishes Chayil Story

Dedicated by her daughter, Terri Klein

Be Good and Be Kind!

A TRIBUTE TO

Perl, Pauline Wolfman OB"M

by Terri Klein

Pauline Wolfman, Perl, daughter of Elise and Jack Latner, embodied the life of an *Aishes Chayil* from the early age of sixteen, when she suddenly lost her very own *Aishes Chayil*, her dear mother. A beautiful woman inside and out, a devoted daughter and wife, an unconditionally loving mother and grandmother, and a kind and nurturing human being, my mother stepped into all of these roles with dignity and grace. A natural empath, she was a deep listener and a compassionate soul—a truly unique *neshama*.

"Like the merchant's ships bringing her bread from afar," she always found a way to nourish others physically, emotionally, and spiritually.

In her life, my dear mother faced medical challenges, yet she was a warrior and her courage and resilience prevailed. She cared for people from a genuine place, and her ultimate mission was to serve. With a solid foundation of faith, her circle of love continued to expand. She instilled in her family the power of prayer and tradition.

The Sabbath and High Holidays were a sacred opportunity to bring family together around an immaculate table adorned with exquisite food and smiling faces. Pauline put the needs of her family and friends first. "Like the merchant's ships bringing her

Pauline in front of a painting of herself

bread from afar," she always found a way to nourish others physically, emotionally, and spiritually.

My dear mother was also a poet, and her favorite teaching was:

Be good and be kind, keep this always in mind
And life will be happier, I'm sure you will find.
Never be greedy, selfish or untrue
Keep G-d and love with you, in all that you do.

The legacy of this *Aishes Chayil*, my darling mother, lives on today in her beautiful children, grandchildren, and now great-grandchildren. It was an honor and a privilege to be her daughter. My prayer is for this very special *Aishes Chayil*'s Legacy to live on and carry forward in me and my daughter, Leorah, and for generations to come.

Thank you for always being with us.
It felt so nice to feel heard and be seen.
To know you was to love you,
Our Precious Pauline.

You are the wind beneath our wings,
the air within our breath.
With you as our guardian angel,
we will be forever blessed.

Your eternal and unconditional love
continues to flow through our veins.
Your lessons and messages will guide us,
and your legacy will always remain.

GROW as an Aishes Chayil

Gratitude: **I am grateful for my physical, emotional and spiritual nourishment. I am grateful for...**

Recognition: **Recognize how your life is similar to a journey on a ship. Where is your ship headed? Write a poem, if you wish.**

Oneness: **How can you go the extra mile to share empathy and unconditional love with those around you?**

What actions can you take to actualize Rachel's dream of her children returning to the Land of Israel with the redemption?

Wish: **What is a personal dream that you wish for?**

ו

A Thread of Nourishment

"She rises while it is still nighttime, and gives food to her household and a portion to her maids."

Digging Deeper

What does this verse mean?

The *Aishes Chayil* is a hard worker and awakens before sunrise, while it is still dark, to offer nourishment to her family and hired help.

Throughout the generations, the Jewish woman has fueled faith through serving Kosher food to her household. Her challah and chicken soup for Shabbos, Hamantaschen for Purim, donuts for Chanukah and other treasured recipes nourish both the body and soul of those who enjoy them.

"*Ta'amu ure'u ki tov Hashem* — Taste and see that G-d is good."[1] Reb Elimelech of Lizhensk interpreted this to mean, "Taste and see that all goodness is, in fact, G-d!" He explained that one can taste G-d's presence within the food itself, as hinted by the verse, "*B'chol derachecha de'eihu* — In all your ways know [G-d]."[2]

The *Aishes Chayil* demonstrates how the pleasant flavors become holy when eaten "for the sake of Heaven." The Baal Shem Tov taught that in this way, one weaves together the physical and spiritual while eating.[3]

What is the deeper explanation of this verse?

"She rises while it is still nighttime" refers to the darkness of exile, which conceals the light of G-d. The *Aishes Chayil* awakens from the emptiness and chaos of the world to perceive G-d through the darkness.

She accomplishes this by giving "*teref l'veitah* — food to her household," meaning Torah, which is food for the mind and soul. Like food, knowledge is something external that is consumed and made part of oneself.

She also provides "*chok l'na'aroseha* — a portion to her maids" by employing the material world to perform "*chukim*," which are mitzvos. In the service of G-d, the material is elevated to holiness.[4]

The Aishes Chayil uses her gifts to nourish bodies, minds and souls, physically and spiritually. Through family traditions, stories, songs, art, and other creativity, she dishes out Torah values in a way that others can digest, absorb and enjoy.

As a result, she instills faith in those around her, empowering them to pierce through the darkness of exile to connect with G-d through Torah study and mitzvos.

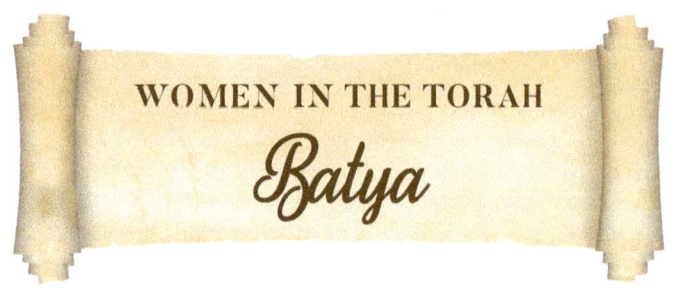
WOMEN IN THE TORAH
Batya

Batya was the daughter of Pharaoh who became a Jew. Batya's name is mentioned among the righteous women since she took care of Moshe and therefore merited to enter Gan Eden alive.[5]

Why did Batya take care of Moshe?

When Pharaoh's wise men foresaw that a baby boy

---
1 Tehillim 34:9
2 Mishlei 3:6
3 Toldos Yaakov Yosef, Parshas Va'eira

4 Malbim
5 Midrash Shachar Tov

would grow to overcome him, he ordered that all male Jewish infants be thrown in the Nile River. During this decree, Yocheved, daughter of Levi and wife of the Jewish leader Amram, gave birth to a son whom she hid for as long as possible. Soldiers came searching after three months, so Yocheved set the baby afloat in a basket on the Nile River while his sister Miriam watched from a distance. As the basket floated, "Pharaoh's daughter went down to bathe… Her maidservants were walking along the Nile River and she saw the basket amid the reeds," but it was far from the shore.[6]

How did Batya finally reach the distant basket?

"*Vatishlach es-amasah* — She sent *amasah* (אמתה)," which Rashi explains to mean 1) "her maidservant," whom she asked to bring her the baby, or 2) "her arm," which G-d miraculously extended many lengths.

Basket in hand, "She opened it and saw him… he was a weeping boy and she had pity on him and she said, 'This is one of the Hebrew children!'" When he refused milk from Egyptian women, Batya accepted Miriam's offer to bring her own mother as a nurse to feed him. When he grew old enough, Yocheved returned him to the palace. There, Batya nurtured him as an adoptive son and named him Moshe, meaning

"I drew him from the water."[7]

How was Batya rewarded?

She rose above the dark ways of Egyptian society, converted to Judaism, and risked her life to disobey her father's decree. She saved the future redeemer of our people. In reward for her kindness, the Torah calls Moshe only by the name she gave him, although he had many names.[8] G-d said to Batya: "Moshe was not your son, yet you called him your son. You are not My daughter, but I shall call you My daughter" — Batya, "daughter of G-d!"[9]

How do the two meanings of "amasah" teach us how to tackle a task?

1. Maidservant: Batya delegated the task of retrieving the basket to her maidservant, showing us the value of working with others to achieve a common goal. We can accomplish much more as a team than possible alone when we share our time, energy and strengths.

8 Midrash Shemos Rabbah
9 Midrash Vayikra Rabbah

6 Shemos 2:5
7 Shemos 2:6-10

Remember the acronym H.A.N.D. to get

Help from your team,
Ask for ideas,
Negotiate, and
Delegate tasks!

2. Arm: Batya stretched out "her arm," and it miraculously extended, showing us how once we do a good deed, G-d helps us succeed. Even when our goal or someone who needs help is beyond our reach, we do our best and entrust the rest to G-d. He is infinite and the source of all our strengths and success. With faith in Him, we can achieve more than we ever imagined!

Who else rose amid the darkness of Egypt to nourish faith in G-d?

During their enslavement, Jewish women drew water from the river and G-d prepared fish in their buckets. They would cook some and sell others, buy wine, and feed their husbands and treat their wounds in the fields where they worked. After they had eaten, the women would gaze into their copper mirrors with their husbands and say, "I am more beautiful than you." This aroused their husbands' desire, and as a result, they were fruitful and multiplied and gave birth to multitudes of Jewish children.[10]

When the weary men despaired about the future and feared Pharaoh's threats to their children, they wanted no more. With beautiful optimism, the women nourished their husbands' faith in building their families and in G-d's promise of Redemption.

At great risk, these women instilled faith in their children, who recognized G-d first at the Splitting of the Sea. Infants raised their heads from nursing, babies in the womb "sang," and children pointed with their fingers, proclaiming: "*Zeh Keili v'Anveihu* — This is my G-d and I will glorify Him!"[11]

How were these women rewarded?

When Moshe collected materials for the construction of the *Mishkan*, the women donated their copper mirrors to be fashioned into the *kiyor*, or washstand.

"G-d spoke to Moshe... 'You shall make a copper *kiyor*... and you shall put water therein. Aharon and his sons shall wash their hands and feet from it.'"[12]

Initially, Moshe questioned the placing of mirrors in the sanctuary since they are used for vanity. G-d replied, "These are more precious to Me than anything, for through them, the women set up many legions [of children] in Egypt."[13] This is why the *kiyor*'s dimensions could be as large as necessary to accommodate every precious mirror.

Later in the wilderness, the women's faith remained strong. When the scouts returned from Israel to report on how unconquerable the land seemed, the men wanted to return to Egypt. The women, however, trusted in G-d's promise of the land.

---

10 Talmud Sotah 11,b
11 Shemos 15:2; Talmud, Sotah 30b
12 Shemos 30:17-20
13 Rashi, Shemos 38:8

How do the women in Egypt inspire us to nourish our faith?

- Pray to Hashem daily
- Nourish yourself and others with Kosher Food
- Recite blessings on food
- Study Torah and nourish the soul
- Use the gift of creativity to nourish our faith
- Perform good deeds
- Recognize G-d in the details of life, marvel at the numerous ways He interacts with our world.

STRETCH OUT YOUR HAND

By Racheli Jacks

Stretch out your hand
Cause all it takes is one good deed
Stretch out your hand
And try to think what others need

An action so small
Seems like nothing at all
Yet it's the pivotal turn
That makes a difference to the world

Chorus:
Oh-oh-oh
Reach out, and lend a hand
Compromise and understand
Remember to try your best
And know that *Hashem* will do the rest

There's nothing that you cannot do
Ask — your friends have ideas too
Negotiate and Delegate
Hashem will help — do it all the way!

COPPER MIRRORS

Lyrics by Fruma Schapiro
Produced by Ohel Chana High School, Los Angeles

Peer into the copper mirror
Tell me, tell me, what you see
Do you see a slave girl or one who is free?
Am I free to use my mind, follow my heart, do what is right?
Reflected in this mirror's deepest parts

In the copper mirror look into your eyes
Understand the sacred task where my identity lies
A Jewish mother I can be
Generations we will see
Reflected in this mirror's deepest parts

We know we must, with firm belief, sacred trust
A woman uplifts her home with courage and care
Let the mirror play its part
Kindle hope in aching hearts
In the face of darkness and despair

To my dear mother,

Daniella Katzenberg שתחי׳

"She rises while it is still nighttime, and gives food to her household..."

Thank you for being a shining example of an Aishes Chayil and for creating a beautiful Jewish home. Your kindness, strength, and unwavering faith inspire us all. We are grateful for the nourishment, prayers, and resourcefulness you've woven into our lives. Your light guides us on our paths. We wish you many more healthy years filled with nachas from your children, grandchildren, and great-grandchildren.

With heartfelt appreciation,
Nechama Dina Laber

Eilu, Eilu Chavivin Olai Min Hakol[14]
I will let my mirror play its G-d-given role
Holy enduring beauty binds us to *Hashem*
Each child born is another precious gem

Our intentions pure, with copper mirrors we secure
The future of our people despite this slavery
Bizchus, Bizchus Noshim, Noshim Tzidkaniyos
In merit of the women's bravery

Hashem will extol
Eilu, Eilu Chavivin Olai Min Hakol
Mesiras Nefesh shining in the form of the *Kiyor*
You overcame inflicted pain
To carry on a precious chain
Your mirrors will now shine forever more

Eilu, Eilu Chavivin Olai Min Hakol
I will let my mirror play its G-d-given role
Holy enduring beauty binds us to *Hashem*
Each child born is another precious gem

Our intentions pure, with *Mesiras Nefesh* we secure
The *Geulah* of our people as we march to victory
Bizchus, bischus noshim, noshim Tzidkanius
In merit of the women's bravery

We know we must, with firm belief, sacred trust
A woman uplifts her home with courage and care
Let the mirror play its part
Kindle hope in aching hearts
In the face of darkness and despair

---

14 "These are more precious to me than everything"

Pearls of Wisdom

TASTE
and see that
G-D IS GOOD

-Tehillim 34:9

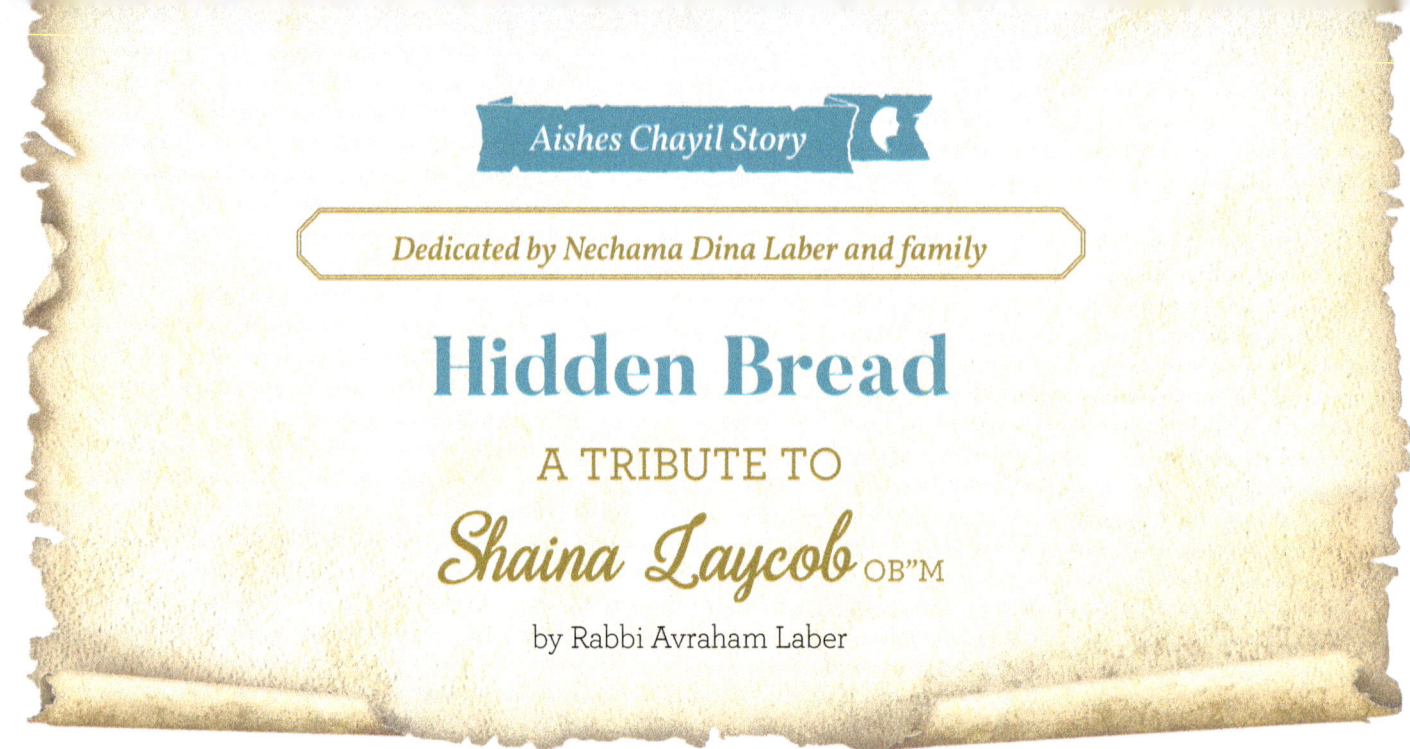

Hidden Bread

A TRIBUTE TO

Shaina Laycob OB"M

by Rabbi Avraham Laber

Shaina Laycob lived in Russia during World War I. She was known as a terrific baker. The occupying German Army ordered her to bake bread and pastries for the soldiers.

The Aishes Chayil "rises while it is still nighttime, and gives food to her household," Shaina woke up early in the morning to bake extra for the hungry in the local synagogues. Her husband, Azriel Yitzchok, would hide freshly-baked goods between layers of clothing he wore, so the Germans wouldn't detect his bread giving. In this quiet joint activity, they risked their lives to save Jewish people from starvation during the war.

One day, German soldiers caught Azriel Yitzchok smuggling bread, and they were ready to kill him. His wife Shaina walked forward and firmly declared "If you kill him, you'll have to kill me too." Slowly, the soldiers lowered their guns, since they didn't want to lose their baker!

Baruch Hashem, the Laycob family immigrated to America after World War I. Aboard the ship, nine-year-old Lyka Laycob gazed out at Ellis Island. She, along with her mother, Shaina, father, Azriel Yitzchok, grandmother Raizel, and her nine siblings weathered a long tumultuous journey from their home in Lithuania to America.

Arriving in Ellis Island was an answer to their prayers. In America, when her mother gave her an orange, Lyka was incredibly excited because she'd never seen one before. "It was beautiful," she remembers.

Inspired by her parents' selflessness during the darkest of times, Lyka, called Lillian, dedicated her life to the service of others. As a private nurse, she provided comfort and care to those in need, embodying the spirit of the Aishes Chayil who "gives food to her household."

> *In America, when her mother gave her an orange, Lyka was incredibly excited because she'd never seen one before.*

She worked the night shift, allowing her to be home in the morning for her 4 sons, Robert, Danny, Leonard and Azriel Wasserman. When asked what brought her the greatest joy, she replied with a smile, "My children and grandchildren."

Despite the profound grief of losing her youngest son, Rabbi Azriel Yitzchok Wasserman ob"m, at just thirty-seven, Lillian rose above the darkness of sorrow. She continued to nourish her family with the same unconditional love and dedication as her parents, Shaina and Azriel Yitzchok Laycob.

In a poignant twist of fate, Lillian (Bubby Wasserman) passed away on the 5th of Shevat, which also happens to be her son Azriel's birthday. It is a day that symbolizes the enduring connection between generations.

Bubby Wasserman's life echoed the enduring legacy of her parents, bridging the past and present through acts of kindness and resilience honoring the memory of her parents and their sacrifices during a time of great adversity.

Above: Shaina the baker, and her husband Azriel Yitzchok; Right: Bubby Wasserman

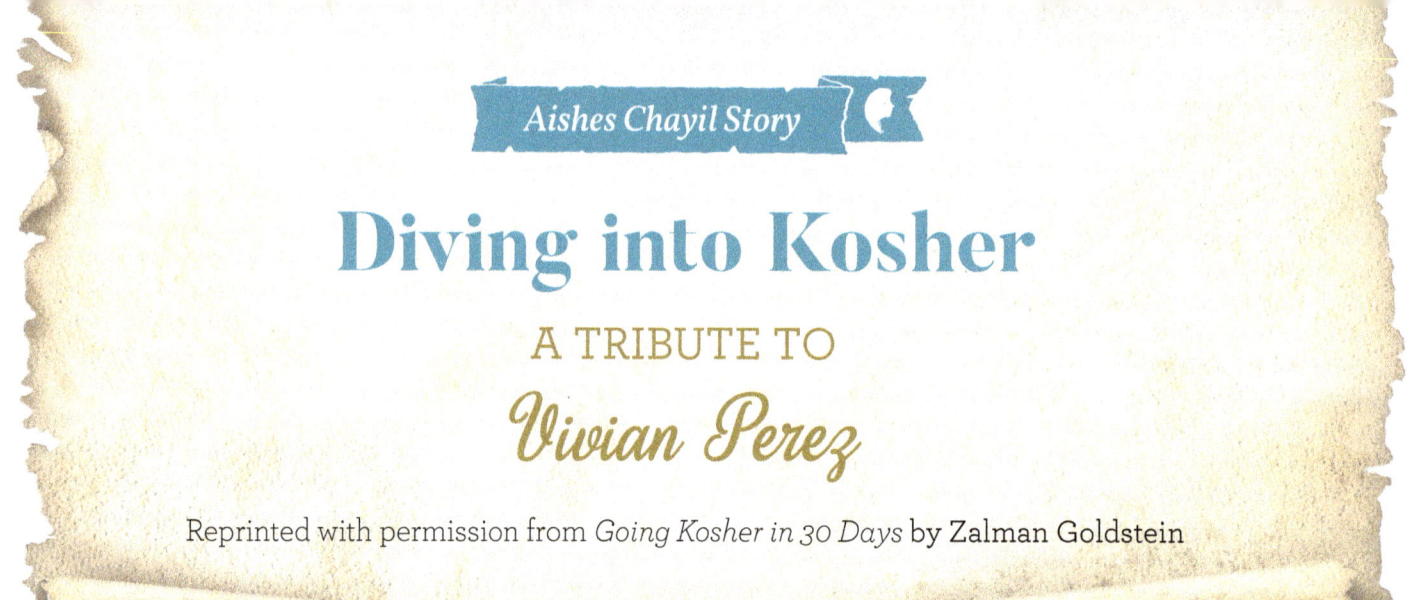

Aishes Chayil Story

Diving into Kosher

A TRIBUTE TO

Vivian Perez

Reprinted with permission from *Going Kosher in 30 Days* by Zalman Goldstein

Vivian Perez could never understand the reasons behind keeping Kosher. She questioned Rabbis who patiently explained the meaning of *Kashrus* to her. Still, none of the reasons seemed good enough to justify changing her eating habits and her kitchen. One day, something inside her compelled her to begin keeping Kosher, and she decided to "take the plunge."

Vivian later reflected on her decision to keep Kosher: "As anyone who has ever gone deep-sea diving knows, it is only after you're enveloped by the sea that you begin to see and appreciate its hidden beauty. Only after I actually started feeling beholden to and observing the Kosher dietary laws did the answers begin to come. Surprisingly enough, they didn't come from outside; they came from somewhere within. The more meticulously I kept Kosher, the deeper the answers from within resounded."

Through the act of "jumping into Kosher," Vivian internalized the answers. Every time she ate she was reminded of her soul. She practiced self-control and commitment and turned a mundane act into a way of serving G-d. She now sees keeping Kosher as freedom for her soul, even though on the surface it may seem to carry a lot of restrictions.

Vivian rose above the darkness to nourish her household with Kosher food. She said, "To think of the Kosher dietary laws as just a grueling regimen with routine requirements and regulations, is like telling a professional diver in full scuba gear to stay close to the shore, to not dive beyond the shallow waters. That's how frustrated my soul felt when it was not given the fuel needed for its realization. So, take the dive. Once you do, keep on going, deeper and deeper. Allow yourself to become enwrapped in the ocean and to see what magical beauty will reveal itself from within your own soul that you may never have known you had."

GROW as an Aishes Chayil

Gratitude: **Express gratitude for a special food or delicacy that is a tradition in your family. I am grateful for…**

———————————————
———————————————
———————————————

Recognition: **Does your family have a special recipe that has been passed down from your mother or grandmother? What is the story behind this dish?**

———————————————
———————————————
———————————————
———————————————
———————————————
———————————————

Oneness: **How can you foster faith and connect to your legacy through food for the body and soul?**

———————————————
———————————————
———————————————
———————————————
———————————————
———————————————

Wish: **What is your wish from G-d?**

———————————————
———————————————
———————————————

זָמְמָה שָׂדֶה וַתִּקָּחֵהוּ מִפְּרִי כַפֶּיהָ נָטְעָה כָּרֶם.

ז

A Thread of Planting

"She considers a field and acquires it; from the fruit of her hands, she plants a vineyard."

Digging Deeper

What does this verse mean?

When the *Aishes Chayil* plans to buy a field, she does not rest until she buys it.[1] From the profits of her work in the field, she plants a vineyard.[2]

What is the deeper meaning?

The *Aishes Chayil* plants the seeds of Judaism in her children and ensures the future of our people, who are likened to a vineyard.

As the prophet Yeshaya declared, "For the vineyard of the Lord of hosts is the House of Israel."[3]

Why are the Jewish people compared to a vineyard?

A vineyard is where grapes grow to produce wine. Wine holds a dual nature: it can be elevated when used for performing Kiddush and other mitzvos, sanctifying life-cycle events. However, wine can also be misused and lead people astray.

This choice presents itself to us every day:

Will we choose to utilize the material world for holiness, or will we allow it to pull us down?

The transparent skin of grapes reflects a time when the Divine energy infused in everything will be visible. Our mission is to elevate the physical world and reveal the hidden G-dliness within.[4]

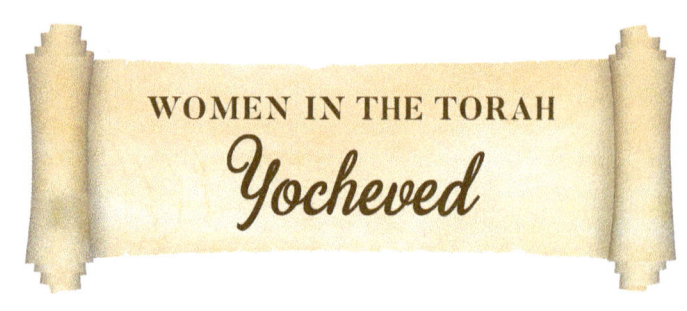

WOMEN IN THE TORAH
Yocheved

Yocheved gave birth to Moshe, who is equivalent to all of Israel and is referred to as a vineyard, as it states, "For the vineyard of the Lord of Hosts is the House of Israel."[6]

How did Yocheved's "planting" affect the future?

As the mother of Moshe, the redeemer of the Jewish people, who are compared to a vineyard, Yocheved played a crucial role. Just as a gardener protects crops during storms, Yocheved ensured the survival of the nation during the turbulent times in Egypt. When life seemed dark, dangerous, and chaotic like a jungle, Yocheved envisioned a garden for G-d, where Jewish children would flourish.

As a midwife alongside her daughter, Miriam, she protected numerous innocent babies from Pharaoh's evil decrees to kill or assimilate them into Egyptian culture. If a child's health was at risk during birth, they prayed: "*Hashem*, You know we disobeyed the evil king's instructions, endangering our lives. Please spare this infant so that people do not slander us, claiming that we tried to harm him."[7]

Despite Pharaoh's decrees, women even gave birth

---

1 Metzudas Dovid
2 Malbim
3 Shemos 5:7
4 Based on teaching from the Rebbe, Parshas Shelach

5 Yeshaya 5:7
6 Midrash Shachar Tov
7 Rashi on Shemos 1:15, Midrash Shemos Rabbah

to six babies at once. "The Israelites were fertile and prolific; they multiplied and increased very greatly, so that the land was filled with them."[8]

Yocheved was a gardener who lovingly tended to each child like a seedling. She strengthened their roots of faith in G-d and enabled them to flourish physically and spiritually. In Yocheved's hands, the Jewish population continued to grow.

What happened to the newborn children?

Many mothers were forced to secretly give birth and hide their babies from soldiers in the fields of Egypt, where the *Shechinah* protected and nurtured them. When the Egyptians discovered them, G-d caused the ground to miraculously swallow the newborns to protect them. When the Egyptians gave up plowing the soil to unearth them, the children sprouted from the ground like grass. As G-d said: "I caused you to multiply like the plants of the field."[9] Furthermore, G-d miraculously provided oil and honey from two stones for the infants' nourishment.

Once they were old enough, these children returned home. And at the awe-inspiring miracle of the Splitting of the Sea, they recognized G-d first, exclaiming,[10] "*Zeh Keili V'anveihu*—This is my G-d and I will glorify Him!"[11]

Yocheved planted the vineyard of our people and bravely risked her life to raise a generation of faithful children.

What is the meaning of Yocheved's name?

Yocheved's name contains the three letters of the Hebrew word "*kavod*" (כבד) which means "honor or glory." Her face reflected G-d's glory because she honored Him through her good deeds.

Yocheved's professional name was Shifra, meaning "beautified," while Miriam's name was Puah, meaning "cooing." As midwives, they provided clothes, food and shelter to mothers and newborns. Shifra would beautify the newborns, and Miriam would soothe them with her words.[12] Additionally, the name "Puah" alludes to Miriam's role as a prophetess.

The Kli Yakar also adds that Shifra means "youth," as

[12] Shemos 1:15, Rashi

[8] Shemos 1:7
[9] Yechezkel 16:7
[10] Shemos 15:2
[11] Midrash Tanchuma; Talmud, Sotah 11b

Yocheved appeared like a young woman at 130 years old when she gave birth to Moshe.

What was Yocheved's reward?

G-d blessed her with the spiritual wealth of her son Moshe, who was equal to the entire people of Israel. Through her son Aharon, she also became the Matriarch of the House of *Kehunah*, or the priestly family, and the House of Levi. Additionally, G-d blessed both Yocheved and Miriam with great material wealth.[13]

"From the fruit of her hands" signifies that the reward of Yocheved's deeds was her planting a vineyard.[14] Working in her field as a midwife, Yocheved cultivated a vineyard of children, including our redeemer Moshe, who chose to sanctify G-d's name.

How does Yocheved empower us today?

Yocheved empowers each of us to plant the seeds of Judaism and nurture today's children, who are the Jewish future. As a result, we preserve the existence of the Jewish people and bring redemption closer.

When G-d instructed Moshe to prepare our people for the giving of the Torah on Mount Sinai, He told him, "Thus shall you say to the house of Yaakov and tell the sons of Israel… You have seen what I did to the Egyptians and how…I brought you to Me…You will be to me a treasure from among all the nations."[15]

Our Sages comment: "Say to the House of Yaakov" refers to the women, and only afterward should Moshe "tell the sons of Israel," referring to the men.[16] G-d instructed Moshe to speak to the women first because they play a special role in raising the next generation.

Just as the Exodus from Egypt occurred in the merit of the women, our future redemption will also be in the merit of the Jewish women today.

LOOKING BACK

By Racheli Jacks

Looking back over so many years
Generations survived through hardships and tears
And yet there remained a spark of hope
Ignited by Jewish women throughout times

Chorus:
In the past they pulled us through
In the future we will too,
Bizchut Noshim Asidin L'higael[17]
We eagerly await the eternal *Geulah*
Please *Hashem* hear our cry *Ad Mosai*?

Founding a home is her primary role
With devotion, she instills a love for *Yiddishkeit*
In so many ways, she gives of her life,
To ensure that *Klal Yisroel* stays alive!

Chorus

---

13 Shemos 1:21, Rashi
14 Metzudas Dovid
15 Shemos 19:3-5
16 Shmos 19, 3-4 Rashi

17 In the merit of women, in the future we will be redeemed.

L'SAKEN OLAM

Lyrics by Sarah Leah Eber

Looking back over the years
Jewish women prevailed
Brave and modest bold and kind
Their faith has never failed

From Devorah's wisdom to Chana's prayer
Esther's self-sacrifice Rochel's care
Rivkah's kindness and Sara's modesty
Leah's gratefulness Yael's bravery

In Egypt they suffered through hardships and tears
It lasted for so many years
They kept their names, their dress stayed the same
Keeping their souls aflame

Yocheved and Miriam
The future they did see
Saving Jewish babies
'Gainst Paroh's decree

The faith they instilled
Gave courage to withstand
They danced to *Geulah*
Tambourines in hand

Chorus:
Jewish women we have the key
There's much we have to uphold
Using our inner strength from the past
As the future we now mold

Their depending on us to work to achieve
Igniting the sparks that are left to retrieve
United we stand together as one
Perfecting the world *L'Saken Olam*
End of Chorus

We may think just who are we
This task is way too great
Keep in mind you're one of a kind
Your faith you can't understate

Just like a midget though small in size
On giant's shoulders we are tall and wise
Perfecting the world through our nurturing role
With mitzvos with kindness we'll achieve our goal

Chorus:

They look down at us beseeching us to hear
Their plea to us women that the future we bear
United we stand together as one
Perfecting the world *L'Saken Olam*

Pearls of Wisdom

Divine Providence brings every Jew to his dwelling place in order to strengthen Yiddishkeit and disseminate the study of Torah.

When you plow and sow, *things will grow.*

-Hayom Yom 25 Cheshvan

Aishes Chayil Story

Without a Title, an Institution of Her Own

A TRIBUTE TO

Morah Raizel Wolvovsky OB"M

By Dovid Margolin

Raizel Wolvovsky was many things to many people.

To the hundreds of children she taught over her decades as a preschool teacher, she was the loving, imaginative *Morah* who made Judaism come alive at the most formative stage of their lives. To others, and there were many, she was the hostess whose Crown Heights, Brooklyn, home was as good as theirs on visits to the hub of the Chabad-Lubavitch movement—the place where there was somehow always room to sleep, eat, have a cup of coffee or a listening ear. And then there were the countless beneficiaries of her many extracurriculars, which were in fact a part of her daily routine: She was a matchmaker who paired hundreds of young couples; a *bikur cholim* (caring for the ill) volunteer who cooked meals to their exact specifications; and a friend, neighbor and community

Raizel Wolvovsky receives a dollar and a blessing from the Rebbe, as her husband, Monya, looks on. (Photo: Wolvovsky family/JEM)

Her warmth was combined with creative and progressive methods of communicating the lessons to children.

member who went out of her way to interact with everyone around her, always adding some touch no one else thought of.

Raizel Wolvovsky, who passed away on Nov. 21 (18 Kislev) at the age of 66, did it all—with her husband Monya's (Mordechai) tireless assistance—while serving as a hands-on mother to 11 children of her own.

In the early 1980s, Raizel started a new preschool named Gan Chinuch with the Rebbe's blessing, although it was mostly known as "Morah Raizel's." For the next three decades, Wolvovsky nurtured generations of children in this preschool and, through her classic "*Now I Know My Aleph Bais*" video, passing on to her young students her own deeply held love of Jewish tradition and learning in a way children would remember for years to come. Later, she became the inaugural director of the preschool division at Bnos Menachem girls' school.

Her warmth was combined with creative and progressive methods of communicating the lessons to children. "Everything was tangible and touchable, it wasn't common in the early '90s," said one former student of hers. On the Chassidic New Year of 19 Kislev, she'd pull out a treasure box in which she stored a Tanya, the foundation text of Chabad thought, given to her by the Rebbe. If she was telling the story of Jonah, she'd create an interactive Lego display—boat and fish and all. "When I became a preschool teacher 20 years later," the student said, "I did the same thing, because I still remembered how Morah Raizel taught it."

"The Torah likens a human being to a tree," the Rebbe wrote in a 1965 letter, noting that this lesson pertained in particular to children's education." When the tree is young, especially when it is still in the stage of a seedling, every good care given it in that early stage, however insignificant it may seem, is an investment which in due course amplifies itself many times, and the full effects become evident in the mature, fruit-bearing tree.

"Likewise is the minute attention given to a child, even where the benefit for the moment appears to be quite small. For even a 'small' benefit may with time turn out to be of a lasting quality and extraordinary proportions, impacting the daily conduct according to the Torah and Mitzvot…"

This was a mission Morah Raizel took to heart, and it was apparent in the hundreds of children who passed through her classroom.

Later, as her children married and many of them established Chabad centers from California wine country to the hills of Tuscany, Italy, she became an active member of each of their growing communities, forming relationships with people based not on externalities but a connection to the soul.

"She saw something in me and was always able to tell me things I needed to hear," wrote Andrea Rubenstein, a member of the Chabad of Sonoma County community in Northern California led by Wolvovsky's son and daughter-in-law, Rabbi Mendel and Alti Wolvovsky. "She was one of the guiding lights in my return to Judaism. I will miss her in a way words cannot express."

> *She became an active member of each of [her children's] growing communities, forming relationships with people based not on externalities but a connection to the soul.*

This ability to see something in each individual and have just the right word or gesture for them made Raizel Wolvovsky a powerful force for good far beyond her immediate surroundings.

"You can't overestimate how powerful of an influence she was on so many," observed her son, Rabbi Berel Wolvovsky. "Without holding a position or a title, she was an institution of her own."

Raizel embodied the verse, "she considers a field and acquires it," as each day she planted seeds of Judaism in her students, children, guests, and everyone she helped. From the fruit of her hands, she planted a vineyard. Her good deeds will continue to blossom into countless fruits through all those who continue to grow, thanks to the seeds she planted.[1]

---

1. Copyright and reprinted with permission of Chabad.org

GROW as an Aishes Chayil

Gratitude: **Which parent or educator planted seeds in you which you are grateful for today?**

_____
_____
_____

Recognition: **Can you recognize someone who is successfully planting seeds of Judaism in children today?**

_____
_____

Recognize a situation you have been in where a small deed blossomed into a much greater result.

_____
_____
_____

Oneness: **How can you nurture children today, physically, emotionally or spiritually?**

_____
_____
_____
_____
_____

Wish: **What is your wish from G-d?**

_____
_____
_____
_____
_____
_____

חָגְרָה בְעוֹז מָתְנֶיהָ
וַתְּאַמֵּץ זְרוֹעֹתֶיהָ.

ח

A Thread of Readiness

"She girds her hips with might and strengthens her arms."

Digging Deeper

What does this verse mean?

"Girding the hips" refers to wearing a belt, which is a sign of readiness. Soldiers wear weapons on their hips to indicate their readiness for the mission. Similarly, an *Aishes Chayil* prepares herself by acknowledging that her success comes from G-d. She doesn't say, "my strength and the might of my hands has produced this valor for me."[1] She recognizes that G-d's strength surrounds her like a belt, empowering her to resist the temptations of the evil inclination and fulfill her life's purpose.[2]

To further fortify herself, she "strengthens her arms" through learning Torah, which invigorates her actions. As a result, she is ready to fulfill mitzvos with greater diligence and agility.[3]

WOMEN IN THE TORAH
Miriam

Miriam prophesied, "In the future, my mother will give birth to the savior of Israel."[4]

Miriam's father, Amram, had separated from Yocheved because of Pharaoh's decrees to drown the baby boys. Since they were Jewish leaders, all the married men followed his example. However, Miriam foresaw the birth of her brother Moshe, who would redeem them from Egypt, so she urged her father to reunite with her mother and have more children.

Amid a joyous celebration, Amram remarried Yocheved, and Miriam, along with her brother Aharon danced with a tambourine as she sang, "My mother will give birth to a son who will set Israel free!" Miriam cherished this tambourine throughout the difficult years in Egypt.

When Moshe was born, the entire house filled with light and Amram exclaimed, "My daughter, I see your prophecy is coming true!" However, when Moshe was hidden in the Nile and Pharaoh's decrees became harsher, Amram questioned Miriam, "What has become of your prophecy?" Nevertheless, even at the age of six, Miriam became more determined to see how her prophecy would be fulfilled. She faithfully "stood from a distance"[5] to watch over her brother.[6]

How does Miriam the Prophetess show readiness?

Miriam actively prepared for the redemption. As a midwife, she courageously defied Pharaoh's decrees and refused to participate in the drowning of baby boys in the Nile River. Instead, she soothed and comforted the newborns, ensuring their well-being.[7]

Miriam took decisive action to ensure the fulfillment of her prophecy through the birth of Moshe, the future redeemer. From the banks of the Nile, she vigilantly watched over Moshe, ready to call her mother to nurse him when Batya discovered the floating basket.

With unwavering confidence in the forthcoming

---

1 Devarim 8:17
2 Alshich
3 Metzudas Dovid, Ibn Ezra, Malbim
4 Midrash Shachar Tov
5 Shemos 2:4
6 Talmud, Megillah 14a and Sotah 13a; Pesikta Rabbati
7 Shemos 1:15, Rashi

redemption, Miriam prepared her tambourine, which symbolized her readiness to offer heartfelt praise to G-d. Finally, at the age of eighty-six, Miriam's prophecy came to fruition. She led the women's song of redemption during the awe-inspiring splitting of the sea. The Torah recounts, "And Miriam the Prophetess, the sister of Aharon, took the tambourine in her hand; and all he women went out after her with tambourines and dances."[8]

The tambourine, known as '*et hatof*,' indicates a special significance. It is the very same tambourine that Miriam used at her parents' wedding. She is identified as Aharon's sister, (*Achos* Aharon) emphasizing her role as a prophetess who foresaw the coming Redemption even before Moshe's birth.[9]

[8] Shemos 15:20
[9] Talmud, Megillah 14a; based on the talks of the Lubavitcher Rebbe for Shabbos Mevorchim Iyar 5736, 1976

Why did all the women have tambourines?

As the entire nation hurriedly left Egypt, they didn't even have time to bake bread for the journey to freedom. Despite this, they were prepared with tambourines. Rashi highlights the remarkable faith of the righteous women of that generation.

"The righteous women of that generation were so confident that the Holy One, Blessed be He, would make miracles for them that they took tambourines out of Egypt."[10]

Their unwavering trust in G-d's promise of redemption guided them to prepare in advance, firmly believing that there would come a time when they would sing, dance, and express their profound gratitude through the uplifting rhythms of tambourines.

[10] Shemos 15:20, Rashi

How was Miriam rewarded for paving the joyful path to Redemption?

G-d bestowed goodness upon the midwives, and the people multiplied and became very strong. It was because the midwives feared G-d that "He made houses for them."[11]

Yocheved, mother of Miriam, and Aaron, was blessed to mother Moshe thanks to Miriam's prophecy. From her children descended the House of Levi and Priests (*Kohanim*). Miriam, known as Puah, was privileged to mother the royal dynasty, the "House of David," from which the future redeemer, Moshiach, will emerge.[12]

Additionally, Miriam's grandson, Betzalel, was imbued with a spirit of wisdom and skillfully built the Mishkan, the holy sanctuary.

In Miriam's merit, a wellspring flowed and miraculously followed the Jews for forty years in the Wilderness. It was called "*Be'eras* Miriam — Miriam's Well."[13] From Mount Carmel, one can view the Mediterranean Sea and notice a sieve-like rock known as *Be'eras* Miriam.[14][15]

What is Miriam's message for us today?

Miriam serves as an inspiration to us by not merely hoping for redemption, but to actively prepare for it with determination. Despite living in challenging times, Miriam "strengthened her arms" and remained alert, ready to play her part. Miriam's example empowers us to demonstrate readiness and make choices today that contribute to the future of our people. When we encounter personal "Egypts" or limitations, we can choose not to succumb to fear but to approach the situation with confidence and prepare ourselves for our own redemption.

The initial redemption from Egypt took place due to the unwavering faith of righteous women who anticipated it by preparing their instruments during the period of exile. So too, the ultimate redemption, our *Geulah*, will be brought about through the *Nashim Tzidkaniyos* —the righteous women who are actively preparing for redemption and expressing their faith through dancing with their tambourines today.

Meaningful Melody

BEZCHUT NASHIM

Composition by Shmuel Marcus
Lyrics by 8th Day, Yosi Friedman
Rivkah Krinsky — granddaughter of Assia New ob"m

I know you although we've never met
A legacy we will not forget
A common thread since ancient times
Generations you've defined
Your image embedded in my mind

Sarah's candle's still burn bright
Rivkah's kindness brings the light

---

11 Exodus 1:20-21
12 Shemos 1:21, Rashi

13 Talmud, Taanis 9a
14 Talmud, Shabbos 35a
15 It is customary to drink a cup of hot tea on Motzei Shabbos when, by Jewish tradition, all natural water bodies are temporarily able to connect to Miriam's Well.

"*Ko tomar l'vet Yaakov*"
Tell them first, they need to know
Rachel and Leah's tears are by our side

Chorus:
Mothers and daughters
Who are reaching out to others
Tell them that it's up to you and me
Pharaoh and the others
Couldn't stop our holy mothers
Now we tell them that it's up to you and me

Bezchut nashim tzidkaniyot nigalu avoteinu[16]

From old to young your story's told
Your strength and beauty forged a mold
Heroines in daily life
Our anchor in times of strife
Your courage made us who we are

Devorah tell us prophecy
Miriam lead us in melody
Souls of then are souls of now
We are one and we'll witness how
Our faith brings redemption to the world

Daughters of Israel can you hear me?
Esther go and tell the king
Yehudit save your Maccabees
Daughters of Israel can you hear me?
Take this song for all to sing
It's our time in history

16 In the merit of the righteous women our ancestors were redeemed.

GOT TAMBOURINES!

Content and arranged by: Mrs. Esther Chanowitz
Lyrics: Chana Zirkind
Sung by: Mrs. Rachely Jacks
Music: Chanale Fellig Harel
Ttto: V'hu Yigaleinu

Miriam *Haneviah* knew it all along,
With her tambourine, her *emunah* stayed strong.
We have their *neshamot*, we will persevere!
Moshiach's almost here!

Miriam *Haneviah* knew it all along,
With her tambourine, her *emunah* stayed strong.
We have their *neshamot*, we will persevere!
Wave it in the air!

Od tadi tupayich,
Let's beautify our tambourines!
Veyatzat bimchol mesachakim,
Come on, let's dance and sing!

Od tadi tupayich,
Our tambourines are beautifying us,
Veyatzat bimchol mesachakim,
And unifying us!

Pearls of Wisdom

In the merit of the righteous women of that generation, our forefathers were redeemed from Egypt **and in the merit of the women today, we will be redeemed in the future.**

–Talmud, Sotah 11b

Aishes Chayil Story

The Face of a Believer

A TRIBUTE TO

Assia New OB"M

By her son, Rabbi Ruvi New

Two hundred and ten years of slavery had taken its toll on the Jewish men in Egypt. Such that even when Moshe first arrived on the scene to announce that redemption was near, "They didn't listen, because of brokenness of spirit." It was hard for them to imagine a life beyond slavery.

The women: different story. Slavery couldn't break their faith in redemption, nor their resolve to keep bringing Jewish children into the world, despite the risks, the danger, the darkness. While yet in Egypt they were preparing their tambourines for the anticipated celebration of redemption they never stopped believing in. These are the tambourines of resilience, of faith, of courage, of daring to believe in the possibility of a brighter tomorrow. And these were the tambourines with which they sang and danced when the redemption finally came.

During the Shiva after my mother's passing, Leah Zelwer, a family friend from Israel, showed me a tambourine that my mother had given to her. She said, "Your mother asked me to hold on to it and keep it for her, so that she will have a tambourine in Israel with which to sing, dance and celebrate when Moshiach comes."

A family friend from Israel showed me a tambourine that my mother had given to her. She said, "Your mother asked me to hold on to it and keep it for her, so that she will have a tambourine in Israel with which to sing, dance and celebrate when Moshiach comes."

Allowing that to sink in, it struck me how my mother's

faith in redemption was reminiscent of the Jewish women of Egypt. She too was raised in an "Egypt" of sorts – Communist Russia, where people were slaves to the state, under tyrannical dictators like Pharaoh. It was where harsh decrees were imposed upon the Jewish people to demoralize and destroy Jewish life, particularly targeting Jewish children, just as Pharaoh had done in his day.

Many succumbed to the power of the state, unable to fight back, unable to believe redemption was possible

> *She too was raised in an "Egypt" of sorts – Communist Russia, where people were slaves to the state, under tyrannical dictators like Pharaoh.*

"from shortness of spirit." Despite the odds stacked against her, my mother never lost her faith, optimism, or belief in redemption. She defied compulsory school attendance on Saturdays and Jewish holidays in Russia, risking severe consequences.

Forced to leave her home in Leningrad in 1941 with the onset of the war, embarking on an arduous journey to Tashkent where the family lived in one room with a mud floor until their return to Leningrad in 1945, the hardship of it all, never crushed her spirit. She was the big sister caring for her younger siblings, one of whom was Nechama who passed away in Tashkent after contracting pneumonia.

In 1946 my mother's family was part of what came to be known as "The Great Escape." The Polish government was allowing Polish citizens displaced by the war to return from Russia, back into Poland and Chabad activists were able to obtain hundreds of Polish passports for dozens of Chabad families. The escape was fraught with danger, as none of these Russian citizens were "Polish nationals" or could speak Polish. With faith and fortitude they miraculously crossed the border and after a brief stay in Vienna, were transferred to Paris.

After two years in Paris, the Previous Lubavitcher Rebbe directed his *Chassidim* to take up permanent residency in different places. My mother's family and four other Chabad families were encouraged to settle in far-off Australia to help build Jewish life in Australia.

After my family's resettlement in Australia, my mother became a pillar of the local Jewish community. She was fluent in multiple languages, and her elegance and poise were unparalleled. Despite all the demands on her time, she never stopped helping others, from cooking and baking to teaching and singing.

My mother possessed a beautiful operatic voice, which she put to use for charity concerts. Her repertoire of old Yiddish classics and contemporary Jewish and Israeli songs delighted her audiences, bringing them great joy and happiness. She recorded two studio albums: "Assia Sings."

She organized large-scale events to raise money for Children of Chernobyl, and her performances galvanized the emerging Jewish communities in Russia and Ukraine in the early nineties.

Although she never saw her music as a career, it was an essential part of her efforts to inspire others and raise money for worthy causes. Even in her sixties, my mother remained undaunted and unafraid, continuing to perform and inspire others. And there in her hand, as she sang and inspired, was her tambourine.

Thus, throughout her life, my mother's faith remained unshakable. Her tambourine was more than just a percussion instrument; it was a symbol of her resilience, optimism, and faith in redemption. She eagerly awaited

My mother possessed a beautiful operatic voice, which she put to use for charity concerts.

the arrival of Moshiach and the end of exile and pain. There was hardly a conversation that took place without her concluding the conversation with a wish that *"Moshiach zol shoin kumen,"* Moshaich should come already.

GROW as an Aishes Chayil

Gratitude: **Which choice are you grateful for?**

_____
_____
_____

Recognition: **Recognize the wise choices you can make today to shape your future.**

_____
_____
_____
_____

Oneness: **What is one positive action you can choose to prepare for the redemption?**

_____
_____
_____

What is a goal you have for the next two months? Next year? In five to ten years? What is one step you can take today towards your goal and to show readiness?

_____
_____
_____
_____
_____
_____

Wish: **What is your wish from G-d?**

_____
_____
_____
_____

ט

A Thread of Faith

*"She senses that her trade is profitable,
so her lamp is not extinguished at night."*

Digging Deeper

What does this verse mean?

The *Aishes Chayil* knows that her merchandise is good and so she works even at night.[1]

What is the deeper meaning?

We can understand the verse more deeply with the analogy of a business owner who invests money to buy merchandise. One will experience *pizur hanefesh*, "bitterness of spirit," due to not knowing if the venture will earn a profit. When one sells one's merchandise at a higher price than the initial investment, one rejoices and is comforted over the earlier pain. The profitable result was worth the risk.

What is analogous to the above scenario?

The investment of a soul in a body at birth is like a risky business venture. Just as one invests money into a business with pain, the soul within the body carries the burden of meeting its physical needs in a dark and difficult world.

The *neshama* experiences distress, yearning to succeed in its earthly mission yet wondering whether it will be spiritually profitable.

When is life in this world profitable for the soul?

Chassidus teaches that at the time of creation, sparks of G-dliness were scattered and hidden throughout the world. When we observe mitzvos, the sparks are elevated. When we reveal those sparks, our soul's descent becomes profitable, and it shines brighter than before it entered this world.

Torah study, too, is our merchandise and trade. In the night of *golus*, the unwavering trade of Torah empowers us to persevere and illuminate the darkness.[2]

"*Ki neir Hashem nishmat adam* — The soul of a person is G-d's candle."[3] Despite the challenges a person faces, the soul, which is "truly a piece of G-d above,"[4] can never be extinguished. Just as a flame persistently flickers upward toward its source, the *neshama* always strives to reach closer to G-d.[5] This powers each soul to reveal the Divine sparks in this world.

"If a person finds himself in a situation he feels he cannot handle, he has to remember that he has a part of G-d that is "*Ein Sof* — unlimited," the essence of his soul. By tapping into the unlimited soul, he can handle any situation."[6]

When will the soul receive its full reward?

We have endured the exile and been scattered, with the purpose of elevating the hidden sparks of G-dliness in this world. With the arrival of Moshiach, all the light we have generated in the darkness will be revealed. This revelation, the profit of our investment during exile, will surpass even the G-dly revelations in the days of the Holy Temple and the giving of the Torah. Let us fervently pray to G-d and declare our unwavering readiness to celebrate the abundance of our spiritual wealth with the coming of Moshiach, when we will joyfully proclaim, "It was all worth the trouble!"[7]

---

1 Metzudas Dovid
2 Alshich
3 Mishlei 20:7
4 Tanya, chapter 2
5 Tanya, chapter 19
6 Rabbi Greenglass of Montreal, ob"m
7 Toras Chaim by the Mitteler Rebbe, page 198

WOMEN IN THE TORAH
Chana

"*Ta'amah ta'am tefillah* — Chana tasted the flavor of prayer," as it is written,[8] "And Chana prayed, 'My heart exults in G-d.'"

As a result, she merited a son who was equal to Moshe and Aharon, illuminating Israel like candles, as it is stated:[9] "Moshe and Aharon among his priests, and Shmuel among those who call His (G-d's) name." Furthermore, it is written about Shmuel:[10] "The lamp of G-d had not yet gone out, and Shmuel was sleeping in the Temple of G-d."[11]

What was Chana's deepest wish?

Chana experienced the pain of being childless and yearned deeply to become a mother. She faced the taunts of Penina, her husband Elkanah's second wife, who had seven children. In a world that seemed dark, Chana's unwavering faith kept her inner flame burning bright. Through heartfelt prayer, she revealed a great light.

Elkanah, trying to console Chana, asked her, "Chana, why do you weep? Why do you not eat? Why is your heart sad? Am I not better to you than ten sons?"[12] In his questions, Elkanah implied that if G-d had not granted her a child, perhaps there was another purpose for her soul to fulfill in this world.

How did Chana respond to her husband?

Chana did not reply to her husband's comment, as she understood that his suggestion was misguided. While she appreciated her husband's compassion, she knew deep within that her wish for children was essential to fulfilling her soul's mission. The faith and yearning within her soul, her inner flame, remained unextinguished, and she continued to fervently pray.

Where and how did Chana express her prayer?

Chana's family arrived in Shiloh on a pilgrimage to

---

8 Shmuel I 2:1
9 Tehillim 99:6
10 Shmuel I 3:3:
11 Midrash Shachar Tov

12 Shmuel I 1:8

the *Mishkan*, where the *Shechinah* dwelled before King Shlomo established the *Beis Hamikdash* in Jerusalem.

Chana's anguish over her childlessness stemmed not only from personal yearning but from a deeper desire to serve G-d with her entire being, to fully use all of her organs for Him. This included the gift of motherhood and nursing a child.[13] She promised to dedicate her son to G-d by bringing him to serve in the Sanctuary.

She prayed to G-d, weeping profusely: "Master of Legions, if you take note of the suffering of your maidservant, and You remember me, and give your maidservant a son, then I shall dedicate him to G-d all the days of his life."[14]

How did the High Priest respond to Chana's prayer?

Eli the *Kohain Gadol* observed Chana praying before G-d. Her lips were moving but her voice was not heard, so Eli thought she was drunk. He said to her, "How long shall you be drunk? Put away your wine!"[15]

How could Eli accuse Chana of being drunk?

He was implicitly asking her, "Why are you drunk by indulging in your personal wants and desires on Rosh Hashanah, when we crown G-d as King? How can you be so selfish as to stand on the holiest place on earth and ask for your personal needs? And if you must ask for them, is this the time and place to pray with such passion?"

How did Chana respond to Eli?

"You misunderstand me," answered Chana. "I am a woman of sorrowful spirit. I have not drunk wine or strong drink, but I have poured out my soul before G-d."[16]

She explained that her request stemmed from her soul so that she might dedicate a son to G-d for all the days of his life.

What was Chana's greatest "profit"?

Despite the darkness, Chana tasted the gift of prayer with faith in her soul's mission. She merited a son, the prophet Shmuel, who, like Moshe and Aharon, brought light to Israel!

What does Chana teach us about prayer?

Chana serves as a powerful example of the essence of prayer. Her story teaches us that our physical needs are not separate from our spiritual ones; instead, all the gifts we receive from G-d can be used to serve Him. This concept is beautifully expressed in the prayer "*Nishmat Kol Chai*," which acknowledges that "the limbs that You have arranged within us, the spirit and soul that You have breathed into our nostrils, and the tongue that You have placed into our mouth, they all shall thank, bless, praise, glorify, exalt, adore and proclaim the kingship of Your name, our King..."[17]

When we pray to G-d, we ask for financial resources to contribute to charity (*tzedakah*), strength to build a sukkah, and nourishment for our bodies and souls. We recognize that these physical necessities enable us to create a "dwelling for G-d" on earth. Our wishes and needs are a reflection of our soul's deep yearning to serve G-d.

For instance, we may find ourselves drawn to a specific

---

13 Talmud, Berachos 31,b
14 Shmuel I 1:11
15 Shmuel I 1:14

16 Shmuel I 1:15
17 Shabbos Liturgy

garment because our soul senses a hidden spark of G-dliness within it, waiting to be revealed. Our unique tastes and desires are manifestations of our individual missions in life, and they express the unwavering flame of our soul burning within us.[18]

Is it important for women to pray?

Chana's story demonstrates to us the power of a woman's prayer. In the following story, the Lubavitcher Rebbe provides encouragement to Mrs. Chaya Hecht ob"m, to engage in prayer.

Mrs. Chaya Hecht, a mother of several young children, was asked by the Rebbe, "Do you pray every day?" She responded that she recites the *Shema* and the Morning Blessings daily but does not have the opportunity to complete the entire prayer service due to her responsibilities in caring for her children. She explained, "I need to be in tune with them, so I don't have the time to concentrate properly on my prayers."

The Rebbe replied, "If you would ask me if you should pray, then I would tell you that, yes, you should pray every day, from beginning to end. The best way is to do it a little bit at a time, adding more each day until you can complete all the prayers. Do that every day. Don't be concerned with the children when you are praying — find somebody to watch them for that amount of time."

The Rebbe's words were a source of strength and inspiration for her. She made a firm commitment to pray every day, and this decision had a profound impact on her life. Reflecting on her experience, she remarked, "The Rebbe ensured that I took care of myself both physically and spiritually by urging me to pray daily and maintain a connection with G-d. He set my life in front of me, guiding me through all the years I've been on this earth."[19]

---

18 Adapted from Likkutei Sichos, vol. 19

19 Copyright and reprinted with permission of Chabad.org. Source: JEM

Meaningful Melody

VATISPALEL CHANA

by Chanale Fellig

On a mountain of Israel, two women are known One walks with children, while one walks alone Day after day turns to year after year
The burning inside turns to pain she can't bear

No words can console her, no love can replace Her arms start to tremble, her whole body shakes
A womb oh so empty, a heart filled with pain Her grief knows no boundaries and tears pour like rain

Vatispalel Chana, she prays all the while
Have I been forgotten, don't I get a child?
I don't ask for many, just give me one
And in return your maid Chana, will give You her son

Eli Ha'Cohen watches from far
Daughter of Israel tell me who you are
Your whispers have traveled; your home will be blessed
So now go in peace, for He'll grant your request

Her *Tefilos* accepted, her prayers are heard
He gives her a child, she gives Him her word
A son only borrowed, a son she won't raise
Her joy knows no boundaries, and G-d she does praise

Vatispalel Chana she turns to the sky
Hashem is my Savior, *Hashem* upon high
En Tzur Kelokainu, Hashem You are One
And blessed be Your Name, for You gave me a son
And blessed be Your Name, now I give You my son

Dedicated in honor of a true Aishes Chayil,

Nechama Dina Laber

our remarkable and inspirational mentor.

We thank you for your tireless efforts, your tenacity, your unwavering emunah in all possibilities, and your dedication to Hashem, your family, and your JGU girls!

We love you, Yaffah and Shoshana Ferber

Pearls of Wisdom

The mission of every human being is to bring the many things of this chaotic world into harmony with their inner purpose and the oneness that underlies them. To do this, each of us must have those elements related to our mission: our family, our health, our homes, our income.

We pray for these things from our innermost heart; our soul pours out in yearning for them—

because our soul knows that without them, she cannot fulfill her mission in this world.

-Copyright and reprinted with permission of Chabad.org

Aishes Chayil Story

Dedicated by Goldie Tennenhaus, Azriel & Chana Wasserman, children and grandchildren of Miriam Fellig

Be A Warrior, not a Worrier!

A TRIBUTE TO

Miriam Fellig OB"M

By Mendel Super

It was 1951. Eighteen years old, newly married and expecting her first child, Miriam Fellig was alone. She had her husband, Joe (Yosef Mordechai) Fellig, but all her family had perished in the Holocaust. She traveled from her home in Montreal to meet the Rebbe — Rabbi Menachem M. Schneerson — who had only recently assumed the leadership of Chabad-Lubavitch.

She confided in the Rebbe, telling him about her dreams and fears. She wanted to have a large family, she told the Rebbe, but she had no family to help her. Would the Rebbe adopt her? Without hesitation, the Rebbe answered in the affirmative, and thus began a decades-long relationship between a young mother and a leader of world Jewry.

Miriam Fellig "recognized that her trade is profitable,"

Miriam Felling and her husband

the value of investing time and resources in raising a family. Despite facing darkness and loss, "her faith is not extinguished" and she declared, "I am going to have as many kids as I can because I will never talk about the Holocaust, but I have to do something about it."

Miriam, who passed away on November 12, 2021 at the age of 89, told the USC Shoah Foundation in an interview, recalling her words to her newlywed husband. "And I am going to have a name for everyone in my family so they will never be forgotten, and I am going to have children that will want to have children. I am going to do to Hitler what he did to me. He took everything away, and I am going to bring it back. I am not going to just be defeated and talk about it, cry about it, light candles; I am going to have living monuments… 10 months after [marriage], I had my first son."

As she had no parents, aunts or uncles, the Rebbe was the only person Miriam had to show her children off to. Every year, the family would drive from Montreal to Brooklyn and proudly present the children to the Rebbe. The Rebbe listened to her worries, fears and challenges, and counseled her as a parent would.

"Be a warrior, not a worrier," the Rebbe told Miriam in a private audience, her daughter wrote in the N'shei Chabad Newsletter. When she told the Rebbe that no matter how hard she tried, she couldn't keep her house neat and tidy with her growing young brood, the Rebbe gently replied, "But I see your husband, and he looks happy."

> *"I am not going to just be defeated and talk about it, cry about it, light candles; I am going to have living monuments…"*

It was the Rebbe's fatherly guidance and care that helped Miriam cope with the loss of her entire family. "She would ask the Rebbe whatever she wanted," says her son-in-law Raphy Tennenhaus. "How do you still thank G-d after you lost everything?" a granddaughter once asked her. Miriam replied that it was the Rebbe's love for her that got her through it.

Her devotion to her family and her connection with the Rebbe helped her secure a signed letter from the Rebbe in honor of her son—in-law's and daughter's new Chabad center in Hallandale, Florida. "The Rebbe's secretariat told us that the Rebbe wasn't sending personalized letters anymore for these occasions," notes Goldie Tennenhaus, but her mother persisted. "My son-in-law works so hard," she told the Rebbe's secretary Rabbi Binyamin Klein. "Maybe the Rebbe can send us a letter?"

Beginning in 1985, they received personalized letters for their annual dinners from the Rebbe. The last letter they received, in 1992, was in fact the last letter the Rebbe signed—the secretariat later informed Tennenhaus—just hours before he suffered a major stroke while visiting his father-in-law and predecessor's graveside in Queens.

"My mother showed us how to fiercely love, protect and fight for our spouse and family. She taught her children and grandchildren to believe in G-d, to hold the Torah dear, and to love the Rebbe and trust in his words."[1]

[1] Reprinted with permission and copyright of Chabad.org.

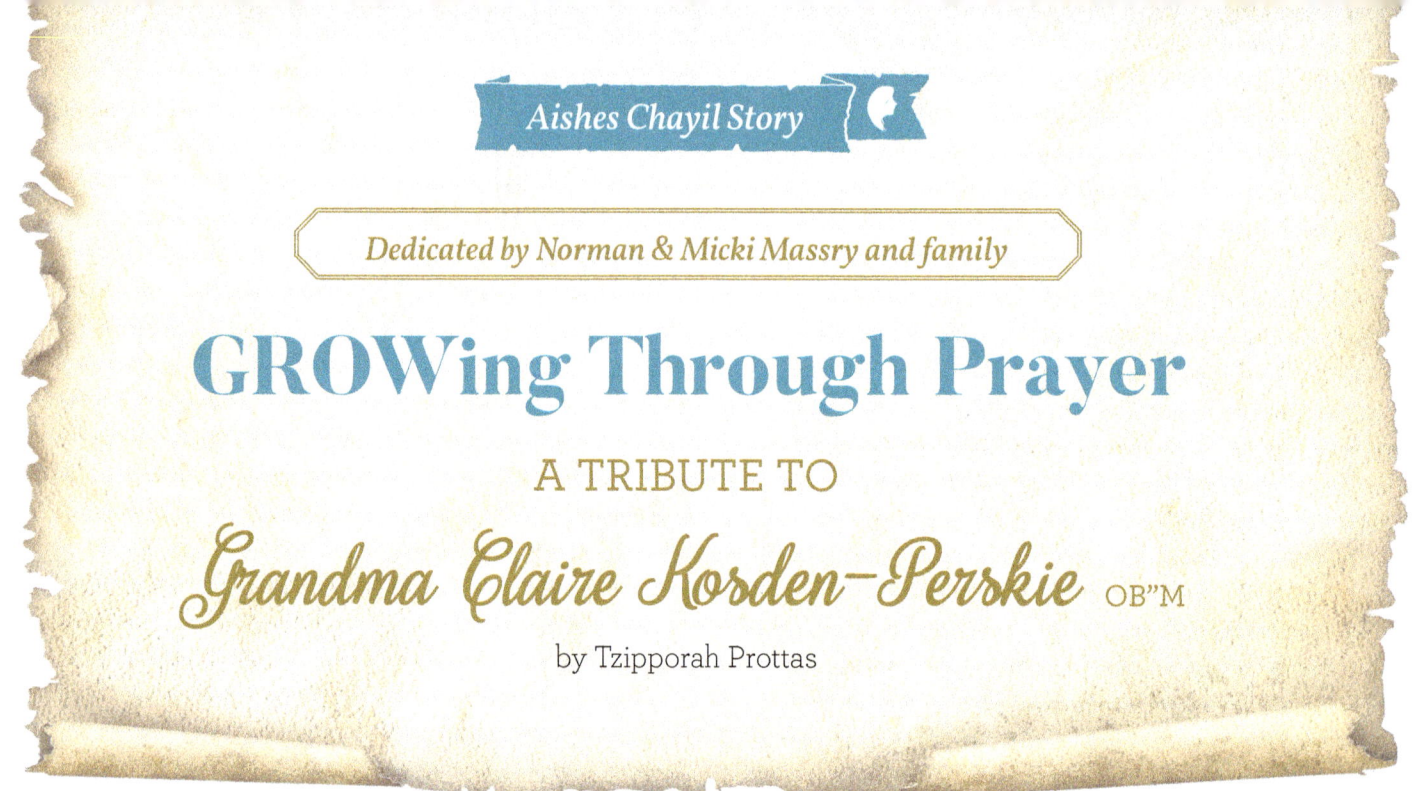

GROWing Through Prayer

A TRIBUTE TO

Grandma Claire Kosden-Perskie OB"M

by Tzipporah Prottas

As the first Yartzeit approached, Micki Massry wanted to honor the legacy of her mother, Claire Kosden-Perskie ob"m — a Holocaust survivor who exemplified faith, fortitude and connection to family. As the daughter of a renowned *chazzan* of Prague's *Altneuschul* ("Old-New") Synagogue before World War Two, Claire was infused with a love for faith and prayer from her earliest youth.

Micki shared with Nechama that despite all the difficulties her mother lived through, she was the most loving mother to her daughters and their children. She spoke the language of connection, praying for them and showering them with unconditional love.

Each day, even when she wasn't well, she would recite the *Shema*, proclaiming faith in One G-d; and each Friday, she kindled her Shabbos lights with personal prayers.

Micki told Nechama that in her later years, Claire asked her daughters Sheryl, Micki, and Ava, "Who will say Kaddish for me? Who will pray for me?"

"I will," Micki answered. "I will make sure we pray and say Kaddish."

Micki shared that she deeply misses her mother's connection. She also yearns to connect with the words of the Hebrew prayers more meaningfully.

As Nechama heard more about Micki's wish and her mother's request to her three daughters, she knew that

In her later years, Claire asked her daughters Sheryl, Micki, and Ava, "Who will say Kaddish for me? Who will pray for me?"

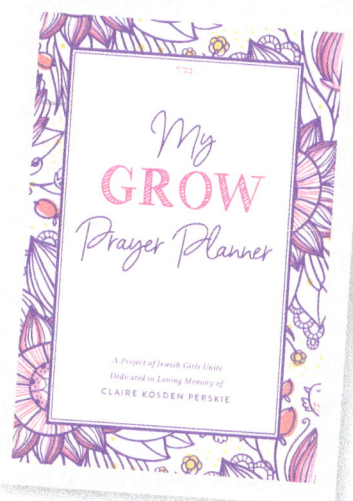

Nechama Laber training educators in the GROW Method, in memory of Claire Kosden-Perskie

developing the GROW Method would be a fitting legacy for Claire Kosden-Perskie — Chaya bas *Hachazzan* Yaakov V'Esther.

The GROW Method of Prayer is an acronym for Gratitude, Recognition, Oneness, and Wishes. It is designed to help individuals personalize their prayer experience by incorporating these four concepts into their daily practice. The method is universal, meaning it can be used by anyone regardless of age, personality, or background. By following the GROW Method, individuals can deepen their connection to their Core, Creator and community.

Since its launch by JGU in August 2021, the GROW Connection Network has grown into a global initiative empowering women and students worldwide, with expanding GROW Connection Circles and GROW Mentors leading in their schools and communities. The network also provides creative resources published by the JGU Press, including GROW planners with short reflections, writing prompts, and doodling space to apply the GROW Method of Prayer to life.

GROW Mentor Terri Klein says, "At GROW Circle, women of all backgrounds belong. It is a judgment-free and safe space for moving from a place of disconnect to connection." GROW Mentor Shaindel Leanse adds, "When I come [to this group], I feel connected to the whole, to the Oneness in me."

Ultimately, the story of Micki Massry and her mother reminds us that even in the face of challenges and loss, we can choose to approach life with a spirit of gratitude and a willingness to grow. Life is not always perfect, but we can always turn to prayer and GROW through it. The power of prayer gives us the strength to transform life's irritations into pearls and inspire others to do the same.

"My grandmother loved life, and when her grandchildren would visit she made sure they had a wonderful time interacting with her. Most important to her was that we continue to follow along her path of connection to our faith," recalls her granddaughter, Julie.

GROW as an *Aishes Chayil*

Gratitude: **What are the blessings that you prayed for that you can be grateful for today?**

_____
_____
_____
_____

Recognition: **What are ways that you fuel your inner candle, your soul?**

_____
_____
_____
_____
_____
_____

Oneness: **Gaze at a burning candle and feel your soul, your inner flame, flickering. If it could speak, what is the mission it is yearning to fulfill? What is your next step?**

_____
_____
_____
_____
_____
_____

Wish: **What is a physical item that you need in order to fulfill your soul's mission?**

_____
_____
_____

A Thread of Feminine Strength

"She puts her hand to the spindle, and her palms support the distaff."

Digging Deeper

What does this verse mean?

Although the *Aishes Chayil*'s mind is on her business ventures, she does not neglect her skills and uses her tools for weaving.[1]

What are a spindle and distaff?

Throughout history, spinners have used a device called a distaff which is a wooden board to which the fibers of raw material are tied and prepared to be spun.[2]

Kishor is a spindle, the tool used by the spinner.[3] Spinning is the action of twisting fiber, such as wool, cotton, or flax, into thread to be woven, knitted, or crocheted into fabric. The spinner draws the fibers from the distaff and spins them with a spindle.

The Hebrew word "*kishor*" (כִּישׁוֹר) is derived from "*kisharon*," (כִּשָׁרוֹן) meaning skill and talent. G-d endows each person with a unique set of tools and talents, and the woman of valor utilizes hers while also providing for her family. She fulfills the Divine mission of weaving G-dliness into the physical world with her unique abilities. In partnership with G-d, every Jew has a role in weaving the tapestry, which will be completed with the redemption.

WOMEN IN THE TORAH
Yael & Devorah

In the war with Devorah and Barak, Yael killed Sisera with a tent peg using the strength of her hands. Why did she not use a typical weapon? She fulfilled the mitzvah,[4] "There shall not be the vessel of a man on a woman," which prohibits women from wearing men's military garb.[5]

When did Yael use her feminine strengths with Devorah the Prophetess?

In the period when judges ruled Israel, Devorah led the Jewish people for over forty years. During her leadership, Israel was subject to King Yavin of Canaan and his cruel general, Sisera. Her husband, Barak, was the commander. In a decisive battle at the foot of Mount Tabor by the brook of Kishon, G-d delivered Yavin's armies into Jewish hands. Sisera fled the battlefield on foot and sought refuge in the tent of Yael, a righteous non-Jew.

"Give me now a little water to drink, for I am thirsty," he said. Instead, she gave him a flask of milk and covered him to make him drowsy. Once he fell into a deep sleep, Yael took a hammer and tent-peg and drove it through Sisera's skull, and he died.[6]

---

1 Metzudas Dovid
2 Rashi
3 Metzudat Tzion

4 Devarim 22:5
5 Midrash Shachar Tov
6 Shoftim 4:1-21

We see that she did not require masculine weapons of war to save the Jews — only a simple tent peg in her own home.

How did Devorah use her feminine strengths?

Devorah modestly counseled her people from under a palm tree, which is straight, tall, and shadeless, so she would not be secluded with men.

As a skilled wick-maker, Devorah spun wicks for the lamps in the *Mishkan*. She encouraged her husband to deliver the wicks so that the holy environment would kindle his flame of inspiration for Torah learning. Thus, he was called "*Lapidot* — Torch." G-d rewarded Devorah's actions with the gift of prophecy, saying, "Since you desired to increase My light, I will increase your light." Her spiritual light shone over the Jewish people as a warrior and the only female judge in Jewish history.[7]

Yael and Devorah demonstrate how our creative, feminine strengths can shape the Jewish future.

How did Devorah praise Yael?

After leading Israel to a miraculous military victory, Devorah praised G-d with her own song, in similar fashion to Miriam's Song at the Sea.

"Blessed by women is Yael; by women in the tent she will be blessed," Devorah sang. "Sisera requested water; she gave him milk. In a stately saucer she brought cream. Yael stretched her hand to the peg and her right hand to the workman's hammer. She hammered Sisera, pierced his head [with the peg], smashed and pierced his temple."[8]

In the song, Devorah also described her own leadership, saying: "I arose, Devorah, I arose as a mother in Israel."[9]

This is puzzling, as we have no commentary discussing her children or whether she had any. It would make more sense for Devorah to describe herself as a general, leader, judge, and prophetess.

What can we learn from Devorah who chooses the title of "Mother in Israel"?

Devorah's message to all Jewish women is that we are first and foremost **mothers!**

7 Rashi, Shoftim 4:4; Eliyahu Rabbah, chapter 9
8 Shoftim 5:24-26

9 Shoftim 5:7

In her various leadership roles, she exemplified feminine, mother-like qualities.

As a wife at home, she spun wicks for her husband to bring to the *Mishkan*, where he was able to grow in Torah.

As a prophetess and judge under her palm tree, she supported the Jewish people spiritually and emotionally and raised them to become "a light unto the nations."

As a military general on the battlefield, she fought like a mother for the Children of Israel, for their peace and security so that they could fulfill their potential.

We are all mothers when we nurture others with our Divine feminine gifts, as Yael and Devorah did. We educate and empower others to shine, create a peaceful environment, and inspire love and connection to G-d.

What does the Lubavitcher Rebbe say about Chassidic Feminism?

"A man's mission in life is to "conquer" the material world and transform it into a home for G-d. This is not to say that the woman is not involved in the transformation of the 'outside' world. In addition to her primary role of nurturing holiness within herself, her home and her community, her influence extends beyond these realms. But also when she ventures out, she does so with 'innerness,' with her distinctively feminine traits of modesty, dignity and gentleness."[10]

WOMEN IN THE TORAH
Desert Women

How did the Jewish women contribute their feminine strengths to build the Mishkan?

They gave their precious jewelry, mirrors, and talents to build G-d's home in the desert. The Torah states, "And the men brought donations, in addition to the women."[11] This means that the women gave first, and their donations were greater than the men's donations.

Why was the quality of the women's donations superior?

In addition to giving their jewelry and mirrors, the talented women demonstrated their exceptional craftsmanship by fashioning gifts with exquisite care. Remarkably, they even "spun the goat hair" while it was still on the goats, showcasing their unique skill and great joy in fulfilling this challenging task. Their contributions reflected the devotion and dedication of the women in building the *Mishkan*.[12] [13]

A closer look...

Women are not obligated to fulfill time-constrained positive mitzvos, such as the construction of the *Mishkan*. Their participation involved mitzvos that

---

10 From an address by the Rebbe, autumn 1989 (free translation)

11 Shemos 35:22
12 Rashi on Shemos 35:26, quoting Talmud, Shabbos 74b
13 The men's gifts were only inanimate matter, yet the women's gift of spun goat-hair, still attached to the animal, held the elevated status of a living being. -Likkutei Sichos: vol. 7 — Shemos for Parshas Vayakhel

included them. For instance, they could contribute materials for constructing a roof, allowing them to bring offerings inside the building. The Lubavitcher Rebbe questions, why the women would weave goat-hair curtains if the *Mishkan* already had a cover?

At first glance, these curtains may seem excessive or even contradictory to the technical laws. However, the Torah commends the women's donation because it falls under the mitzvah of offering their time and talents to serve G-d.

What is the takeaway for our lives?

The women's donation of woven goat-hair curtains demonstrates that our G-d given talents and tools are meant to be utilized to serve G-d. When we use our unique instruments for holiness, we weave G-dliness into the physical world. And when we accept the responsibility to utilize our strengths, G-d gives us the ability. We all have a part in building G-d's home, and we are obligated to use our talents to contribute to that holy endeavor.[14]

14 Likkutei Sichos, vol. 26, Parshat Vayakhel

ONE MORE LIGHT

This song launched the JGU One More Light Campaign
Written and composed by Rivka Leah Popack

Did you hear the story told
As each soul comes to this world
It answers the purpose of creation

Do you believe that it could be
A single soul, like you or me
Could change the world and all we see forever

Plant a seed and watch it grow
Drop a stone, the ripples flow
Farther than you'd ever know

The sea is vast, the ocean's wide
But greater is your will inside
A simple act can change the tide

Yes I believe, like the sunrise each day
You light up the world each time that you pray
I believe like a flame burning bright
You shine through the darkness with each Friday light
A moment the world is waiting for
For you and your one more

Your one more light (4X)

Reach within to find your art
The colors that define your heart
Each of us can paint our part

Inspire me, I'll inspire you
You'll hit a wall, I'll pull you through
Heart and soul in everything we do

A million beats of a million hearts
Flames collide and outshine the stars
One melody with a thousand parts

Yes I believe, like the sunrise each day
You light up the world each time that you pray
I believe, like a flame burning bright
You shine through the darkness with each Friday light
A moment the world is waiting for
Let us light just one more

Sheker hachen vehevel hayofi,
Isha yirat Hashem he tit'halal
T'nu la mipri yadeha,
Vi'yhaleluha bashearim maseha

[Charm is deceptive and beauty is naught
A G-D fearing woman is the one to be praised
Give her praise for her accomplishments
And let her deeds laud her at the gates]

Chorus

I believe, like the sunrise each day
We'll light up the world

Pearls of Wisdom

Your talent is G-d's gift to you. *What you do with it* is your gift to G-d.

-Leo Buscaglia

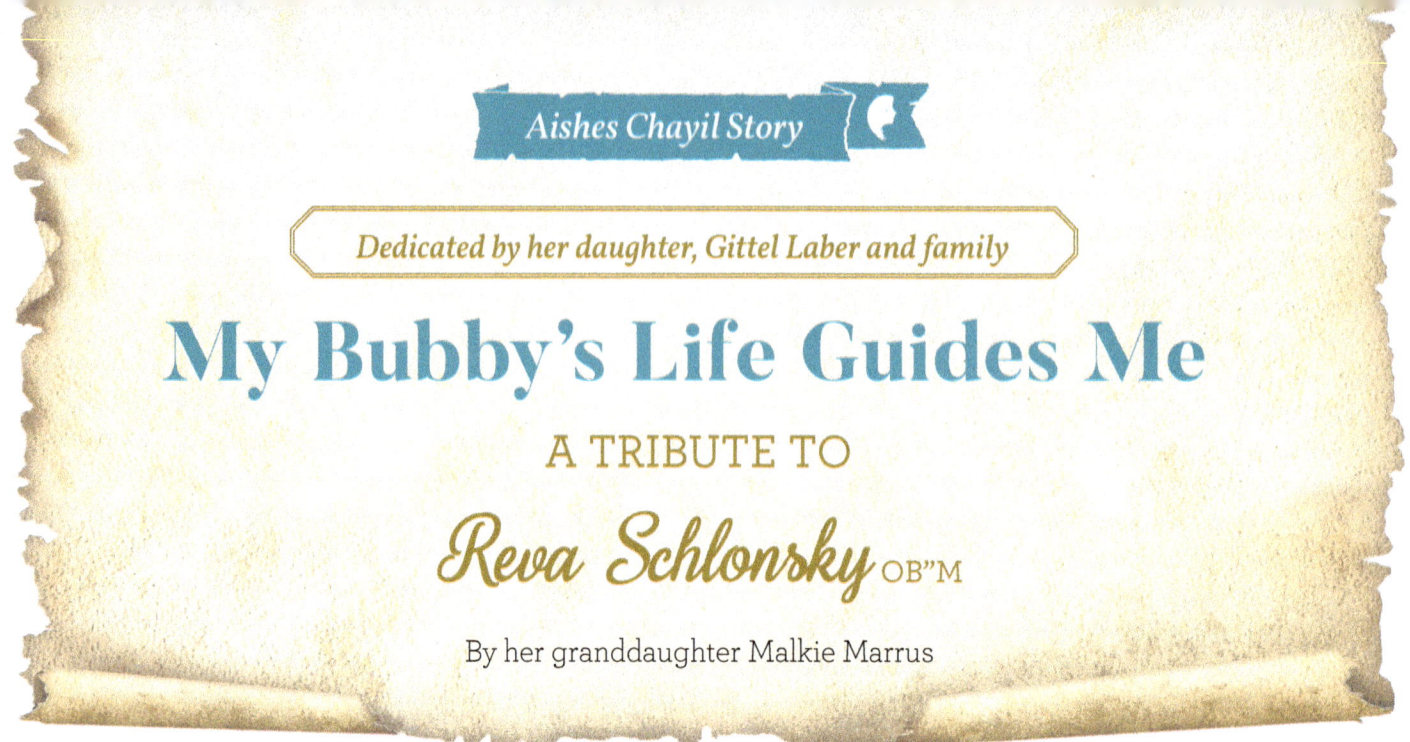

Aishes Chayil Story

Dedicated by her daughter, Gittel Laber and family

My Bubby's Life Guides Me

A TRIBUTE TO

Reva Schlonsky OB"M

By her granddaughter Malkie Marrus

I felt Bubby's love every time we were together, even when it was over FaceTime or a phone call. I wish to love my children fiercely and express my love and excitement.

When I started to bake challah for the public, Bubby sent me an article about a man who baked bread for others and how much joy it gave him. I was so touched that she took the time to encourage my interests and endeavors. I wish to be real, and make connections like she did.

At every wedding, and I have 8 siblings ka"h, Bubby exclaimed, "I hope I can make it to the next one." She made it to her great granddaughter's wedding, that of Chaya (Laber) Shepherd in NY. I wish to participate in as many family Simchos as I can.

Bubby was a ferocious reader. She wrote poetry and essays, and some were published. She belonged to a writers' club and explored different styles of writing. I wish to read and write more!

Bubby participated in family Zoom meetings. My 99 1/2 year old grandmother had Facebook, WhatsApp and even an Instagram account to stay connected to her family and friends. She loved to follow our activities and always commented on posts and pictures. I wish to learn new technologies and apps.

Bubby and her first husband, Emil, opened a business

Every time one of her children posted a fundraiser for their Shul or school, she was one of the first to contribute.

called "Reitman's Cameras and Cards." She supported his passion for boating. He suffered a heart attack on his boat when I was six years old and unfortunately passed away. Despite this loss, she remarried a few years later and built a beautiful life with her second husband, Dave Schlonsky. She became a stepmom to three adult children. Estee was a paraplegic, and my grandmother cared for her and loved her like a daughter.

I wish to travel and live life fully!

Bubby mailed checks every Chanukah for every grandchild and great-grandchild. Every time one of her children posted a fundraiser for their Shul or school, she was one of the first to contribute. I wish to give Chanukah Gelt to my grandchildren and great-grandchildren, G-d willing. I intend to give to as many charities as I can.

Bubby managed the greeting cards at the Milwaukee Jewish Home gift shop for many years. Every day of the week there was something specific she was involved with. I wish to volunteer and contribute to my community.

My great-grandmother Anna Selensky had scoliosis and needed care in her later years. She lived in the Jewish Old Age home and Bubby would spend time with her mother every day! She would take us often to visit her. She modeled love and respect for parents. My mother, Gittel, FaceTimed her mother every day.

Bubby dancing with her great granddaughter Chaya (Laber) Shepherd

I wish to share a bond with my mother as Bubby modeled for me.

Bubby had so many close friends over the years, who truly cared for each other like sisters. When Bubby's friends passed on, she was very pained. She said she knew she was getting old when her friends were the age of her daughter. I wish to invest in my friendships!

Dear Bubby, I'm so grateful that you were such a huge part of my life for so many years. I wish to continue giving you *nachas* as you smile with pride at your family forever.

"She stretches forth her hands to the spindle, and her palms support the distaff." Bubby used her talents and the tools she was given, including technology, to support and spread love to her family and friends until her passing at the ripe old age of 99 years old.

GROW as an Aishes Chayil

Gratitude: **I am grateful that I am...**

I am grateful that I have...

I am grateful that I can...

I am grateful that I feel...

I am grateful that I think...

I am grateful that I was...

Recognition: **Recognize two skills that are important for a Jewish woman to have today and explain why.**

Recognize your own skills and talents.

Oneness: **How can you use your unique tools and talents in partnership with G-d?**

Wish: **What is your wish from G-d?**

כ

A Thread of Tzedakah

"She spreads out her palm to the poor and extends her hands to the needy."

Digging Deeper

What does the repetition in this verse mean?

After we describe the *Aishes Chayil*'s business ventures and feminine strengths, we praise her dedication to *tzedakah*.

"She spreads out her palm to the poor" means that the *Aishes Chayil* opens her hand so the poor can take her gift and does not close her hand to keep it for herself.

"She extends her hands to the needy" means that she is sensitive to the needs of the people in her life and reaches out to those who are ashamed to ask for support.[1] When the needy suffer at home and do not ask for help, she discreetly brings them food. The Sages say that a woman's charity is more significant because she offers prepared food, which gives the recipient pleasure.[2]

The *Aishes Chayil* skillfully extends her hands to weave and sew clothing for those in need, offering her help without waiting for requests. In Hebrew, '*Oni*' (עוני) signifies a person facing financial hardship, while '*Evyon*' (אביון) refers to someone even more impoverished. Her assistance to the '*Oni*' is symbolized by the use of her '*Kappa*' (כפה) – one hand – and for the '*Evyon*' (אביון) she employs '*Yodeha*' (ידיה) – two hands – emphasizing her commitment to giving even more generously.[3]

What does the word "tzedakah" mean?

Tzedakah in Hebrew means "justice." The act of giving charity is different from the act of giving *tzedakah*. Charity means giving in order to be nice and to consider oneself as sweet and generous. *Tzedakah*, an act of justice, focuses on the obligation to help others in need.

By giving to others, we declare that the money does not belong to us, but rather is to be shared. When we struggle to part with our wealth, we are holding onto the belief that it is ours to keep. However, recognizing that everything comes from G-d to share with others empowers us to be giving and generous.

A stingy person is compared to a wire trying to hold on to electricity. This would be absurd, since the whole purpose of the wire is to conduct electricity. However, a person who gives generously understands that he is plugged into G-d, the source of all blessings, and a portion of one's wealth is meant to be passed on.[4]

Commentaries[5] remark that *tzedakah* is the only mitzvah by which G-d allows us to test Him, and He promises us abundance in return.

What are the eight levels of giving tzedakah?

In his *Mishneh Torah*,[6] the Rambam defined the following eight levels of charity, each higher than the next:

1. Giving a poor person work or loaning him money to start a business so he will not have to depend on charity.
2. Giving *tzedakah* anonymously to an unknown recipient.
3. Giving *tzedakah* anonymously to a known

---

1 Metzudas Dovid
2 Chomat Anach, Ibn Ezra; Talmud, Taanis
3 Alshich

4 Excerpted and adapted with permission from Seeing G-d by Rabbi D. Aaron
5 Malachi 3:10
6 Hilchos Matanos Aniyim 10:1,7-14

4. Giving *tzedakah* publicly to an unknown recipient.
5. Giving *tzedakah* before being asked.
6. Giving adequately after being asked.
7. Giving willingly, but inadequately.
8. Giving unwillingly.

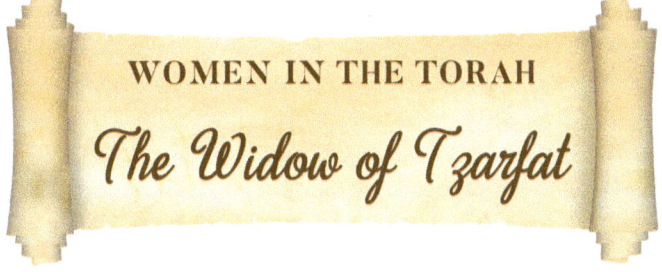

WOMEN IN THE TORAH
The Widow of Tzarfat

She was a paradigm of generosity, who sustained the Prophet Eliyahu in a desperate time with bread and water.[7]

When and how did the Widow of Tzarfat sustain Eliyahu?

G-d had struck Israel with famine brought on by drought as punishment for becoming caught up in idolatry. At this same time, Eliyahu, a G-d-fearing prophet, was a fugitive from the wicked King Achav who sought to kill him. He fled to a brook near the River Jordan, where G-d sent ravens to miraculously smuggle him food.

Eventually, G-d directed Eliyahu to Tzarfat, where a widow would continue to assist him. She kindly drew water for the thirsty traveler, but hesitated when he requested some bread: "If I have a morsel, it is nothing but a fistful of flour and a bit of oil in a flask. I am gathering two twigs, and I will come and make this for my son and myself. We will eat it, and G-d should have pity on us, or then we may die of hunger."

"Go home, knead and bake the flour and the oil," Eliyahu replied, "then bring me a loaf. Thereafter, you and your son shall eat."[8]

What was the widow's reward for giving a stranger her last piece of bread?

G-d reassured her through Eliyahu that he would never let her flour or oil run out until the rains returned. Indeed, her vessels stayed continuously full until food was no longer scarce. In gratitude, she begged Eliyahu to lodge in her home and fed him for as long as he wanted to stay.

7 Midrash Shachar Tov

8 Melachim I, chapter 17

This special woman's name is never openly mentioned; she did not search for fame or recognition for her generosity.

How does the Widow of Tzarfat inspire us today?

As an *Aishes Chayil*, we can each uplift those in need with sensitivity and generosity and bring them joy. We can answer the call of those who reach out for help and extend ourselves to those who hesitate to ask. And as we give, we truly gain: "Great is *tzedakah*, for it hastens the Redemption!"[9]

SILENT PRAYER

by Rivka Leah Popack

As you embark upon this journey
And I won't be there
I close my eyes and turn away
To pray this silent prayer

That you find the strength within you
To be more that you are
And the faith to believe
It's how you travel far

And whatever comes to pass
And where you might be
I pray you see the reason at the heart
To know it's meant to be

And when it seems that life's too much
I just hope you see it's true
That G-d wouldn't make you face a test
You couldn't follow through
May you discover the gift in giving
And find your peace of mind
Know that you're never alone
G-d is by your side

Find the will to make a difference
The will to live and learn
See the good in others
And do kindness in return (chorus)

Make the most of what you're given
And what comes your way
Send off your own prayer
Live with purpose every day

And though the nest seems so much safer
Than the endless stretch of sky
I pray for you the courage
To spread your wings and fly so high

You can fly so high
You can reach the sky
There is nothing you can't do
When you know G-d believes in you

יהי רצון מלפניך ה׳ אלקינו ואלקי אבותינו
שתשמע קול תפלתי כי אתה שומע תפלת כל פה

As you embark upon this journey,
And I won't be there
I turn around and walk away
And send you with this prayer

9 Talmud, Bava Basra 10a

Pearls of Wisdom

We MULTIPLY OUR BLESSINGS BY DIVIDING THEM WITH OTHERS.

Our Sages teach, "*Tzedakah* saves a person from death," and citing the remarkable story of Rabbi Akiva's daughter as evidence.[1]

A star-gazer told Rabbi Akiva that his daughter would die on her wedding day. The sage replied that an event need not occur just because it is written in the stars. Our choices can change our destinies.

On the big day, as the young bride was preparing herself, she did not notice a poisonous snake slithering into the room and up the wall behind her. As it was poised to bite, she removed a pin from her headdress and stabbed it into the wall — right through the eye of the snake.

Later, the bride was still unaware of her narrow brush with death when the lifeless snake was found pinned to the wall. Rabbi Akiva turned to his daughter and asked her, "What did you do such that you merited to save yourself from death?"

She recalled a moment from earlier in the day. As everyone in the house was busy preparing for the wedding, she alone responded to a knock at the door. She rose from beautifying herself to greet a poor, hungry man in the doorway and offered him her own food. Rabbi Akiva nodded knowingly: "*Tzedakah* saves a person from death."

Rabbi Akiva's daughter was certainly an *Aishes Chayil* and this verse of the song may also be attributed to her.

Did you know?

It is a Jewish custom for the bride and groom to give an increased amount of their own money to *tzedakah* on their wedding day. Parents, grandparents, siblings, relatives and friends are encouraged to also give *tzedakah* in honor of the bride and groom, accompanied by prayerful wishes for their eternal well-being; that the mitzvah of *tzedakah* will bring blessings and their joy will be unbounded and everlasting.[2]

---

[1] Talmud, Shabbos 156b; Mishlei 10:2

[2] Simchas Olam, pages 71-73

Aishes Chayil Story

Dedicated by Chana Zeldy (Rubashkin) Minkowitz

In Business to Feed the Hungry

A TRIBUTE TO

Rivka Rubashkin שתחי׳

In the early 1960s, Avraham Aaron Rubashkin expanded his businesses and opened Crown's Deli on 13th Avenue in Boro Park, which initially was meant to be an additional business. The restaurant went through a number of cooks in a short amount of time. Rubashkin's wife, Rivka, together with another woman, took over, turning the deli into the equivalent of a soup kitchen. Anyone and everyone knew that if they were hungry, they could go to Crown's and fill up on a hearty meal, paying whatever they could or nothing at all. The restaurant, which closed around the year 2008, never made a profit.

Rivkah Rubashkin recognized that to live is to give and she set an example for her children and many descendants. She lived the verse, "she spreads out her palm to the poor and extends her hands to the needy."

Everyone knew that if they were hungry, they could go to Crown's and fill up on a hearty meal, paying whatever they could or nothing at all.

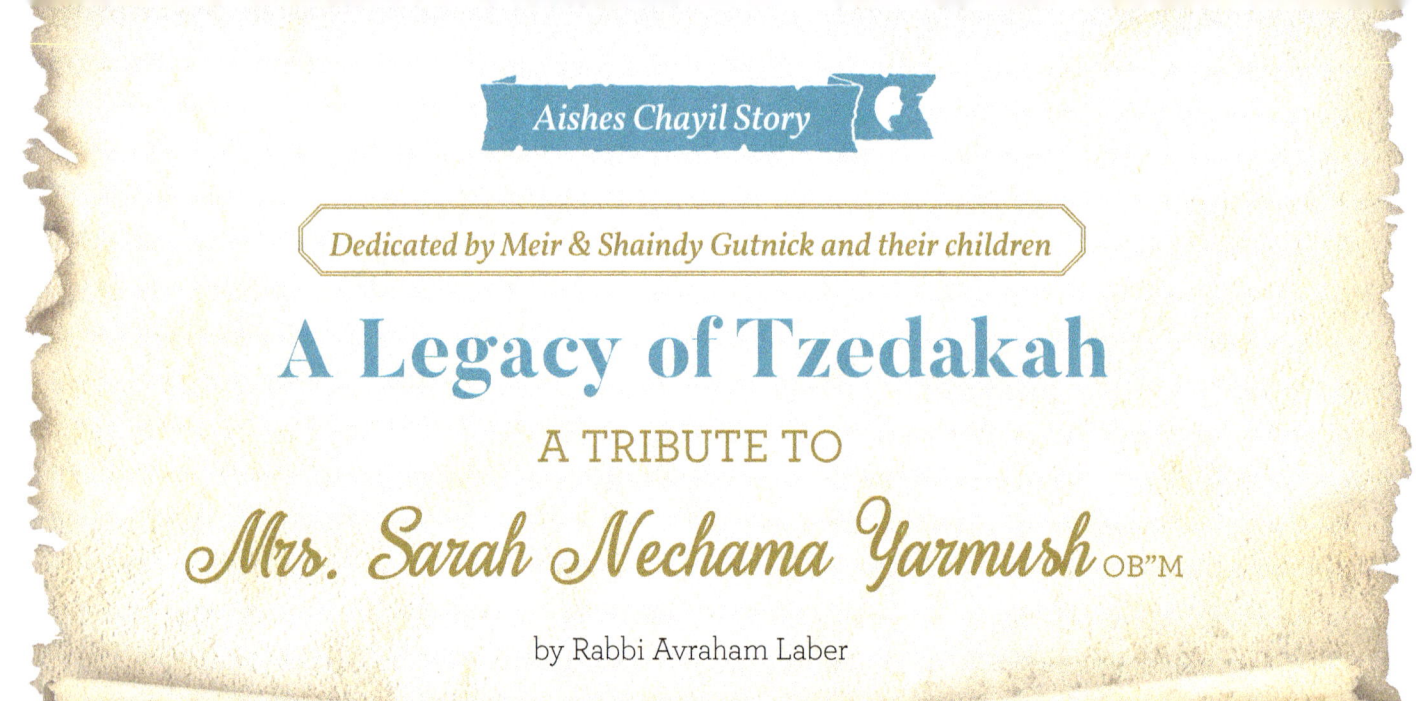

Aishes Chayil Story

Dedicated by Meir & Shaindy Gutnick and their children

A Legacy of Tzedakah
A TRIBUTE TO
Mrs. Sarah Nechama Yarmush OB"M

by Rabbi Avraham Laber

In the summer of 1964, during a public *Farbrengen* in honor of his father's *Yahrzeit* on Menachem Av 20, the Lubavitcher Rebbe shared that recently he received a surprising letter and donation from a young, American-born mother of a large, blessed family.

She wrote that after teaching for some time in a Jewish school, they fell behind in paying her salary. Years later, the school finally paid her the entire accumulated sum of $5,000. As the money was unexpected, and she and her husband David Aryeh had been managing without it for several years, she decided with his consent to joyfully send it to the Rebbe as *tzedakah*.

She did not want any recognition for this donation. On the contrary, she requested that it remain a secret, and therefore insisted on not receiving a receipt, to avoid the donation becoming known to the office employees.

The Rebbe explained the significance of her gift. "The young woman and her husband are blessed with a large family, both of them work hard, and they struggle to cover their expenses. I am almost certain that this couple does not have personal savings of this $5,000 amount for their future. When she finally received money owed to her,

> *The woman never spoke of her deed, and even her own children were unaware of it. This incident only became known after her passing.*

When she finally received money owed to her, she could have donated a portion of it and retained most, or at least a portion, to pay her own children's tuition bills. Yet, with great joy she donated the entire sum to tzedakah!

Mrs. Yarmush receiving a publication from the Rebbe

she could have donated a portion of it and retained most, or at least a portion, to pay her own children's tuition bills. Yet, with great joy she donated the entire sum to *tzedakah*!

"In addition, she and her husband were not raised in Russia where people are accustomed to a life of *mesiras nefesh* (self-sacrifice). They were both born and raised here in America, which is a more materialistic country, where people do anything to earn another dollar. Nevertheless, she was infused with the spirit of Torah and self-sacrifice and was so determined to give this major gift happily."

The Rebbe concluded: "I decided to use this money to establish a special fund to assist Jewish teachers, and let her actions serve as a good example to all people to give *tzedakah* generously, to the point that it is a sacrifice equivalent to hers, and to do so with joy!"

The woman never spoke of her deed, and even her own children were unaware of it. This incident only became known after her passing at age ninety-one in the year 2017, when Rabbi Yehudah Krinsky, one of the Rebbe's secretaries, visited the Shiva home. He told the family that their mother was the woman the Rebbe spoke about in 1964.

Her name is Mrs. Sarah Nechama Yarmush, whose legacy of "extending her hands to the needy" is a source of pride and inspiration for her many descendants and us all.

GROW as an Aishes Chayil

Gratitude: **What are the blessings you are grateful for?**

_____
_____
_____
_____
_____

Recognition: **Recognize a time you helped someone and, in the process, gained more than you gave.**

_____
_____
_____
_____
_____

Oneness: **List eight ways that you can reach out to others in need. Write a poem about helping others with eight verses, corresponding to the eight levels of tzedakah.**

_____
_____
_____
_____
_____
_____
_____
_____

Wish: **What is your wish from G-d?**

_____
_____
_____

לֹא תִירָא לְבֵיתָהּ מִשָּׁלֶג
כִּי כָל־בֵּיתָהּ לָבֻשׁ שָׁנִים.

ל

A Thread of Courage

*"She has no fear of the snow for her household,
for all her household is dressed in scarlet wool."*

Digging Deeper

What does this verse mean?

In the merit of weaving clothes for the needy, the *Aishes Chayil* is unafraid of the snow because her household is dressed in colorful wool clothing.¹ Reds, such as scarlet, are associated with heat and warm the person wearing them.²

The word "dressed — *lavush*" is singular to express equality; the *Aishes Chayil* prevents cold jealousy between siblings by dressing them equally, as if each one is her only child.³

What else does the cold snow represent?

Cold represents the spiritual cleansing of the soul in the afterlife.⁴ However, cold also symbolizes discomfort, fear, bitterness, death, jealousy, and indifference to Torah and mitzvos.

The plural form of the word "scarlet," *shonim* (שנים), derives from the word *shnayim* (שניים), or "twofold," alluding to the performance of two mitzvos: Shabbos and circumcision. These protect the *Aishes Chayil*'s family from the "cold."⁵

Additionally, the plural "*shonim*" hints to the doubled expressions in mitzvos to help others:⁶

"פתוח תפתח" — You shall surely open [your hand to the needy]."⁷

"נתון תתן" — You shall surely give [to him]."⁸

"העֲנֵק תַעֲנִיק" — You shall surely provide [for him]."⁹

The *Aishes Chayil* is unafraid since the warmth of her generosity and mitzvos serves to protect her family.

WOMEN IN THE TORAH
Rachav

When Israel came to destroy Jericho, Rachav did not fear them since they gave her a sign, as it is written,¹⁰ "this line of scarlet string..."¹¹

What was Rachav's first encounter with the Israelites?

The miraculous salvation of the Jewish people from Egypt struck the world with awe. Forty years later, the world watched as they prepared to enter the Promised Land. After Moshe's passing, his successor, Yehoshua, appointed Pinchas and Calev as spies. Their task was to enter the land to determine how to best conquer it.

They crossed the Jordan River and lodged in the city of Jericho at the inn of Rachav. She was a Gentile known for her beauty, but lack of modesty, as she hosted crowds and entertained kings. It was the perfect decoy: Canaanite soldiers would not expect to find Jews there.

---

1 Rashi, Malbim
2 Metzudas Dovid
3 Alshich
4 Rashi
5 Midrash
6 Rashi

7 Devarim 15:8
8 15:10
9 15:14
10 Yehoshua 2:18
11 Yehoshua 2:18

Despite the spies' efforts, the king of Jericho learned of their presence and sent messengers to the inn. Instead of exposing the spies, Rachav hid them on her roof and reported to the messengers: "It is true; the men did come to me, but I do not know from where they were. When the city gate was about to close at dark, the men went out; I do not know where they went. Pursue them quickly, for you can overtake them!"[12]

Why did Rachav risk her life to protect Pinchas and Calev?

One might expect her loyalty to lie with her own nation. However, reports on G-d's wonders for the Jewish people deeply influenced Rachav's awe and respect for them. She further believed that the Jews had a right to the land. Rachav promised Pinchas and Calev that if the conquerors spared her family, they would convert to Judaism and live a moral life.

She approached the spies' hiding place and pleaded, "Swear to me by G-d, since I have shown kindness to you, that you will also show kindness to my father's household and give me a true sign that you will save our souls from death."[13]

The spies gave her a sign with the instructions: "Behold, when we arrive in the land, you shall bind this line of scarlet thread in the window where you let us down; and you shall bring your father and your mother and your brothers and all your father's household home to you." [14]

"She replied, 'According to your words, it shall be.' She sent them off, and they departed, and she tied the scarlet cord in the window."[15]

How was Rachav rewarded for her courage?

True to her word, Rachav converted to Judaism at fifty years old and ultimately married Yehoshua. Our Sages tell us that she merited to become the ancestress of eight prophets, including Yirmiyahu and Yechezkel.

From the depths of an unholy environment and while facing a difficult and uncertain situation, she courageously sought a connection with G-d.

How can we tap into Rachav's courage within us?

It may be challenging to recognize an area where growth is needed and embark on an unknown journey of personal change. However, when one makes an effort to grow, G-d sends a guide, perhaps in the form of a person, life situation, book or even a song. As it says, "Along the

12 Yehoshua 2:4-5

13 2:12-13
14 2:18
15 2:21

path a person desires to go, he is led." [16] When Rachav sought to transform her life, G-d sent her two guests who embodied a life of Torah and holiness.

Growth is the result of a gradual process within ourselves, which includes making daily choices in the direction of our goal. We have free will to either make excuses that discourage us from growing or to take responsibility and notice the opportunities coming our way.

How can we live without fear in our homes?

Rachav did "not fear the cold" of danger, since the merit of her courageous deeds protected her household, symbolized by the sign of "scarlet" thread. Similarly, we affix a *mezuzah* to our doorpost as a sign of G-d's protection.

In a cold and dark world, we learn from Rachav to courageously choose faith over fear. Our good deeds spiritually protect us and increase light in the world. As it says, "*Teshuvah*, *tefillah*, and *tzedakah* avert the evil decree."[17]

Let us each remember always: "G-d is with me and I shall not fear!"[18]

---

16 Talmud, Makkos 10b
17 Yom Kippur Liturgy
18 Adon Olam, Morning Blessings

Meaningful Melody

LIGHT UP A CANDLE

By Thalia Hakin ob"m
Melody Composed by Rivka Leah Popack
Produced by Sam Glaser

When you light up a candle
You light up your *Neshama*
You light up the world
And when you light up the world
You make it a better place
Like for you, me and everybody

Now the world, the world is dark
But soon to be bright for us
Imyirtze Hashem Moshiach will come

Light light up light up a candle
Light light up light up the world
Light light up light up a candle
Light light up light up the world

So let's light up a candle
We'll light up our neshamas
We'll light up the world
And when we light up the world
We'll make it a better place
For you, me and everybody

So let's light light up light up a candle
Light light up light up the world
Light light up light up a candle
Light light up light up, light up the world

Pearls of Wisdom

THE WHOLE WORLD IS A VERY NARROW BRIDGE

BUT THE MAIN THING IS TO NOT BE AFRAID AT ALL!

Aishes Chayil Story

Dedicated by Sarah Freedman and her grandchildren, Shaina and Nechama Freedman

A Fearless Mother
A TRIBUTE TO
Maryasha Garelik OB"M

By Henya Laine as told to Rishe Deitsch (Chabad.org)
Candle lighting story by Blumah Wineberg, with assistance from Mrs. Devorah Alevsky

The Communist regime in Russia mandated that all Jewish children attend public school and be indoctrinated in Communist ideology, with the aim of eradicating religion from future generations. *Bubbe* Maryasha and her husband Yitzchok Elchanan Shagalov were determined to raise their children in accordance with Jewish tradition and refused to send them to public school.

Under Communism, all businesses were confiscated by the government and every individual was dependent on government aid for food, clothing, and shelter. *Bubbe* Maryasha and her family was evicted from their home one bitterly cold winter day and forced to live in the synagogue, using benches as beds and tables. Life became even more difficult when her husband Elchanan was arrested for spreading Judaism which was considered an illegal activity under communist rule, and she was left to raise her six children alone.

Bubby Maryasha saw how sad her children looked. She, too, felt sad, but refused to allow her feelings to stand in the way of G-d's will. *Bubbe* Maryashe prepared

> *Bubbe Maryasha and her family was evicted from their home one bitterly cold winter day and forced to live in the synagogue, using benches as beds and tables.*

Life became even more difficult when her husband Elchanan was arrested for spreading Judaism which was considered an illegal activity under communist rule, and she was left to raise her six children alone.

Bubbe Maryasha Garelik with her daughter Shula Kazen, her son-in-law Rabbi Zalman Kazen and their children.

the Shabbat candles and said to her children, "For this Father has sacrificed and was taken away. We will now do the mitzvah to light the Shabbat candles!" The mother and her daughters lit the candles despite the dangers. She then said to her children, "Today is Shabbos and on Shabbos we are not allowed to be sad. Come children, let's hold hands and we will dance around the Shabbos *lichtelech* (candles)". She took her children's hands and together they made a circle and sang Shabbos songs.

Bubby Maryasha taught her children: "The Russians can take everything away from us, but they cannot take our spirit!" That indomitable spirit of transforming darkness into light remained with her throughout her life.

Together with a neighbor, she planted potatoes in the back of the synagogue to sustain her children. The potatoes were growing nicely, carefully tended by *Bubbe* Maryasha and the neighbor. Then one day the Jews were informed: tomorrow, all prayer books and Torah scrolls will be confiscated and burned. Late that night, Jews came running anxiously to the synagogue to save the Torah scrolls and holy books. Of course nobody wanted to be seen coming in the front door so everybody ran back and forth using the back door and carrying heavy loads.

Bubbe Maryasha and her neighbor had drawn a line down the middle of their garden to designate each one's portion of the potato crop. The neighbor stood guard over her portion and would not allow the running Jews to ruin her tender plants. She greatly slowed them down, but at least they could run freely over Bubbe Maryasha's part, for, as she said as she watched her garden become completely trampled and ruined, "To save holy books, I can give up my potatoes."

The next morning as Bubbe Maryasha and her partner were surveying the damage, the neighbor commented quite bluntly, "Well, I'm sure glad we know which half is mine! I wouldn't let those men in their heavy boots ruin my crop." Well, harvest time came. The neighbor's potato crop grew to a normal size. *Bubbe* Maryasha's potatoes grew huge and strong and brown. *Bubbe* Maryasha had enough to feed her children for a long time, and enough left over to give to needy friends and to sell on the thriving "black market," too.

After selling her surplus, she came "home" to the children in the synagogue, with a hundred rubles in her hand, an incredible profit. As she came to the door of the synagogue, the *shul* caretaker ran towards her and began speaking fast and anxiously. "They're coming to board up the synagogue. They're condemning the place, because the roof leaks. Nobody has money to fix it, so this is the end of the synagogue. What will you do?!" *Bubbe* Maryasha handed the *shul* caretaker the entire hundred rubles and said, "Go fix the roof."

Finally the Communist government had had enough of this courageous young family. Evicting them into the snow didn't break their spirit. Arresting the father didn't break their spirit. Threatening to close down the synagogue on a pretext didn't break their spirit. There must be some way to get those kids into school! So they informed *Bubbe* Maryasha that the next morning armed KGB men would be coming to personally escort every one of the children to school.

Quickly, *Bubbe* Maryasha divided up the children between relatives and friends, so the Communists wouldn't be able to find them. Then she took the two youngest ones and went to the big city of Moscow, where she tried to get "lost". Many, many times over the years in Moscow they were forced to move from one home to another, either because they were evicted from a home or because a location became too dangerous.

Slowly but surely, *Bubbe* Maryasha married off the children, one by one, without their father, and they made it out of Russia and away from Communist prosecution. She arrived in America in 1953.

Bubbe Maryasha's story exemplifies the strength and resilience of the human spirit in the face of adversity. Despite living under a repressive Communist regime, she chose faith over fear. Her determination to raise her children with Jewish values eventually led to the flourishing and growth of her family for generations to come.

She lived until the ripe old age of 107. She has countless great-grandchildren and many great-great-grandchildren. Four generations of her descendants are Chabad-Lubavitch emissaries in the United States, Australia, China, England, France, Panama, Poland and South Africa.

> *Her determination to raise her children with Jewish values eventually led to the flourishing and growth of her family for generations to come.*

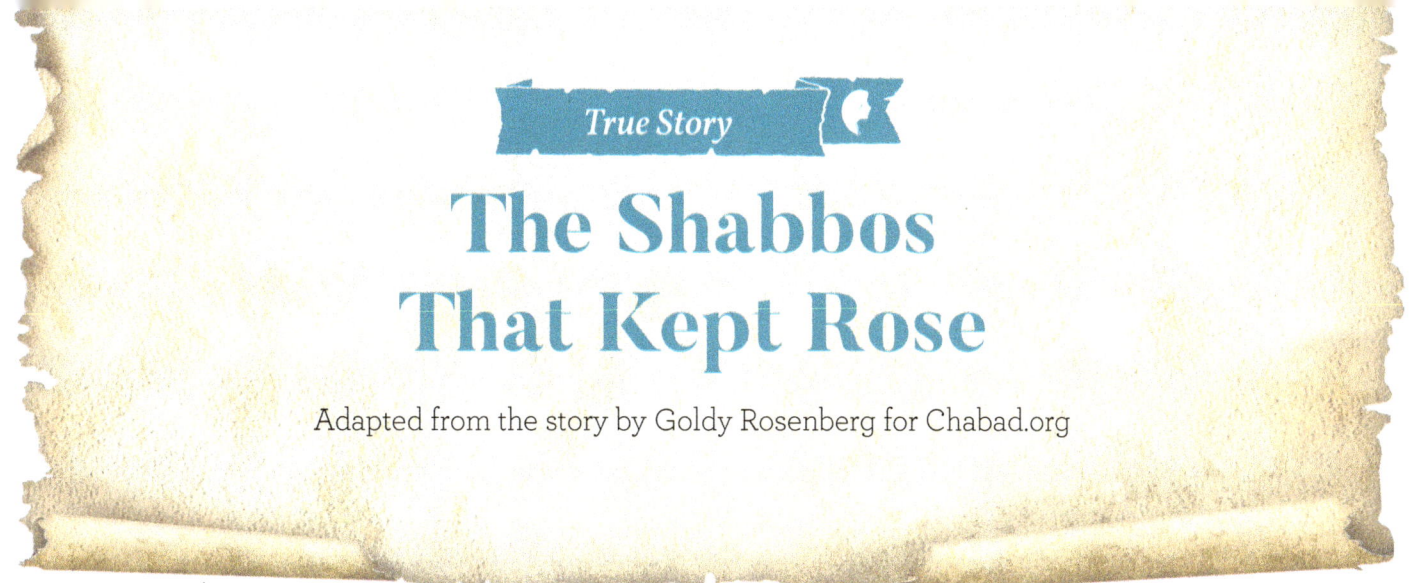

True Story

The Shabbos That Kept Rose

Adapted from the story by Goldy Rosenberg for Chabad.org

Twelve-year-old Rose stood near a Polish harbor, awaiting her voyage to America. As the youngest of nine children, she was chosen for the single ticket her family could afford. The "Golden Land" promised an escape from constant hunger and tribulation in Poland; a chance to start life anew.

Rose's father hoisted her trunk upon the deck of the ship, though the agony of parting with his child filled his eyes with sadness. He held Rose close and murmured, "My child, remember G-d watches over you every step of your way. Remember His laws and keep them well. Never forget that more than the Jews have kept the Shabbos, the Shabbos has kept the Jews. It will be hard in the new land. Remember who you are and keep the Shabbos, no matter what you must sacrifice." Father and daughter embraced tearfully.

As her relatives eagerly welcomed her on American shores, all of Rose's racing thoughts and uncertainty subsided. Soon, she found work as a sewing machine operator. At her "modern" relatives' insistence, Rose began gradually shedding her old clothing, accent, and traditions to keep up with her strange, new lifestyle. However, she never forgot her father's parting words and never gave up on Shabbos. She unfailingly devised a new excuse for her employer each week as to why she did not clock in on Saturdays. Once he noticed a pattern, he took Rose aside. He liked her and her work but if the Sabbath

> *Never forget that more than the Jews have kept the Shabbos, the Shabbos has kept the Jews. It will be hard in the new land. Remember who you are and keep the Shabbos, no matter what you must sacrifice.*

business did not stop, she must look for a new job.

Of course, her relatives urged her to comply, but the echo of her father's words left her conflicted. "Papa is not here to help me be strong. I want to please everyone and fit in this new land, but how can I forget Shabbos?" Rose felt the pressure mount and, late on Friday afternoon, as the time for a decision whirred nearer like the constant hum of the sewing machine before her, she knew it was not a question: she was a Jew who kept Shabbos.

> *Rose felt the pressure mount and, late on Friday afternoon, as the time for a decision whirred nearer like the constant hum of the sewing machine before her.*

Instead of facing her relatives, Rose left early Shabbos morning and strolled around the Lower East Side, softly singing to herself the Shabbos melodies of her childhood. "Papa, this song is for you," she whispered, tears in her eyes. Night descended, signifying the end of Shabbos and Rose's triumph — but only at a high cost. As she trudged home, someone shouting her name pierced her daze. It was her cousin Joe. "What will become of me, Joe?" she wept. "I kept Shabbos but lost my job." He peered at Rose quizzically.

"Rosie," he said gently, "there was an awful fire in your workplace. Few survived — there was no way out of the building. People even jumped to their deaths. Don't you

Firefighters battling the fire at the Triangle Shirtwaist Factory

see? Because you kept Sabbath, you are alive. Because of your Sabbath, you survived."

Out of 190 workers, Rose Goldstein was among the minority who survived the infamous Triangle Shirtwaist Factory fire on March 25, 1911, where 146 immigrant workers perished. Because it had been Shabbos, Rose Goldstein was not there, for "more than the Jews keep the Shabbos, the Shabbos keeps the Jews."

GROW as an Aishes Chayil

Gratitude: "*I am grateful for the courage I did not know I had.*" *Why are you grateful for the trait of courage?*

Recognition: Recognize who or what helps you tap into your courage.

Recognize how Shabbos and other mitzvos protect or enhance your life.

Oneness: What is a tip for overcoming fear or taking a leap of faith?

Wish: What is your wish from G-d?

מ

A Thread of Modesty

*"Bedspreads she makes for herself;
linen and purple wool are her clothing."*

Digging Deeper

What does this verse mean?

מַרְבַדִּים *Marvadim* — bedspreads adorn the bed, as we see from an expression with similar wording: "*Marvadim revad'ti* (מרבדים רבדתי) — I have bedecked my bed with covers."[1]

The *Aishes Chayil* takes time to adorn herself and her home to befit G-d's presence. Her beautiful garments reflect her *malchus*, or royalty, symbolized by the color purple.

It says in *Tehillim*, "*Kol kvuda bas-melech pnima* — כָּל־כְּבוּדָּה בַת־מֶלֶךְ פְּנִימָה All the glory of the King's daughter is her inwardness," meaning her modesty.[2] This trait is her crown of royalty.

She refines her inner thoughts, speech and deeds, which are the garments that "dress" and thereby express her soul.[3] Pristine clothing is a symbol of fine character traits, while "*begodim tzoyim* בגדים צואים — soiled clothes" symbolize distasteful traits.[4] An *Aishes Chayil* chooses to dress beautifully on the inside and out.

What is the Jewish perspective on modesty?

Modesty is a way of life that expresses the holiness and inner beauty of the soul — one's true self. The prophet Micha included it as one of the keys to unlock the Jewish people's potential to fulfill the Torah: "What does G-d require of you, but to do justice, to love kindness, and to walk modestly with your G-d?"[5]

Why is an Aishes Chayil praised for her bedspreads and clothing?

An *Aishes Chayil* engages with the material world by creating useful items such as bedspreads and clothing, all for a spiritual purpose. She decorates her home to create a warm and loving environment. She wears beautiful clothing to honor the Shabbos or *Yom Tov*. Recognizing that her soul requires a healthy body to fulfill her mission, she sets aside time for self-care and fitness. In this way, she brings heaven down to earth and fulfills the purpose of creation. From the *Aishes Chayil*, we learn how to forge a partnership between the physical and spiritual aspects of our lives.

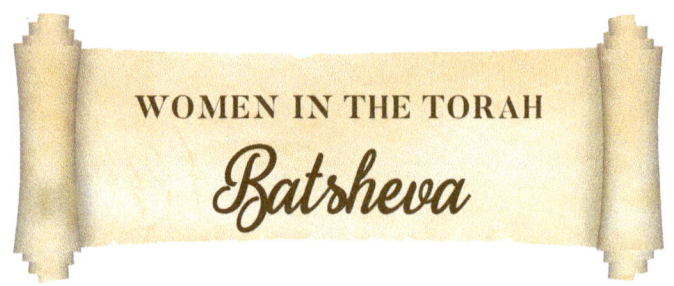

WOMEN IN THE TORAH
Batsheva

As King David's queen, Batsheva dressed modestly in royal linen and purple and ruled from one end of the world to the other. Due to her noble ways, her son, King Shlomo, attained greatness.[6]

Which other women in Torah exemplified regal modesty?

Sarah: When angels came to announce the long-awaited birth of Avraham and Sarah's son, they were served a sumptuous feast, yet the hostess was unseen.

---

1 Mishlei 7:16, Rashi
2 45:14
3 Tanya, chapter 4
4 Ralbag

5 Micha 6:8

6 Midrash Shachar Tov

The angels asked Avraham, "Where is Sarah, your wife?" Without having to investigate, he replied: "*Hinei ba'ohel* — Behold, in the tent." Rashi explains that his simple reply meant, "She is modest."[7]

Rivkah: The Torah says,[8] "No man had known Rivkah," but what does this mean? Other girls would mingle with men at the well. For this reason, Rivkah did not often visit, except for when she met Eliezer according to G-d's plan.

Devorah: She counseled her people under a palm tree, which is straight, tall, and shadeless. This protected Devorah from any improper seclusion with men.

Queen Esther: Her name derives from the Hebrew word "*hester* — hidden" and expresses her inner being.

Modesty, which includes knowing what to say and when to say it or to be silent, guided her choices. For example, she concealed her identity from Achashveirosh as advised by Mordechai.[9] Once the proper moment arrived to save her people from Haman's evil plans, she revealed herself.[10]

Ruth: Modesty was the first trait recognized by the judge and landowner Boaz in the righteous convert, Ruth.

As she gleaned abandoned grain in his field among the needy, she stood out in her dignified conduct.[11]

Kimchis: It is related that Kimchis had seven sons, all of whom merited to serve as Kohanim Gedolim. The Sages asked her, "What have you done to deserve this?" She answered: "The rafters of my home have never seen the braids of my hair."[12]

Her modest conduct of covering her hair even while at home alone spiritually elevated her sons and grandsons to the role of Kohanim Gedolim.[13]

How do these women of valor empower us today?

Each of these women empower us to choose how we wish to dress our body and soul and influence our environment.

Let us each ask ourselves: "Do I present myself as befits a daughter of G-d?"

As an Aishes Chayil, we each are a "*Bas Melech* — princess," whose home, clothing, and conduct reflect our royalty. We dress not to impress but to express our

7 Bereishis 18:9
8 Bereishis 24:16

9 Esther 2:10
10 Esther 7:3-4
11 Midrash Ruth Rabbah
12 Talmud, Yoma 47a
13 Excerpted from the Talks of the Lubavitcher Rebbe for 18 Elul 5742

Divine souls. When we are conscious of our thoughts, speech and deeds, our outer layers reveal our inner beauty. This awareness allows us to impact everyone around us.

The previous Lubavitcher Rebbe recalled his father saying: "A chassid creates an environment. If he does not, he had better check his own baggage carefully, to see whether his own affairs are in order. The very fact that he fails to create an environment should make him as broken as a splinter. He must demand of himself: 'What am I doing in this world?'"[14]

If one wishes to make a positive impression on one's environment, it may be time to focus inward. *"Kol kvuda bas-melech pnima* כָּל־כְּבוּדָּה בַת־מֶלֶךְ פְּנִימָה — The glory of the King's daughter is her inwardness."[15] Our strength is the ability to master our inner world and, from there, influence others.

THREE MALACHIM CAME

By Racheli Jacks & Ziva Katzenberg

Three *Malachim* came
When Avraham was in pain
Each one on a *Shlichus* of his own
Fulfilling their task
Where's Sarah they asked?
Modestly, she remained in her tent

On a camel she rode Rivka left her abode
Yitzchok she saw from afar
She covered her face
Her veil fell in place
Now each Jewish bride does the same

Chorus:
Oh *Bnos Yisroel* look back and see
The women of our ancestry
They lived modestly and we can do the same
Oh *Am l'vadad Yishkon*

Styles may come and style may go
But as Jewish daughters we know
Modesty (*Tznius*) in thought, in action and speech
With bring the *Geula* with speed

---

14 Based on Hayom Yom for 30 Adar I, Rosh Chodesh
15 Tehillim 45:14

Pearls of Wisdom

Modesty means knowing and communicating to others that **your identity equals your innermost self.**

The way to project this message is to transform the outside layers of yourself into an expression of your inside.

-"Outside Inside" by Gila Manolson

Aishes Chayil Story

A Private Life of Public Service

A TRIBUTE TO
Rebbetzin Chaya Mushka Schneerson OB"M

By Eli Rubin

Unlike her husband, Rebbetzin Chaya Mushka did not practice her dedication to the Jewish people in the public eye, but in the privacy of her own home. She never attended her husband's public talks or communal services in the main synagogue. Even on Rosh Hashanah, the Rebbe blew the shofar for her at home, and she always referred to herself as Mrs. Schneerson, never as "Rebbetzin."

Before her husband accepted the leadership of Chabad-Lubavitch, she attended community events and celebrations, and during the public talks of her increasingly frail father, Rabbi Yosef Yitzchak, she stood at the door to ensure the room did not become overcrowded. When her father passed away, and the future of the movement hung in the balance, she told her husband, "If you do not become Rebbe, thirty years of my father's life will have gone to waste."

The strong stance that she took speaks volumes of her courageous commitment to Chabad's continuity. Her older sister had long anticipated that her own husband, Rabbi Shmaryahu Gourary, would become the next rebbe. The Rebbetzin had no desire to compete with her sister, but along with the *Chassidim* she understood that only an individual of her husband's visionary stature could continue her father's mission. The Rebbetzin's sensitivity towards her sister seems to have been one of the factors that led her to evade any public occasion where she might be honored as the Rebbe's wife.

These tensions came to the fore in 1985, when it was discovered that the Gourarys' son Barry was sneaking rare books from his grandfather's library and selling them. When confronted, his mother claimed the books as family property, which her son had every right to sell for profit. Chabad's central organization contested this claim, arguing that the books were the collective property of the Chabad community.

Barry Gourary's lawyers insisted on fighting the case in federal court, and served Rebbetzin Chaya Mushka with a deposition. When asked to whom she thought the books belonged, she replied, "They belonged to the *Chassidim*, because my father belonged to the *Chassidim*." Labeled "the most dramatic moment in the whole proceeding" by Chabad's lawyer, this remark poignantly expressed just how much the Rebbetzin gave up to ensure that *Chassidim* would continue to have a Rebbe.

Rebbetzin Chaya Mushka shunned the limelight to the utmost degree. She once told a visitor, "You can believe me when I tell you that I don't need the honor and that it is absolutely meaningless to me."

> *"You can believe me when I tell you that I don't need the honor and that it is absolutely meaningless to me."*

She would ask to be taken shopping in a location where nobody knew her. She explained, "I cannot shop in stores where people know me, because they think it's necessary to give me special honor, and that is something I don't want at all."

"Linen and purple wool are her clothing," Rebbetzin Chaya Mushka was the epitome of a queen, living each day with dignity, royalty, and modesty.

GROW as an *Aishes Chayil*

Gratitude: **Why are you grateful for your clothing?**

_____
_____
_____
_____
_____

Oneness: **You are a beautiful queen. How do you care for your physical and spiritual self?**

_____
_____
_____
_____
_____

Recognition: **How do you express the colors of your soul and your personality with the clothes you choose to wear? What statement are you making with the clothes you are wearing?**

_____
_____
_____

Wish: **What is your wish from G-d?**

_____
_____
_____
_____

נ

A Thread of Influence

"Her husband is known at the gates, where he sits with the elders of the land."

Digging Deeper

Why does a song dedicated to the Aishes Chayil include a verse praising her husband?

According to Rashi, a man is recognized in public by the beautiful garments his wife makes for him. Furthermore, he is known due to her influence; she inspires him to acquire wisdom.[1] His level of knowledge qualifies him to serve among judges and leaders, who used to hold court at the city gates, as it says,[2] "And the wise men convene at the gates."[3]

The *Aishes Chayil* and her husband embody the adage, "Behind every great man is a great woman."

What do "the gates" represent spiritually?

The *Aishes Chayil* empowers her husband to access the Divine gates of wisdom and understanding with her additional understanding, or *binah yeseirah* – בינה יתירה.

G-d endowed women with this gift when creating Chava, the first woman, from Adam's rib. The Torah states, "*Vayiven...es hatzela* ויבן...את הצלע — and [G-d] built...the rib."[4]

While "*vayiven*" (ויבן) is an unusual term for creation, it derives from the same root as the word *binah* (בינה), since Chava and all women are "built" with a deeper understanding.[5]

With this sense, a woman can discern between good and evil, which became 'mixed up' after Adam and Chava ate of the forbidden fruit of the Tree of Knowledge. This empowers a woman to see beyond the surface and reveal the Divine potential in herself and others.

WOMEN IN THE TORAH
Michal

Michal was King David's wife who saved him from death, as related in chapter 19 of Shmuel I.[6]

How did Michal become David's wife?

As the daughter of King Shaul, who was anointed by the Prophet Shmuel, Michal was a princess and the sister of Merav and Yonasan. Their era was heavy with battles and Israel was in conflict with the Philistines. Shaul declared that whoever defeated their giant warrior Golias would win Shaul's daughter's hand in marriage. Although David was a simple shepherd, he prevailed over Golias with only a rock, and so he married Michal. However, Shaul was intimidated by David, who grew in renown and would succeed him; their relationship was tense. When King Shaul sought to harm David, Michal intervened.

How did Michal save David's life?

When Shaul sent men to slay David at his home, Michal urged her husband to escape through a window. David fled to Ramah, where Shmuel lived, while Michal placed a mannequin in the bed. Despite her insistence that David was ill, Shaul ordered his men to bring him the bed

---

1 Ralbag
2 Devarim 16:18
3 Metzudas Dovid, Malbim
4 Bereishis 2:22
5 Talmud, Niddah 45b

6 Midrash Shachar Tov

with David in it, to kill him. Upon discovering he was tricked, Shaul turned angrily on Michal. She defended herself and appeased him with a story, and Yonasan took over helping David.[7]

How did David become well known due to Michal's influence and support?

When David escaped to reside with Shmuel, he studied secrets of the Torah and became a scholar. After Shaul's passing, David ascended the throne as a mighty and righteous king of Israel. He compiled the book of *Tehillim*, recited by Jews throughout history to bolster their connection with G-d in times of sorrow or joy.

Although David had multiple wives, Michal is credited for his wisdom. She is the only one of whom the Torah says[8] "...and she loved him."[9]

The positive influence of Michal on David stands in stark contrast to the negative impact of Korach's wife, who fueled Korach's discontent and resentment towards Moshe and Aharon, ultimately sparking a rebellion.

How was Korach's wife a negative influence?

Korach, a cousin of Moshe, was one of the Levites, the tribe chosen by G-d to serve in the *Mishkan*. Once, Korach arrived home hairless and explained to his quizzical wife, "All Levites were shaven to purify us for our service."

She retorted, "I do not believe that; Moshe arranged this to make you look terrible!" She resented that her gifted husband was not chosen to be a leader. Already, he envied his cousin Eltzafan, whom Moshe appointed at G-d's word to lead the Levi Kohati family. Korach believed that he, as the son of an elder relative, was rather entitled to this role.

Now, Korach's wife convinced him that nepotism rather than a Divine command influenced Moshe to appoint his brother Aharon as *Kohain Gadol*. They held the highest positions of leadership while excluding Korach. In this way, she incited him to rebel against Moshe, who in truth was motivated by G-d alone.[10]

What was Korach's rebellion?

Korach assembled Dasan and Aviram, Moshe's adversaries, and 250 notable men, mainly from the tribe of Reuvain. They confronted Moshe and Aharon: "You take too much [greatness] for yourselves, for the entire congregation is holy and G-d is in their midst. So, why do you raise yourselves above G-d's assembly'?"

They essentially argued that all Jews should be allowed to become *Kohanim*. However, this implied a rejection of G-d selecting His *Kohanim*. To resolve the debate, Moshe proposed that Korach's assembly and Aharon each offer *ketoret* (incense) before G-d. G-d would

---

7 See the full story in Shmuel I, chapters 17-19
8 Shmuel I 18:28

10 Midrash Bamidbar Rabbah

accept the sacrifice of the one He deemed worthy as *Kohain Gadol*.

On the day of the test, G-d's glory appeared and proved Aharon's worthiness, then caused the earth to open up and swallow Korach, Dasan and Aviram along with their families and possessions, while a Heavenly fire consumed the 250 incense-bearers.[11]

However, On, son of Peles, from the tribe of Reuvain, was saved from this tragic end.

Why was On spared?

Like many women in the Torah, his wife demonstrated a gift of distinguishing between the truth and falsehood. She recognized the lies of this rebellion and was determined to prevent On from joining. She persuaded him that it would be futile and warded off the men who tried to coerce him into rebelling. In her merit, their entire family was saved from destruction.[12]

How do these women's examples influence us today?

These contrasting examples highlight the profound influence that women have in shaping the beliefs and actions of others, for better or worse. As an *Aishes Chayil*, we each possess the spiritual power of binah to influence our family and environment. As it says, *"Nasan Hakadosh Baruch Hu binah yeseirah ba'isha yoseir m'ba'ish* נתן הקב״ה בינה יתירה באשה יותר מבאיש — The Holy One, blessed be He, granted women greater understanding."[13]

It is our choice to search within ourselves to discover the foresight and intelligence required to nurture the good qualities in ourselves and others.

---

11 See Bamidbar, chapter 16
12 Midrash Bamidbar Rabbah
13 Talmud, Niddah 45b

REBBETZIN CHANA

A precious *Neshama* came down to this world
a woman so pious *Hashem* she did serve
dedication so deep to her husband's needs
followed him to exile without a complaint

Chorus
Oh Rebbetzin Chana your flame carries on
It ignites the spark in us all
Your *Mesiras Nefesh* (self sacrifice)
we'll never forget

"Isha Yiras Hashem He Tis-halal"[14]
She picked in the fields some grass and herbs
And ink she did make for her husband's sake
Writing along the side of the page
Reb Levi Yitzchok wrote *Peirushim* (commentaries)

Chorus

Later these *Seforim* were brought
across the sea to her son, the Rebbe in 770
Now we study the books which are so dear
If not for her we wouldn't have them here

---

14 A G-d-fearing woman is the one to be praised.

Pearls of Wisdom

"A king without a queen, the Zohar says,
is neither great nor a king.
For it is the woman who empowers the man to conquer.
And it is the man who empowers the woman to nurture.

And then the man will learn from this woman that he,
too, can reach within others and provide nurture.
And the woman will learn that through nurture,
she can conquer."

-From the wisdom of the Rebbe; authored by Tzvi Freeman

Aishes Chayil Story

Influence with Ink

A TRIBUTE TO

Rebbetzin Chana Schneerson OB"M

by Shmuel Marcus and Avraham D. Vaisfiche

Under the pretext of anti-state propaganda, the Soviet government arrested the Lubavitcher Rebbe's father, Rabbi Levi Yitzchak Schneerson, for religious activities. Once he was sentenced to five years of exile in a desolate region of Kazakhstan, his wife Rebbetzin Chana resolved to accompany him. It was there that she ensured the preservation of his Torah teachings.

Rabbi Levi Yitzchak and Rebbetzin Chana's first home in Chi'ili was a single room in the dwelling of a crude Tatar couple who had a young child. The room had no door, and it was damp, muddy, and filled with swarms of mosquitoes. They lived in extreme poverty and discomfort, with no privacy.

On the 2nd of Nissan, shortly after Rebbetzin Chana's arrival, Rabbi Levi Yitzchak woke up feeling weak. However, as this was the anniversary of the passing of Rabbi Shalom DovBer Schneersohn, he wanted to honor the day by writing some chassidic thoughts. But alas, there was neither paper nor ink to be had.

Deeply troubled by her husband's predicament, Rebbetzin Chana traveled to the nearby city of Kzyl-Orda and returned with two notebooks, some powder that could be made into ink, and a small jar to serve as an inkwell. When this ran out, she somehow managed to obtain additional ink and paper for her husband, despite the shortages and the extreme poverty. When ink was unavailable, Rebbetzin Chana would gather and soak herbs and berries from the field to produce her own ink. Paper was so scarce that her husband wrote in the margins of the books that she had brought with her. The ability to write his Torah thoughts, she would later observe, brought her husband greater pleasure than the bread she would serve him after days of hunger.

Deeply troubled by her husband's predicament, Rebbetzin Chana traveled to the nearby city of Kzyl-Orda and returned with two notebooks, some powder that could be made into ink, and a small jar to serve as an inkwell.

Rabbi Levi Yitzchok passed away at a relatively young age, due to suffering in prison and exile, in the summer of 1944. Rebbetzin Chana carefully preserved her husband's writings. Protecting these writings and traveling great distances with them was quite dangerous. Under the Communist Government of the time, people were arrested for no reason at all. Carrying the name Schneerson was already enough of a "crime", and possessing writings of her husband, who was held as a prisoner under "serious charges," was especially dangerous. When she was finally able to leave the Soviet Union in 1946, Rebbetzin Chana traveled with some of these writings, despite the fact that if she would have been carefully searched, they probably would have arrested and imprisoned her. She also entrusted the remainder of the writings with trustworthy people, and eventually, years later, the writings were delivered to the Rebbe.

Rebbetzin Chana accomplished what seemed impossible.

As it says "Her husband is known in the gates," and in her great merit we are able to study the profound Torah thoughts of her husband until today.[1]

[1] Published and copyrighted by Kehot Publication Society
Copyright and reprinted with permission of Chabad.org

GROW as an Aishes Chayil

Gratitude: **Express gratitude for a Jewish woman who is shaping history with her positive influence.**

Oneness: **How can you be a positive influence on others?**

Recognition: **How does her example have an impact on you?**

Wish: **What is your wish from G-d?**

ס

A Thread of
Resourcefulness

*"Linens she makes and sells,
and she delivers a belt to the peddler."*

Digging Deeper

What does this verse mean?

Even with the strip of material that is left over, the *Aishes Chayil* is resourceful and makes a useful belt.

What accomplishment is this verse praising?

Beyond making what she needs, an *Aishes Chayil* uses the excess material to make a belt. She is not wasteful and finds a purpose for everything in her home.

Where else does the Torah demonstrate avoiding wastefulness?

While the Jewish people traversed the wilderness before entering Israel, they deconstructed the *Mishkan* in order to transport it. The framework, curtains and hardware alone constituted a massive load. Yet, the Levites had only six wagons and twelve oxen donated by the heads of the Twelve Tribes to haul it all![1]

Why were they so scarce?

The *Mishkan* was designed to be a temporary, portable dwelling-place for the Divine Presence. Every slight detail served as a medium to reveal G-d's greatness in this world. It follows that the means of transporting the *Mishkan* furthered this same purpose.

Therefore, the wagons were as large and the oxen as many as strictly necessary for their task. The tribal heads would not allow even an inch of extra space that did not serve a purpose, namely to glorify G-d. And this is true of our entire universe![2]

Every blade of grass, grain of sand, hair on one's head, and unique movement of any creature has a purpose in the grand design of creation.

In the words of the previous Lubavitcher Rebbe, "Ponder this: If the swaying of a blade of grass is brought about by Divine Providence and is crucial to the fulfillment of the purpose of Creation, how much more so with regard to humankind in general and Israel in particular!"[3]

WOMEN IN THE TORAH
Tzlelponit

She was the mother of Shimshon, through whom Israel was saved.[4]

Who was the mother of Shimshon?

Manoach and Tzlelponit[5] were a humble, childless Jewish couple from the tribe of Dan, who dwelled in Zorah. An angel appeared to Tzlelponit to inform her that she would give birth to a son who would save the Jewish people. He instructed her to raise him as a *nazir*, then repeated the instructions to Manoach, and the couple made an offering to G-d.[6] Their child became the great Shimshon who led the Jewish people for twenty years as a judge and a warrior against the Philistines.[7]

---

1 Bamidbar 7:2-8
2 Based on Likkutei Sichos, vol. 28, for Parshas Nasso
3 Hayom Yom, Cheshvan 28
4 Midrash Shachar Tov
5 Talmud, Bava Basra 91a
6 You may find the Biblical source for the obligations of a nazir in Bamidbar 6:1-21. A tractate of the Talmud is dedicated to the nazir, as well. A nazir is a man or woman who "separates" themself by vowing to take on a strict, holy lifestyle characterized by abstinence from all grape products, haircuts, and contact with the deceased.
7 Sefer Shoftim, chapter 13

How did Tzlelponit demonstrate resourcefulness?

Tzlelponit was a role model for the values she wished to transmit to Shimshon. While pregnant, she abstained from wine, since it was forbidden to the future *nazir* and could lead to degrading conduct.[8] Professionally, she made and sold linens to support her son, who later saved the Jewish people.[9]

Rav Aharon Soloveitchik, z"l suggests that Shimshon accompanied his mother to the marketplace to trade with foreigners. This trained him in ethical business and how to deal with other nations in his future leadership. Similar to her creative use of every bit of fabric, Tzlelponit saw opportunities everywhere to teach her son goodness. Since children tend to mirror their parents, every interaction can model how to infuse mundane affairs with connection to G-d.

Life is a classroom!

What is the lesson for our lives?

Tzlelponit demonstrates to us that we can be creative, practical, and intentional in how we use our time, energy, and materials. By doing so, we can transform ordinary moments into extraordinary opportunities to learn, teach, and share with others. We can find a purpose for everything in our home and recognize a learning opportunity in every experience.

Just like an *Aishes Chayil* repurposes a scrap of fabric into a fine belt for sale, we too can optimize what we have and bring redemption to our world by purposefully utilizing the material world to reveal the Divine within it. Whether it is donating spare clothes or refreshing leftover foods, we can all make a positive impact in our own unique way.

8 Shoftim 13:4-5
9 Midrash Aishes Chayil, Yalkut Shimoni

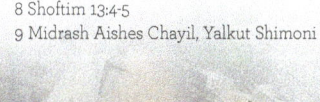

In honor of our Aishes Chayils

Chaya Miriam

and

Leah Shifra

on their Bat Mitzvahs and on

Eliana Sarah's

upcoming Bat Mitzvah.

May they all be a blessing.

Meaningful Melody

HEAVEN ON EARTH

By Racheli Jacks

Does there really exist a place
Where heaven and earth meet
It's here and now, we'll show you how
This oasis you can achieve

Each mitzvah — good deed
Is a piece from above
Which we do down here below
Revealing G-dliness hidden within
The earth will sparkle and glow
The earth will sparkle and glow

Chorus:
We can bring down heaven
Heaven on earth
Through our actions, our mitzvos
Everywhere we go
Everything we do
"Be'chol Derachecha Do'eihu"[10]

Yes there really exists a place
Where heaven and earth meet
It's here and now, we'll show you how
This oasis you can achieve

10. In all your ways know Him. (Mishlei 3:6)

Pearls of Wisdom

Every blade of grass, grain of sand, hair on one's head, and unique movement of any creature **has a purpose in the grand design of creation.**

-Hayom Yom, Cheshvan 28

Aishes Chayil Story

Perfect Porridge

A TRIBUTE TO

Bubby Hinda Deitsch OB"M

by Rabbi Avraham Laber

Reb Mendel and Hinda Deitsch lived with their family in the City of Kharkov in the years 1920-1940 until the War. Their home was always open to guests and people in need. One room was designated as a *shul* for prayer and Torah study, which was pretty dangerous in the Soviet Union. There were Chabad yeshiva students studying in the "illegal" yeshiva on the run, who were always welcomed and happily provided for with daily meals and lodging. Once, a family member asked Reb Mendel, "Are we not doing too much for the guests? He replied, "Our home belongs to them. We are the guests."

In 1942, just before the Nazis marched into Kharkov, the Deitsch family managed to escape to the East by train. After a long and dangerous journey, they reached Samarkand where they lived for two years before settling in Tashkent. These cities in faraway Uzbekistan provided safety from the War, but for many, hunger was a daily challenge. Most of the Jewish refugees evacuated in such a hurry that they were unable to take any possessions with them. In the Soviet Union there were waiting lines where people would present their work identification card, and then receive a small ration of bread. The refugees did not have the cards, and they were starving. Unfortunately, many people died from starvation.

Fortunately, Reb Mendel and Hinda still owned some gold coins saved up from years of business. They used all their savings to feed the hungry refugees. When the money ran out over a period of six months, Hinda would go out to the line and ask people to donate small pieces of bread, which she brought home for the hungry. While she was collecting bread and visiting the sick, Reb Mendel invited guests and served them. He had to learn how to make a porridge out of whatever ingredients were available.

He tried to follow his wife Hinda's instructions, but he had very limited prior kitchen experience. Reb Mendel experienced a learning curve. First, he did not realize that the grains had to be sifted and rinsed. Hinda fed that batch to the animals. Then after getting through the main steps, he did not realize that the pot needed to be stirred. After scraping the hardened porridge out of the pot, Hinda repurposed it into edible latkes.

"A good deed is like making perfect porridge; you have to take the time to do it right."

When Reb Mendel finally mastered the art of cooking porridge, Hinda, the patient wife, sincerely complimented him. Reb Mendel exclaimed, "A good deed is like making perfect porridge; you have to take the time to do it right."

Bubbe Hinda's legacy is in the verse, "Linens she makes and sells, and she delivers a belt to the peddler." She was resourceful and truly cared for others. She ensured precious ingredients didn't go to waste, and that her husband's efforts were recognized and appreciated.

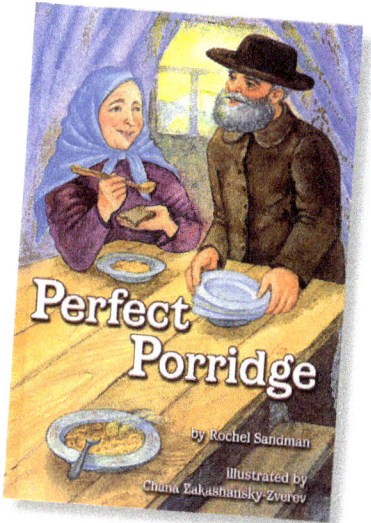

Bubbe Hinda's granddaughter, Rochel Sandman put this favorite family story in writing for children everywhere to enjoy. Perfect Porridge is a warm, spirited book published by Hachai Publishers.
www.hachai.com
Shared here with permission.

GROW as an Aishes Chayil

Gratitude: **What is something you are grateful for that served you well and that you no longer need?**

_____
_____
_____
_____

Recognition: **How can you repurpose or breathe new life into something in your home?**

_____
_____
_____
_____

Oneness: **Share a recipe using leftover foods.**

_____
_____
_____

How can you utilize your time to its fullest?

_____
_____
_____

Wish: **What is your wish from G-d?**

_____
_____
_____
_____

ע

A Thread of Optimism

"Strength and splendor are her clothing, and smilingly she awaits her last day."

Digging Deeper

What does this verse mean?

Physically, an *Aishes Chayil*'s garments are durable and beautiful. Spiritually, she wears her optimism, which is her strength and splendor. Joy is one of her powerful tools to deal with every life situation. As the Lubavitcher Rebbe said, "Joy breaks through all barriers!"[1]

An *Aishes Chayil* smiles and brings joy to those around her throughout her life. She is unafraid of "her last day" on earth, because she lives a life of purpose and accomplishment. She rejoices in knowing that she will depart with a good name.[2]

How does an Aishes Chayil smile each day?

Despite the challenges an *Aishes Chayil* faces, she finds joy in the moment rather than despair. Thoughts create emotions, both negative and positive.[3] The Alter Rebbe explains how to be the master of one's thoughts and not their slave. When a negative thought arises, push it away "with two hands!"[4] And in its place, refocus with optimistic thoughts, words, or actions.

Through her positive perspective, an *Aishes Chayil* gains control over any opposing influences. Her positive energy is contagious, as the *Shechinah* rests where there is joy,[5] and she uplifts her home and those around her.

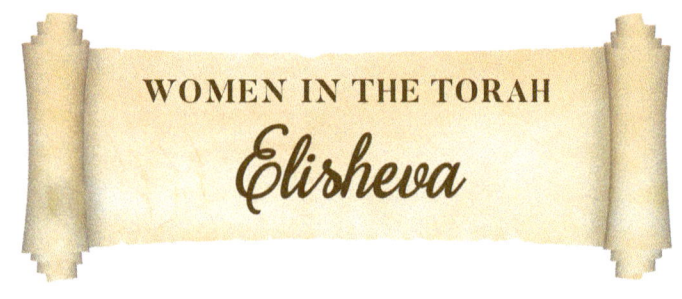

WOMEN IN THE TORAH
Elisheva

Elisheva was the daughter of *Aminadav* and the wife of Aharon, who merited to witness four wondrous occasions on the day the *Mishkan* in the desert was consecrated.

1. Her brother Nachshon brought a *korban* as the leader of his tribe.
2. Her husband became the *Kohain Gadol*.
3. Her brother-in-law Moshe became king.
4. Her two sons became second to the *Kohain Gadol*.[6]

Unfortunately, a dark shadow was cast over the joyful day with the deaths of her two other sons, Nadav and Avihu. The Torah relates that in response, "Aharon was silent," which included Elisheva.[7]

What can we learn from the silence?

When someone is facing a difficult loss on "the last day" of others' lives, all we can do is meet them in their grief with silence, love, and open arms. There are no words to explain the tragedy; it is beyond our grasp. Therefore, silence is a fitting response.

---

1 Likkutei Sichot, Parshas Ki Seitzei 5748
2 Rashi, Metzudas Dovid
3 Tanya, chapter 3
4 Tanya, chapter 27
5 Talmud, Shabbos 30b

6 Midrash Shachar Tov
7 Vayikra 10:3

THE TAPESTRY

This poem is a reminder that everything that happens is part of a Divine design.

The Tapestry
A piece of cloth
With stitches
Stitches on a cloth
Look under the cloth
Snags and knots
Jumbled threads
No order, no pattern!

Now, look at the top
The top of the cloth
Colorful threads, patterns of stitches

A cloth is spread over the world
We from under see confusion
We see snags, we see knots
A jumble we cannot make out

And *Hashem* from above sees beauty
He sees patterns, He sees order
Together, we are Weaving the Tapestry!

How can one live in a state of optimism even when one experiences adversity?

Trust in G-d leads to living with optimism. We bring G-d into our life experiences when we recognize that G-d is Master of the universe, and everything that transpires is willed by G-d, Who does only good. When the good is concealed, we can choose to trust in G-d because we do not see His "bigger picture."

As the Sages said: "One must recite a blessing for the bad just as for the good... and accept both with joy."[8]

We see this concept hinted in the Hebrew word *Golah* (גולה), which means "exile." By inserting the Hebrew letter *Alef*, the *Golah* (גולה) becomes *Geulah* (גאולה), which means "redemption." What does the *Alef* indicate? "*Alufo Shel Olam* — the Ruler of the world."[9]

When one recognizes the *Alef* — the one G-d — and draws it into every aspect of life, one lives in a state of redemption because life is infused with trust in G-d. Many personal redemptions will lead to redemption of the entire world.[10]

What is the takeaway message for our lives?

As we strive to fulfill our life's mission, pain may be a step in the process but never the destination. Sometimes while facing sadness or grief, it is helpful to give ourselves

---

[8] Talmud, Berachos 60b; Tanya, Iggeres Hakodesh, epistle 11
[9] Alef is the first letter and number, the start of everything. Likewise, G-d precedes all existence and is the source of all time and space.
[10] Based on a talk of the Lubavitcher Rebbe, 19 Kislev 5745, 13 December 1984

time to process and validate the pain without shame or guilt. Feeling grief is part of healing and releasing it so that we are free to focus on a brighter future. This process empowers us to refocus on a deeper truth that is a source of profound, inner peace and joy: G-d, our loving Father, guides every detail of our lives. Even pain points us towards our purpose.

Recognizing G-d's presence fosters optimism and joy, which in turn welcomes G-d's presence into our lives[11] in a brilliant cycle. As a result, joy breaks through all barriers, including the barriers of exile, and has the unique potential to bring about the Redemption. This inner joy will surely lead to the ultimate joy, the rejoicing of the Redemption, when[12] "our mouths will be filled with laughter."[13]

A TAPESTRY

Music & Lyrics by Tzirel Liba Greenberg

A tapestry I'm weaving and each day is a thread
Some days are blue or golden
Some days are scarlet red
My tapestry has rhythm
Weave it as I sing
Each thread's another *middah* (trait)
I work on perfecting

Chorus:
Stitch by stitch, thread by thread
I weave and sew where I am led
Day by day, out and in
I weave where I'm going
With where I've been

My tapestry has feelings
Each color is a clue
The pinks of love and caring
Shades of gray when I am blue
My tapestry is growing each time I pass a test
The colors blend in harmony, bringing out my best

Chorus

Underside the tapestry is all I get to see
The threads are crossed and knotted
There is no harmony
But above, there is completion
So I pray with all my might
When both sides of the tapestry
Will reveal Your perfect light

Chorus

Oh, Master Weaver, each thread designed by You
With You is its completion
You will see it through
Oh Master Weaver oooh oooh
Inside, Outside, Upside, Down
It's all You
It's all You

11 Talmud, Shabbos 30b
12 Tehillim 126:2
13 Likkutei Sichos, Parshas Ki Seitzei 5748

Meaningful Melody

ASHIRA (I WILL SING)

By Chavi Rappaport

Have you a song in your heart
Yearning to be sung
A ballad in your soul

A voice you can't control
Ashira sing your tune — *Ki Gamal Alai* כי גמל עלי

Sometimes it's pain
At times it's joy
But it's your melody alone
The notes you own

Chorus:
Let your sorrow become the triumph in your song
Find the joy your harmony to sing along
Blend your music notes together in the greatest symphony
Ashira LaHashem let's raise our voices you and me

I have a song in my heart
Echoing deep in my soul
Ashira I sing
Thank you *Hashem* for everything
The sun the rain the clouds and the storm

Sometimes it's pain, at times it's joy
But it's my own melody, my symphony

Find your song, sing it loud
Sing it strong, it's your song

LIFE

Life is a gift on lend
When to sew and when to mend?
Hashem gives You His hand
So You can reach up in life's demand(s)
He is always there
Even when it is not clear
sometimes
Hidden is the light
In the depths of the plight
The righteous women have the power
It is the call of the hour
Reach up and out to Him
Just let Him in
Then you will experience the win
Outshining the darkness of night
With your Neshama light

Dedicated to

Henya bas Aharon Yosef

by her daughter, Ahuvah Coates

My mother believed in my inner strength and light and in every women's endurance and power to heal this world.

Pearls of Wisdom

Martha Levitt ob"m would tell her daughters that when she disliked her clothes as a child, she was told:

"Put a smile on your face and no one will care what you're wearing."

Dedicated by Chana Rosen in loving memory of her mother

Michla bas R' Moshe Levitt

"My mother uplifted people she knew with her love, warmth, humor and positivity. I honor my mother's legacy with this message: Give an extra smile, a call or text to someone who would appreciate it and brighten their day."

Aishes Chayil Story

Dedicated by Nechama Dina Laber and family

Dancing Through Life

A TRIBUTE TO

Mémé Rachel Bouskila OB"M

by Nechama Laber

During a bleak and cold winter, on the 7th of Shevat, my beloved maternal grandmother, Mémé Rachel, returned her precious soul to her maker. She was 93 years old. My sister-in-law Leah told me that when she notified her family, they immediately asked, "Is that the grandmother who danced at your wedding and was the life of the party?" She rejoiced and danced at all of our family weddings way into her 80s!

Her eyes sparkled with joy as she sang to her grandbabies and danced in the middle of our dining room, turning an ordinary day into an extraordinary one.

"Strength and splendor are her clothing, and smilingly she awaits her last day." This verse encapsulates Mémé Rachel's life. Her family had to restart their life in France after fleeing Algeria because of the Arab militant takeover.

In France, she faced financial struggles and worked hard to raise her three children. Later in life, she faced health challenges and loneliness. Nevertheless, despite all the hardships she encountered, Mémé was always ready to party, and her eyes sparkled with joy as she sang to her grandbabies and danced in the middle of our dining room, turning an ordinary day into an extraordinary one. Later on in life, she even sang and clapped her hands from a wheelchair.

She traveled from France to rejoice in our *simchos* and cried with us in our sorrows. She communicated her tremendous love with her delicious *sephardic* food, open heart, songs and laughter, (even though we didn't all understand French). She inspired us to talk to *Hashem* and say, "D-ieu aide moi! (G-d help me)." She would put aside some of her delicious baked goods for unexpected guests and say, "Cache pour demain (Hide some for tomorrow)." She was the regal matriarch of our family and helped raise her grandchildren and great-grandchildren with love and laughter.

While my mother and extended family were sitting *shivah* in Jerusalem, my eyes filled with tears. Baby Baruch was crying more than usual and my two-year-old son, Schneur, kept asking me, "What happened, Mommy?" I thought to myself, "What would Mémé do right now?" I reached for the beautiful hand-painted tambourines I had made at a camp workshop and offered them to Baruch and Schneur; we danced with Mémé in our hearts, and we sang some of her favorite songs. Baruch and Schneur smiled and laughed, and I knew Mémé was smiling and laughing along with us. We keep Mémé's legacy alive: by singing, dancing, and spreading joy, just like she did, through the highs and lows in life.

Rachel bat Shalom is buried in Jerusalem, Israel near her illustrious great-grandfather, Sidi Bahi Eliyahu Allouche, the Chief Rabbi and Dayan of Constantine (Algeria). Mémé, we miss you, we pray to see your smiling face very soon with the coming of Moshiach.

> *We keep Mémé's legacy alive: by singing, dancing, and spreading joy, just like she did, through the highs and lows in life.*

Mémé resting place in Jerusalem

GROW as an Aishes Chayil

Gratitude: **Write, paint, or draw the things that bring you gratitude, joy and laughter.**

Oneness: **How can you generate an optimistic attitude and increase the joy in any area of your life?**

Recognition: **Recognize G-d's compassion in your daily life or even in challenges.**

Wish: **What is your wish from G-d?**

פ

A Thread of Communication

*"She opens her mouth with wisdom,
and the teaching of kindness is on her tongue."*

Digging Deeper

What does this verse mean?

An *Aishes Chayil* combines her words of wisdom with kindness. She recognizes that words can build or break and change a person's life forever. Her language serves to connect, not just correct; she is wise and knowledgeable without being hurtful or condescending.

She is ready to do acts of kindness while using her wisdom to teach and encourage others to do so, as well.[1]

"She opens her mouth" refers to her "*chochma* — wisdom," while "on her tongue" refers to her binah, or detailed understanding.[2]

Her "*Toras chessed* — teaching of kindness" means that she performs kindness above and beyond the letter of the law, or "Torah."[3]

Does "Toras chessed" imply that there exists a Torah without kindness?

Rather, "Torah of kindness" is the Torah learned with a full, willing heart for the sake of G-d and in order to teach another.[4] It is an act of kindness to share what we know with others.

---

[1] Ibn Ezra, Metzudas Dovid
[2] Malbim
[3] Malbim
[4] Steinsaltz

WOMEN IN THE TORAH

Serach

Serach was the daughter of Asher [and granddaughter of Yaakov]. She was the wise woman who said, "Listen, listen! Please tell Yoav, 'Come over here and I will speak to you.'"[5] With her wisdom, she saved the city where Sheba, son of Bichri, had taken refuge.[6]

When did Serach save a city?

During the rule of King David, Sheba ben Bichri from the Tribe of Binyamin revolted against the king. After quelling the rebellion, David's general Yoav besieged the city of Abel Beth Maachah, where Sheba had fled, threatening to destroy the city unless he emerged. A "wise woman" in their midst, whom our Sages identify as Serach, reasoned that Sheba had forfeited his life when he rebelled against the king. She wisely persuaded the people to comply with Yoav's demand to deliver Sheba to him. The rebel was executed and the city saved.[7]

How did Serach communicate with wisdom and kindness as a young girl?

For twenty-two years, Yaakov mourned his missing son, Yosef; no sound of joy was heard in his home. As a loyal granddaughter, Serach was there to console Yaakov. No one knew at the time that Yosef was alive, promoted from a lowly slave to Pharaoh's viceroy in Egypt.

---

[5] Shmuel II 20:16
[6] Midrash Shachar Tov
[7] Shmuel II, chapter 20

When Yosef finally revealed himself to the rest of the family, Serach was responsible for sharing the news with her elderly grandfather.[8] She lifted her harp, silent in his presence for so many years, and she began to play and sing softly. The notes reached the grieving Yaakov as he wondered about the meaning of it. Filled with joy, he clearly heard Serach say, "Yosef is alive; he rules over all of Egypt!"[9]

The family was reunited.[10]

What was Serach's great reward?

8 Bereishis, chapter 45
9 Midrash Bereishis, Sefer HaYashar on Parshas Vayigash
10 Read the full story online at chabad.org

Yaakov blessed her with long life and prophecy in gratitude to her for bringing him the good news with kindness and wise sensitivity.

Serach never died and was one of nine righteous people who entered Gan Eden alive. At the redemption from Egypt, she revealed to Moshe the hidden coffin of Yosef, who had urged his people to take his bones with them for reburial in Israel.[11] Years later, during King David's reign, Serach saved a city from destruction. She is the only granddaughter mentioned by name when the Torah lists Yaakov's descendants.

What are three tips for effective communication?

PAUSE

Know what not to say, take a breath and pause before responding. Achieving this pause before you speak can at times feel like mountain climbing. When someone finally reaches the top, it is exhausting and exhilarating. Tap into this sense of victory whenever you control your initial reaction and remain silent. Wait until the timing is right to speak.

A helpful acronym to remember this is **W.A.I.T.** which stands for the question:

Why
Am
I
Talking?

11 Talmud, Sotah 13a

TONE

Know your goal when you speak and express it in your tone of voice. If you speak harshly to someone who is doing something wrong, they will not change. It is not a healing approach. It is not only what you say but how you say it.

Ask yourself: What is the best way to express myself to reach my goal? Speaking with calm confidence is much more effective than an angry outburst. One's tone of voice makes a notable difference.

EXPRESS YOUR WISH KINDLY

When describing a problem, use the "I Statement" approach instead of "You." Open with a gratitude statement before you express your wish. For example, instead of accusing the person, "You're so noisy!" try: "Thank you for your lively energy and our conversation. At this time, I need quiet so I can sleep."

What is the message for our lives?

Rabbi Yochanan ben Zakkai once inquired, "Which is the good way to which a person should adhere?" His student Rabbi Shimon replied that "the good way" is to consider the consequences of one's words or actions.[12]

Just as Serach was sensitive to the needs of her listener, we can each practice knowing what to say, when, and how to say it for a positive outcome.

Every time we speak, we make a statement about ourselves because speech is a reflection of our inner selves. As we strive to grow as an *Aishes Chayil*, we can speak with intention and impact others with wisdom and kindness.

Meaningful Melody

PSACH LIBI — I WANT TO GROW

by JGR Camp Staff

Psach Libi — I want to grow
So much that there is to know
Questions waiting to be asked
My thoughts begin to flow

Wider than the greatest sea
Torah is infinity
So how is it that I can grasp
And touch divinity?

A present, an inheritance
To each and every Jew
I can learn and comprehend
Go out and teach it too

If you know aleph pass it on
Reach out apply it too
Never underestimate
The power within you

GROW Circle in JGU
With a special touch
Filled with love I'd never dream
That I would learn so much

Learn it, Love it, Live it, Teach it
Torah never ends
I'll take the knowledge that I've gained
And pass it on to friends

Pearls of Wisdom

In a private audience, the Lubavitcher Rebbe advised Rabbi Azriel Yitzchok Wasserman, ob"m, with three tips for teaching:

1. Words which emanate from the heart, enter the heart.

2. Teach with joy.

3. Be a living example of what you teach!

Aishes Chayil Story

Dedicated by Dr. & Mrs. Edward Jacobs

My Mom's Love
A TRIBUTE TO
Priscilla Jacobs ob"m

by her son Ed Jacobs, MD

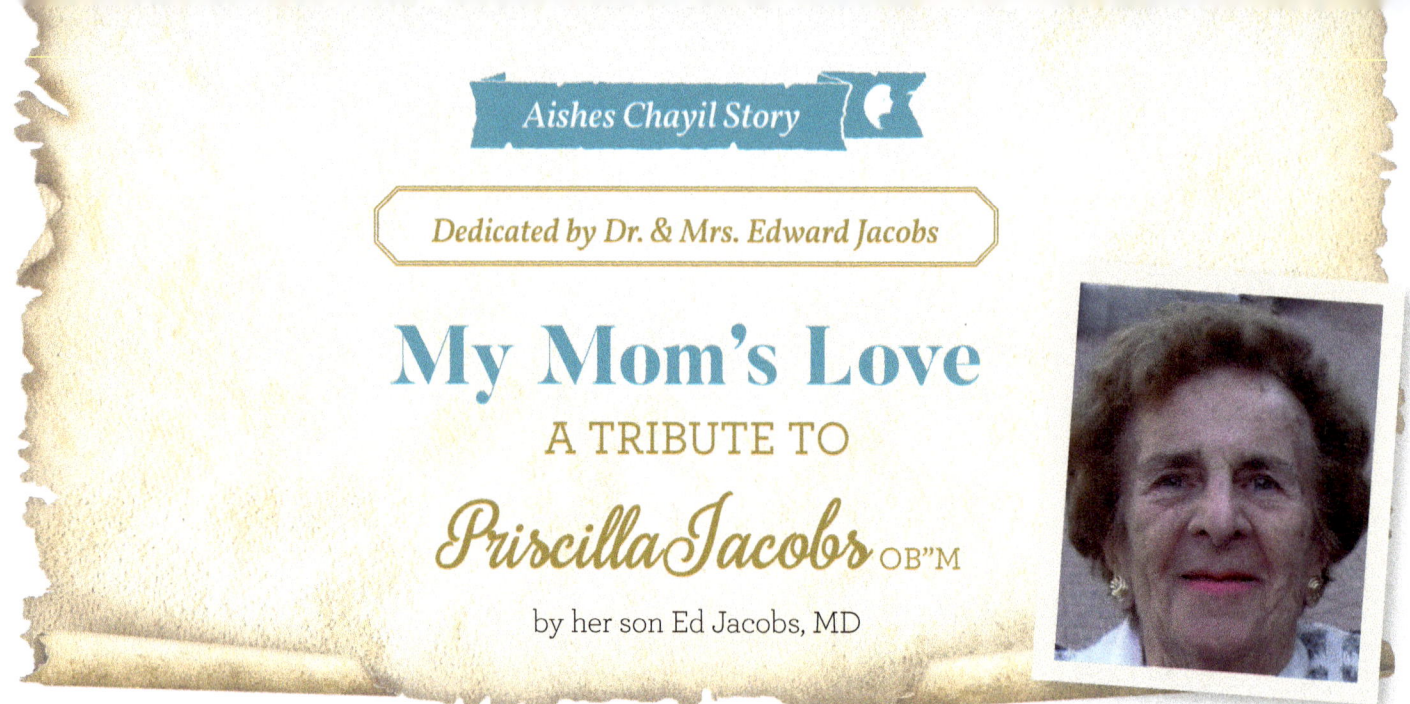

Her eyes always sparkled after she finished *benching licht* on Friday evening ushering in the Shabbos. It was as though she had a direct connection with *Hashem* in those precious moments of candle lighting.

My mom, Priscilla, ob"m, had incredible faith and endless love for her *Yiddishkeit*. She shared her warmth with every Jewish woman in her apartment building: first, on the upper west side of Manhattan, and then, in Hallandale, Florida. She lived the verse, "She opens her mouth with wisdom, and the teaching of kindness is on her tongue." She didn't hesitate to ask a new-found friend if she lit Shabbos candles and offered to teach her if she didn't. Countless Jewish women found the joy of lighting Shabbos candles in no small part due to mom's efforts and loving guidance. She rejoiced in that mitzvah throughout her life.

> She didn't hesitate to ask a new-found friend if she lit Shabbos candles and offered to teach her if she didn't.

It is truly an honor offered by JGU to write about my mother and recall her wonderful traits. She was a warm, compassionate, affectionate mom, wife, grandmother and friend and enveloped us all with her love. She was always drawn to those less fortunate and supported them in many ways.

Her miraculous survival for many years after my dad's passing can be attributed to her faith in *Hashem*, her love for family and the support provided by her Jewish roots. A true woman of valor, a sweet *Yiddishe Mama*, she relished her Jewishness and spread her love of it as far and wide as she could.

May our memories of her always be a blessing in our lives.

GROW as an Aishes Chayil

Gratitude: **Express gratitude for someone's kind words to you.**

_____
_____
_____
_____

Recognition: **Recognize a situation where your choice of words had a positive impact. What helped you choose the right words?**

_____
_____
_____
_____

Oneness: **How can you speak more kindly to create oneness with your family or friends?**

_____
_____
_____
_____

Wish: **What is your wish from G-d?**

_____
_____
_____
_____

צ

A Thread of
Action

"She looks after the conduct of her household and does not eat the bread of laziness."

Digging Deeper

What does this verse mean?

The *Aishes Chayil* takes care of the physical and spiritual needs of her household, overseeing their conduct. She guides her family to act with truth, modesty, and reverence of G-d. Furthermore, "she does not eat the bread of laziness" and avoids wasting time.[1]

What is significant about the word "Halichos"?

"*Halichos*," (הֲלִיכוֹת) meaning "conduct" or "paths," hints to the word *Halacha*, (הלכה) or Jewish law. The *Aishes Chayil*'s actions are in accordance with *Halacha* as she strives to model and uphold Torah values in her home.

In Hebrew, "*lechem* — bread" (לחם) shares the same letters with "*melach* — salt" (מלח). Salt may initially seem bitter, yet it truly brings out the finest flavors in a recipe. Similarly, the details of the Jewish laws may seem restrictive, yet they are G-d's "taste" and add flavor to our lives.[2]

When we structure our actions according to *Halacha*, we convey to G-d: "We recognize how we can give You pleasure through honoring Your tastes, Your preferences, in my home." In this way, we create a comfortable dwelling-place for G-d in this world.[3]

"*Halichos*" (הֲלִיכוֹת) also refers to humans, who are called in Hebrew "*m'halech*" (מהלך)— "a walker." By continually growing, one can attain spiritual heights inaccessible even to angels. Angels are stationary and do not grow. In *Kabbalah* terminology, angels are called "*omed*," ones who stand still, for they always remain on the same level as they were created.

An *Aishes Chayil* knows that growth is the purpose of life. She is not expecting her household members to be angels, but she guides them to GROW! Human beings grow; when their physical growth stops, they continue to grow spiritually.[4]

As the Rebbe says, "Every Living Thing Must GROW!"

WOMEN IN THE TORAH
Ovadia's Wife

Ovadia's wife rescued her sons and saved them from idolatry with King Achav.[5]

How did Ovadia's wife "look after the conduct of her household" and rescue her sons?

The prophet Ovadia and his wife secretly supplied bread and water to many fellow G-d-fearing prophets, hiding in caves from the evil King Achav, who sought to kill them.

Ovadia had owed the royal house a debt but passed away before he could repay it. Now, the king's son, Yehoram, planned to take his two sons as payment. Ovadia's wife recognized the immense spiritual danger her children would face if they lived in the idolatrous palace.

---

1 Rashi, Metzudas Dovid
2 Since the sacrifices in the Holy Temple were brought with salt, when we recite a blessing on bread at our table, which is compared to an altar, the bread is dipped into salt.
3 Likkutei Sichos, Parshas Re'eh 5750

4 Inspired by Rabbi Avraham Twerki, Growing Up
5 Midrash Shachar Tov

Who did she reach out to for guidance?

Ovadia's wife cried out to the Prophet Elisha about her plight. Impoverished, she had nothing with which to repay the debt in her home; all she owned was a single cruse of oil. Elisha instructed her to borrow as many empty vessels as possible and to fill them with oil from her jug. Miraculously, it kept flowing for as long as she could contain it. She then sold all the oil, earning plenty to pay off the debt and secure her family's future for many years to come.[6]

What is the deeper meaning of this story?

The dialogue between the widow and the prophet, who is a G-dly ambassador, mirrors the outcry of the soul and G-d's response to her.

Ovadia's wife to Elisha: "My husband, your servant, has died..."

The soul to G-d: "My service of You is lifeless, uninspired, but I yearn to fill my deeds with purpose!"

Wife: "...and the creditor has come to take my two sons as slaves."

Soul: "But my Animal Soul takes over my emotions, which are called the 'children' of my thoughts. They enslave me to focus only on the physical reality and they cloud my vision of G-d's infinite truth."

Elisha to Ovadia's wife: "What do you have in your home?"

G-d to the soul: "What is left of you?"

Wife: "Your maid has nothing in the house except for a small cruse of oil."

Soul: "Nothing but my pure essence, the bit of fuel at my core which can never be diminished."

Elisha: "Borrow vessels from outside, from all your neighbors; do not borrow only a few empty vessels."

G-d: "Continue to perform many good deeds according to *Halacha*, even when they are 'borrowed' and 'empty'

6 Melachim II 4:1-7

— when you do not 'own' them with a sense of passion and stewardship."

Elisha: "..and pour [your oil] into these vessels..."

G-d: "Sometimes, the first 'vessel' must be a positive action in order to draw down the 'oil' of inspiration from above. When you focus on doing what is right, you will transform your sense of emptiness into a full, illuminating, pleasurable relationship with Me."

What can we learn from Ovadia's wife today?

When we recognize that the Divine is in the details, and we take positive actions according to *Halacha*, we create vessels for G-d's abundant blessings.

G-d has His "tastes" for even the mundane in our lives.

When unsure about a *Halacha*, we can reach out to a Rabbi or mentor for guidance.

When we trust in G-d's will and take a small action, even when we do not yet feel enthusiastic, blessings of connection and inspiration flow.

As the Rebbe Rashab said, "One action is better than a thousand sighs."[7]

BRICK BY BRICK

by Racheli Jacks

Brick by brick and with loving care
With devotion to which nothing can compare
A woman builds her home, her family
Guiding them to be all they can be

So many talents that are necessary
For a mother to fill her role properly
Her expertise and caring thoughtful deeds
With every action, she's planting seeds

Chorus: (2x)
Chochmas Noshim Bansa Baisa[8]
Starting from our Bat Mitzvah
With a woman's wisdom, she's the foundation of the Jewish nation

Learning from the "Women Of Worth"
We contribute to this earth
As we build our home
We build a home for *Hashem*
And the *Mikdash Hashlishi* Amen!

---

[7] Hayom Yom for 8 Adar II

[8] The wisdom of women builds her home. (King Solomon)

Pearls of Wisdom

While the Lubavitcher Rebbe was addressing a women's convention, passionately encouraging listeners to continue their activities on behalf of the Jewish people, he paused to remind them:

"...When a woman dresses her children in fresh clothing, feeds her children nutritious food, and goes around her home at night making sure that the windows are closed and no draft is blowing on her child, this too is avodas Hashem — the holy work of serving G-d!"

Aishes Chayil Story

Dedicated by Ben & Rachel Federman in honor of Mussia Federman's Bas Mitzvah

The Rebbe's Birthday Gift

A TRIBUTE TO

Leah Raizel Shmotkin-Helman OB"M

As told by her daughter Chedva Federman

Leah Raizel Shmotkin-Helman was an extremely kind and intelligent individual who recognized the importance of a solid education. Her emphasis was on instilling strong values and character traits in her children. She believed that while being knowledgeable is valuable, a person's character is of utmost importance.

In the 1960's, she headed *N'shei Chabad* in Kfar Chabad, Israel, with exceptional leadership and love. "She does not eat the bread of laziness." She took action and organized women's events and classes. In 1965, she arranged a birthday gift for the Lubavitcher Rebbe: a gold Kiddush cup from *N'shei Chabad*. Careful not to shame needier residents when she raised the funds, she set up a way for others to privately contribute whatever amount they could. She didn't know the amounts herself and added her own contribution.

She hired a goldsmith from Tel Aviv to design the cup, but the funds were insufficient to buy enough gold to complete the base which was wobbly. So, she immediately donated her gold heirloom watch received from her mother. The goldsmith melted the gold watch to complete the base, and the finished work was sent to the Rebbe with Mrs. Freida Kazarnovsky on behalf of N'shei Kfar Chabad.

Upon receiving the cup, the Rebbe smiled as he studied it and said: "Apparently, business is good in Kfar Chabad, as I wished." He added, "Kesiva Vechasima Tova."

Leah Raizel was *niftar* on *Rosh Chodesh* Adar 2 at the age of eighty years old.

GROW as an Aishes Chayil

Gratitude: **Why are you grateful today?**

Recognition: **Write your own story about an extraordinary woman whose actions shaped you.**

Oneness: **When was a time that you took the right action (halacha) even though you were not feeling inspired?**

Wish: **What is your wish from G-d?**

A Thread of Thanks

"Her children rise and celebrate her; and her husband, he praises her."

Digging Deeper

What does this verse mean?

An *Aishes Chayil*'s family members call her fortunate and praise her for her admirable deeds.[1]

Their praise follows in the next verse: "Many daughters have attained valor, but you have surpassed them all."

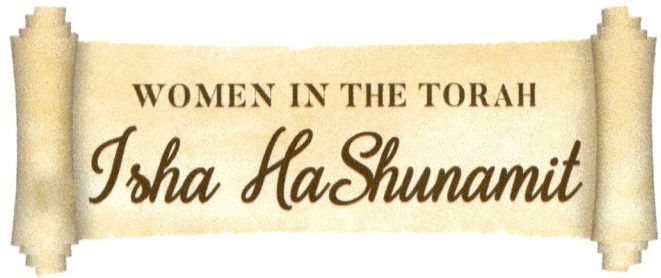

WOMEN IN THE TORAH
Isha HaShunamit

This "Shunamite woman" was called "a great woman"[2] because she pleaded with the Prophet Elisha to be her guest and eat at her home.[3]

What was Elisha's encounter with HaShunamit?

Immediately after assisting Ovadia's wife, Elisha journeyed to Shunam, where a woman offered him food and lodging. Grateful for her hospitality, Elisha blessed her with a son, named Chavakuk.

When he was a young boy, a splitting headache struck Chavakuk while he was out in the field, and he passed away. HaShunamit called her husband and requested a servant and donkey in order to summon Elisha for help. When he inquired what the occasion was for her trip, she calmly reassured him, "Shalom — It is alright."[4] Her calmness exhibited her strong faith that G-d would bring her son back to life.

HaShunamit traveled to find Elisha and begged him to save her child. Through prayer, Elisha revived the boy and she took him home.[5]

How did HaShunamit's son praise her?

Chavakuk grew up to be a great prophet. He praised his mother's faith, which she always lived by and which saved him, when he stated: "The righteous person shall live by his faith."[6] This was the greatest praise he could have given his mother.

What is the lesson for us today?

By living with kindness and faith, we instill it in the next generation. The living example we show each day amid challenging moments will surely leave an impression on children and earn their praise for generations to come.

1 Metzudas Dovid
2 Melachim II 4:8
3 Midrash Shachar Tov
4 Melachim II 4:22-23
5 See Melachim II 4:8-37
6 Chavakuk 2:4

Meaningful Melody

MY DEAR IMA

My dear *Ima* I'm sending this letter
To say the things I've never said
Of my impression as your daughter
These thoughts are running through my head

As far back as I can remember
You said *Shema* with me at night
Each week I saw you welcome Shabbos
I saw your candles burning bright

You made our home a house of Torah
Encouraged Abba to learn each day
You stood behind him through the hard times
You gave him strength in your own way

You taught us all about the mitzvos
Showed us the right way from the start
We always saw your love for Torah
You instilled it in our hearts

Now your children have grown older
Each one has gone their separate ways
But yet we follow in your footsteps
You made us what we are today

Now your daughter is a mother
She does the things you used to do
Not only did you build your own home
But *Ima* you built my home too

Dedicated in honor of the

Aishes Chayils before me:

My grandmother

Ruth Krieger שתחי׳

who chose a life of Torah and Mitzvos,

planting seeds of Yiddishkeit for

many generations to come

and my mother

Evelyn (Chava) Krieger שתחי׳

whose dedication to Jewish education

instilled in me a love for Judaism.

Dedicated by Leah Caras and family

Pearls of Wisdom

Jewish wealth is not houses and gold.

THE EVERLASTING JEWISH WEALTH IS:

Being Jews who keep Torah and Mitzvot, and bringing into the world children and grandchildren who keep Torah and Mitzvot.

—Hayom Yom 9 Nissan

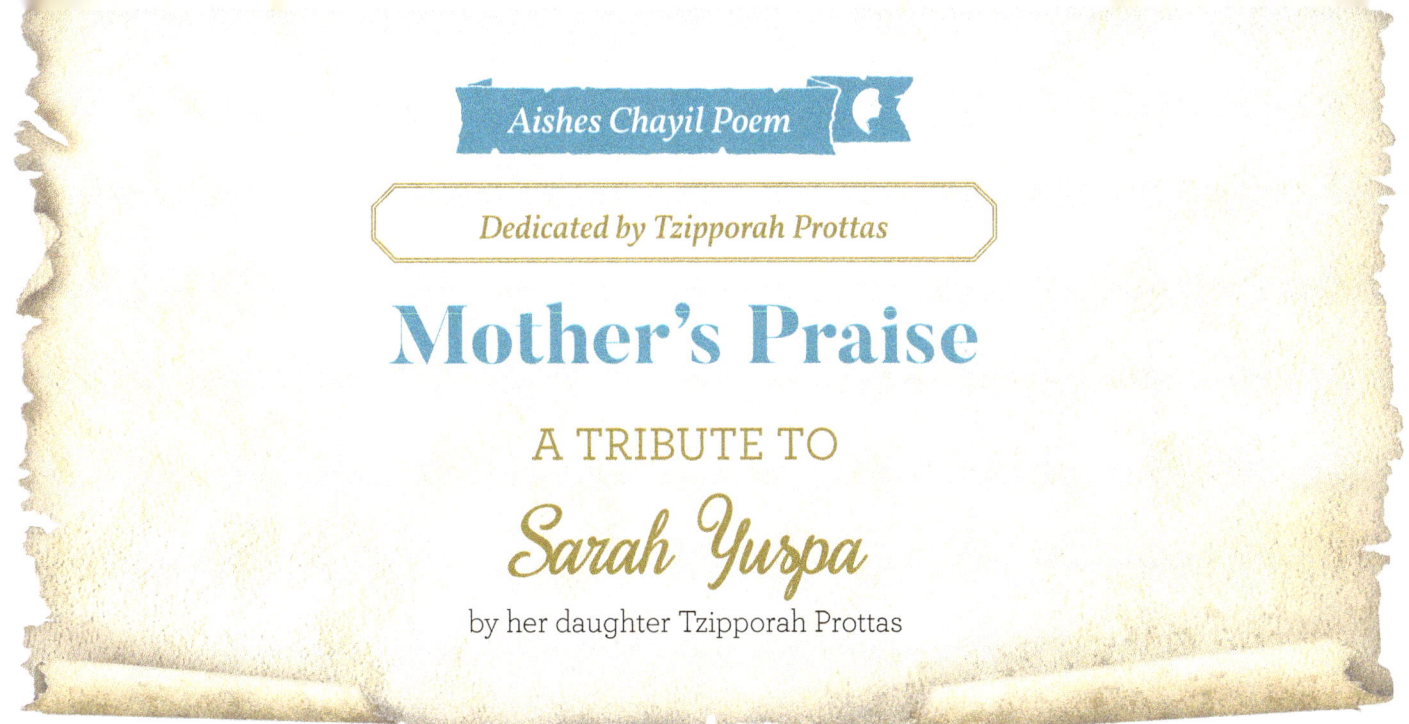

Mother's Praise

A TRIBUTE TO Sarah Yuspa

by her daughter Tzipporah Prottas

Mother, thank you for giving me life
For your loving devotion despite any strife
You birthed me and raised me
You taught me and shaped me
For this, you shall be praised

This poem's a token of gratitude
For your persistent patience despite my attitude
How you intuit my emotions, I haven't grasped
But in your embrace I am warmly clasped
For this, you shall be praised

When tension pervades, it must affect you
Yet you never cease doing what you must do
You stand strong in difficult times
Of juggling many roles, you're a paradigm
For this, you shall be praised

How you weather life's many storms
Causes an impression in my heart to form
Your devotion I wish to emulate
To those who need me; a duty so great
For this, you shall be praised

"Gamalas'hu tov v'lo ra, kol yemei chayeha"
She repays one's good, never their harm
All the days of her life, she is loving, loyal, warm
For this, my dear mother, you shall be praised

Aishes Chayil Poem

Dedicated by Shoshana Fox

My Dearest Mother

A TRIBUTE TO

Shaindel bas Yakov OB"M

by her daughter Shoshana Fox

As I look into the candle light, I see a myriad of colors—deep, nourishing and warm. It has been years since I've seen those colors, the ones coloring my memory of you. When I was four years young, your health began to decline. The bright light of your life dimmed ever so slowly. It put me on a path to discover within: the fabric of light that you had woven.

No, I did not have time to forge many memories or ask you about your life. Who were you? And who did you want me to become?

But, through the darkness, I hear a faint echo of your guiding voice toward light! You lead me on a path ever-so-clear... As I turn to *Hashem* to uncover in prayer, finding the *Emes* that you held so dear.

My prayer is to accept how You, *Hashem*, knowingly run every moment executively...

As best for ALL, with abundance of gifts, even those "faint in the echos..."

In my search through the years, of a living relationship with you — Mama -

Hashem answers my prayers, & opens doors, too!

   I pray for the light of peace that I once knew through you,

That light of warmth that always grew;

The soothing light through winds and thunder.

If loved ones stormed with confusion,

You soothingly brought out their inner cohesion;

I pray to bring out that calm ocean, when things are turbulent outside.

In complete serenity, you also could act quite boldly,

Quick to defend your inner makings.
As a child you committed to your dearest mother,
Who raised you alone, in turbulent weather,
With no father rearing you together,
No one to take you to *shul* as his little daughter.
Easily, you were told, "Make believe you are Ukrainian";
You could not reject your inner making.
In your mother's strength: despite the odds
She told you of your Jewish "Rod."
Speaking up, you stated, "I walk openly as a Jew!"
As you spun through your life of light, came more opportunities to walk above:
Before moving with your *bashert*, Baruch ben Chaim (ob"m), overseas -
Actually two whole months, if you please,
You told your employer of the news,
Who fired you on the spot, due to these.
No, you weren't interested in games of disguise of any kind!
With the same commitment to your mother,
You showed unwavering loyalty towards your beloved:
Years later, we saw how your influence on Papa grew...
He sang to you, his wife, on the day of my *chuppah*
With great emotion for a *Yiddishe Mama*;
And through his tears, came the laughter he once knew
That you brought with the light that he once drew from you!
The path you paved for me to take
Is that *Hashem* always guides my fate.
Into His sturdy, strong hands I can fall,
His faith in me I cannot shake.
Not a broken lantern, overlooked mitzvah,
or parenting mistake.
You did all this, through your loving Gaze!
Please help me, my mother dear:
Through lighting my Shabbos candlessence,
to whisper to our Father in Heaven,
To whom I, too, wish to be transparent.
Please remind me that I, too, have your calm flowing through;
"a healing light shining upon steady waters."
At all times, it is you holding my hand.
When I don't feel it, remind me to reach out to get it.
I can find my voice and talk to you.
I can hear your voice telling me I'm not alone
as I guide my children to the light of Hashem!

Even when I forget this calm, serene love,
All that I must do is see it in the eyes of Shayna,
who's named for you.
    Shayna's inner joy shines through the darkest of times;
    In similar fashion, she "girds her loins,"
    Reaching inward, for her strong voice.
    At times it beholds the Truth quietly;
    At other times, it comes out boldly;
Her joy comes, as yours, from knowing who she is as a Jew!

You gave us a path illuminated with your light,
your deep, nourishing presence
walking with us day and night.
Now, we too, gaze smilingly into the future...!
With tremendous gratitude,
Your daughter, Shoshana Malka

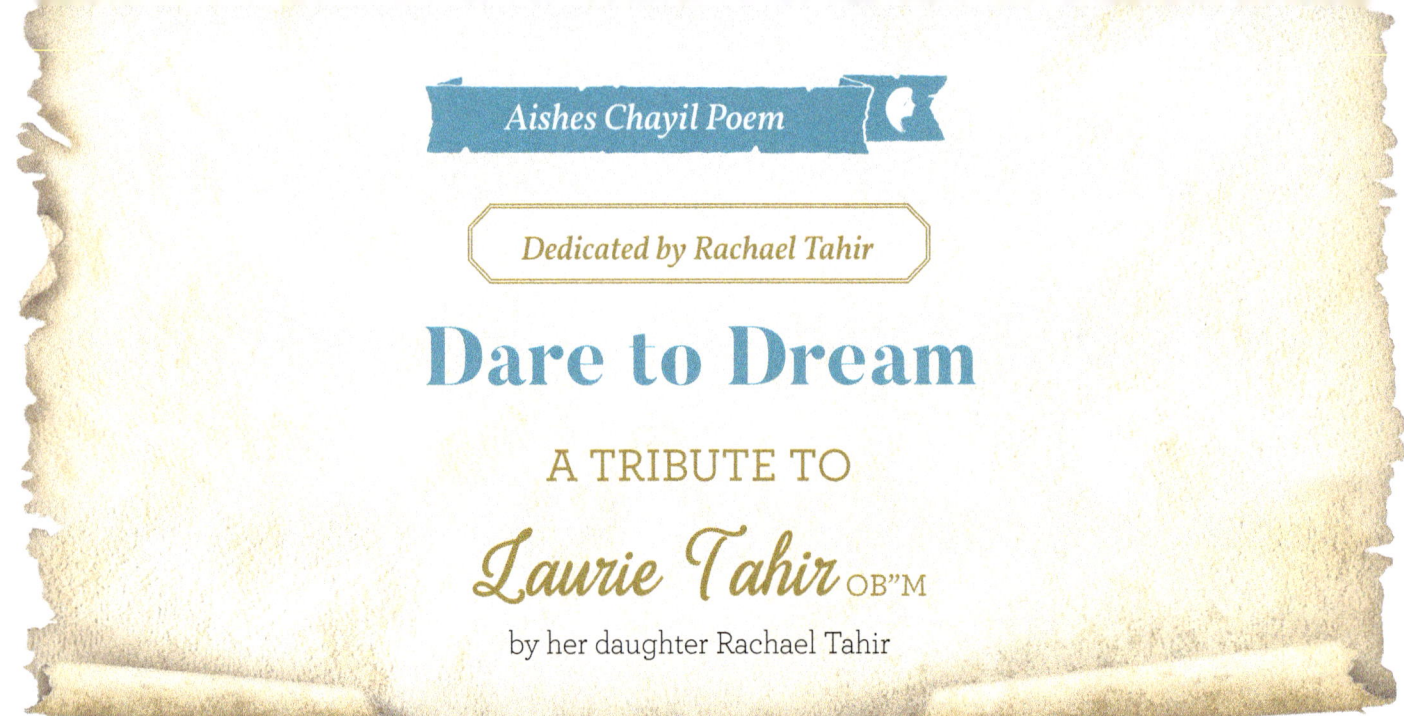

Dare to Dream

A TRIBUTE TO Laurie Tahir OB"M

by her daughter Rachael Tahir

Aishes Chayil Poem — Dedicated by Rachael Tahir

You fought so hard
For me, you did everything
I was your whole world
Because of you, I am who I am today

You helped me find my voice
Taught me to make the best choice
You believed in me

Told me to, "Dare to dream"
We were an incredible team
You will never know how much you mean to me

You influenced the community
Changed a school, it's true
You helped so many; times have changed
But we'll always remember you
An *Aishes Chayil*
You are a woman of valor
A beautiful soul

A woman of strength

We'll never forget you
Your legacy lives on
No matter where I go
You are with me in my heart

Oh, *Hashem*, thank You
Thank You for the gift of life
My mother's life, touching mine

I have the strength to get through
To accomplish almost anything
And it's all because of you, *Ima*
You forever ingrained Judaism in all I do

I miss you so
Your soul touched so many lives
Always in our hearts
I love you Mommy!

GROW as an Aishes Chayil

Gratitude: **Whom can you thank today?**

Oneness: **Write a letter of gratitude to your mother or a woman who cared for you and send it to her.**

Recognition: **Recognize a Woman of Valor in the Torah and how you would like to follow in her footsteps.**

Wish: **What is your wish from G-d?**

ל

A Thread of Success

*"Many daughters have attained valor,
but you have surpassed them all."*

Digging Deeper

What does this verse mean?

This is a continuation of the previous verse in which an *Aishes Chayil*'s husband and children praise her, for she surpasses others in attaining the title "a Woman of Valor."

WOMEN IN THE TORAH
Rus

Rus was a *Moaviah*, who entered under the wings of the Divine presence.[1]

She surpassed women around her, including her sister, Orpah, by recognizing that the true value in life is the fulfillment of G-d's will. Rus gave up a life of material wealth in the idolatrous palace of Moav in order to embrace the wealth of Torah and mitzvos.

What was Rus's journey?

When famine struck the land of Israel, the wealthy Elimelech and Naomi sought relief in Moav. They left behind the starving masses, fearing their endless pleas for help. While residing in Moav, their sons Machlon and Kilyon sought the hands of princesses Rus and Orpah in marriage. Tragically, Elimelech passed away, the family's fortune was lost, then Machlon and Kilyon, too, passed away childless.

One day, Naomi announced to her daughters-in-law that she was returning to her people in Israel. When they tried to accompany her, she refused, instead urging them to rebuild their lives. Persuaded, Orpah returned to a life of luxury in Moav, but Rus surpassed all expectations and clung to Naomi.

She informed Rus of the sacrifices necessary in order to

---

1 Midrash Shachar Tov

commit to a Torah life. Determined, Rus replied, "Wherever you go, I will go; wherever you lodge, I will lodge; your people are my people and your G-d is my G-d!"[2,3]

How did Rus surpass the women around her?

Impoverished, Rus and Naomi returned to Israel. When people saw them, they exclaimed, "Could this be Naomi?" She had changed so drastically from when she was the wealthy wife of Elimelech.

Sustaining herself and Naomi, Rus diligently gleaned grain from the fields left for the needy by Boaz, a righteous relative of Naomi. Boaz observed Rus's exceptional devotion to Naomi and her modest demeanor, which set her apart from the other harvesters.

Guided by Naomi, Boaz married Rus, who gave birth to Oved. From Oved descended David, and Rus witnessed his anointment as king. Furthermore, Moshiach will descend from Rus, Mother of royalty.

What can we learn from Rus's story about true success?

Rus exemplified the verse: "*Tov li Toras picha m'alfei zahav v'kasef* — טוב לי תורת פיך מאלפי זהב וכסף — The Torah of G-d's mouth is more precious to me than thousands of gold and silver."[4]

We, too, have the daily opportunity to recognize that G-d's will defines true value. Amassing Torah and mitzvos — not fame or fortune — constitutes true and lasting success and hastens the arrival of Moshiach!

2 Rus 12:16
3 Continue on to the next chapter for the complete dialogue of Rus and Naomi.
4 Tehillim 119:72

THE PRINCESS

By Sarah Leah Eber

One small voice in the dark
What difference can I make
Which path do I take?
An answer I must find
But wait, there's a voice

That says I should not fear
That voice it sounds so near
It's my *neshama* that I hear

Chorus:
Reach up high
Take a chance
Climb that mountain, here's my hand
Look inside, I'm your guide
To help you learn and understand

Show your face
Know what it takes
To make this world a better place
Your Jewish pride
You can't hide
It's there inside

You're the daughter of a King
A princess to be seen
Stand up tall, be proud and bold
A true *Bas Yisroel* to behold

Congratulations on the wonderful work.

May it bring us to the ultimate light of Moshiach!

Leah & Yitzchok Gniwisch

Of course I know
That you will win
Yagatee Umatzasi Taamin[5]
Reach for the stars
Know who you are
You'll go far.

THE CROWN OF CREATION

Sung by Chanale Fellig

The crown of creation
Lay broken and bent
What once could have been is all gone
But it is in our power to build and carry on

Oh Mother of Royalty
Woman of strength
The message alive in your home
Reveal the dimensions so hidden within
Restoring the crown of women again

Mother of royalty
Woman of strength
You carry the promise *Hachien*
The name that you bore
Will yet shine ever more
Restoring the crown to us again

5 If you try you will succeed. (Megilla, 6b)

Pearls of Wisdom

If a person says, "I have worked hard but have not found success," don't believe him.

If a person says "I have not exerted myself, and I have found success," don't believe him.

If he says "I gave it my all and I have found success, believe him!"

−Talmud, Megillah 6b

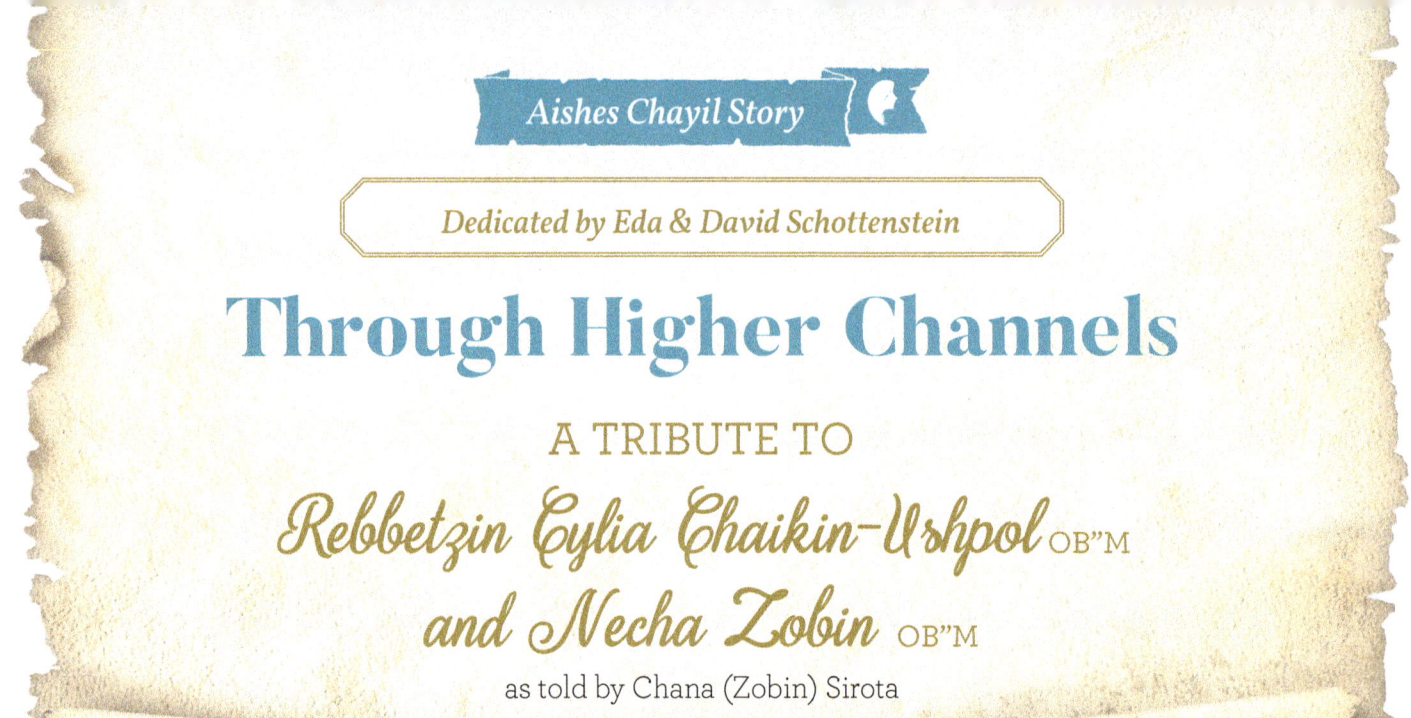

Aishes Chayil Story

Dedicated by Eda & David Schottenstein

Through Higher Channels

A TRIBUTE TO

Rebbetzin Cylia Chaikin-Ushpol OB"M
and Necha Zobin OB"M

as told by Chana (Zobin) Sirota

During the Soviet era, practicing Judaism and learning Torah in secret was considered a crime that could cost one their freedom and even their life. In 1938, the KGB arrested a group of Lubavitcher *Chassidim*, including Tzvi Hersh Zobin, who was newlywed at the time. They were sent to a brutal prison camp in northern Russia, where Tzvi Hersh relied on his sister Cylia for life-saving food parcels and news of home. Cylia informed Tzvi Hersh that his wife had given birth to a baby girl, but tragically, both perished in the Holocaust, along with Tzvi Hersh's father and siblings. Only Cylia and her two sons survived.

Cylia had an opportunity to leave the country with a Polish-Jewish group, but hesitated to leave her brother behind. Tzvi Hersh urged her to leave as soon as possible so that his only remaining family would survive.

After serving his ten-year sentence, Tzvi Hersh was welcomed by Lazer and Raizel Nanos, a Lubavitcher couple in Georgia, who arranged for him to marry their niece, Necha, called Nina. The young couple gave birth to a son named Dovid, and shortly thereafter Tzvi Hersh was arrested again for "anti-government activities." He was permanently exiled to Siberia, and

> *Cylia, now Rebbitzen Chaikin, who was living in Montreal, sent parcels and words of encouragement to the Zobins, which considerably improved their standard of living.*

his loyal wife Necha followed him with their son. There in Siberia, shortly after Stalin's death, they gave birth to a daughter named Chana on Tammuz 12.

After several years of waiting, the Zobins were finally granted freedom, but they endured further hardships once settled in Rostov. They were cramped living conditions, twice-rejected visas to Israel, and constant harassment and persecution. Cylia, now Rebbitzen Chaikin, who was living in Montreal, sent parcels and words of encouragement to the Zobins, which considerably improved their standard of living. She and her sons worked relentlessly to obtain visas on their behalf, finally securing Canadian visas for "sponsored immigrants." However, Russian authorities rejected the Zobin family's third visa application.

The Rebbe guided Cylia every step of the way during these years. In 1972, he advised her to try once again to bring the Zobins to Canada using "higher channels." Strengthened by the Rebbe's encouragement, Cylia refused to give up. With the help of the Montreal Lubavitch community, who gave her invaluable support and strength, she continued to appeal to "higher channels." She managed to contact a member of parliament and gain an audience with Mary McDonald, the administrative assistant of Canada's Prime Minister, Pierre Trudeau. President Alexei Kosygin of the USSR was expected in Canada, and McDonald convinced Trudeau to intervene on behalf of the Zobins. On the day of her remarriage to Rabbi Ushpol, Cylia heard the good news that her brother had received the exit visas, two weeks after Kosygin's return to Moscow.

The Zobins arrived in Montreal, thrilled to live openly

Chana Sirota at her wedding with Bubby Ushpol (top). Nina - Necha - is next to her in the bottom photo.

as frum Jews without fear of persecution. Several months later, they traveled to New York for a private audience with the Rebbe and were overwhelmed to be face-to-face after writing letters for years. The Zobins asked the Rebbe for a *bracha* for his family still in Russia, to which the Rebbe replied: "*Zei vellen kumen balt mit klenere nissim ve eich* — They will come soon with lesser miracles than you." Two weeks later, the relative sent word that his family had obtained exit visas to Israel in one month.

Chana Zobin was in Crown Heights again when she met her future husband, Yisroel Sirota, one Simchas Torah. The Sirotas were originally from Tashkent, where they faced unbelievable hardships, but they were luminous examples of self sacrifice. Yisroel's parents, Mordechai and Rivka, had opened their home in Tashkent as a sanctuary for hundreds of Jews fleeing the Nazis.

With the Rebbe's blessings, Chana and Yisroel married and moved to Montreal, where initially they were the only young, observant Russian Jews. Soon, more Russian immigrants began to arrive, and the Rebbe advised Yisroel to get involved with them as a shliach. One of the young Sirotas' first accomplishments was establishing the Jewish Russian Community Center — a division of the Chai Center of Montreal.

Today, the Sirotas organize communal holiday celebrations for hundreds. They arrange *brissim* and Bar mitzvahs for boys and men of all ages and have also arranged Jewish weddings for couples who had only civil marriages in Russia. As many Russian Jews had not been taught Hebrew, the Sirota's supplied Chumashim and Siddurim with Russian translations and directed a Russian Talmud-Torah for children. Volunteers at the Center pick up leftovers after events and distribute the food to needy immigrant families.

The Sirota's credit their impact to the enthusiasm and compassion of the local Jewish community, full-time *shluchim*, and many volunteers. "Our lives are often stressed and difficult," admits Chana. "But compared to the *mesiras nefesh* of our parents and the hardships still facing our fellow *shluchim* and Jews in Russia, we are indeed fortunate. We know that when we appeal to higher channels, *Hashem* will continue to send us His *brachos* until the coming of Moshiach."

At her Bas Mitzvah, Nina Schottenstein said, "Becoming a Bas Mitzvah means following in the footsteps of the women who have paved the way for us. My great-grandmother Necha, or Nina, is one such role model. She risked her life to be with her husband in Siberia, where my Bubby Chana Sirota was born. My Bubby and Zaidy, as well as my parents, have also been influential role models in my life.

For my Bas Mitzvah project, my mother partnered with Nechama Laber of Jewish Girls Unite to publish a journal of self-discovery called Seven Voices of Leadership. By studying the Prophetesses Sarah, Miriam, Devorah, Chana, Avigail, Chuldah, and Esther, girls can learn from these role models to become the best version of themselves and create positive change in the world."[1]

> *"Becoming a Bas Mitzvah means following in the footsteps of the women who have paved the way for us."*

Eda Schottenstein, mother of Nina, was a student of Nechama Laber when she was just 12 years old in Beth Rivkah, Montreal. Eda comes from a long line of strong and valiant women and she continues to inspire others to cultivate trust in G-d and to seek guidance from higher sources. As a testament to this, she sponsored The GROW Trust Planner, a journal inspired by Shaar Habitochon, The Gate of Trust, in honor of her daughter Aliyah's Bas Mitzvah in 2023. Both publications are available for purchase.

[1] Abridged version from an article in the N'Shei Chabad Newsletter, December 2000

GROW as an Aishes Chayil

Gratitude: **Express gratitude for something you are proud of.**

Oneness: **What is something you can do today for which your future self will thank you? What is your next step towards success?**

Recognition: **How do you define true success? What is your vision for success?**

Wish: **What is your wish from G-d?**

ש

A Thread of
True Beauty

*"Charm is false and beauty is vain;
a G-d-fearing woman, she should be praised."*

Digging Deeper

What does this verse mean?

Charm and beauty are empty when they do not accompany reverence. Yet in a world where *"sheker hachein,"* falsehood has charm and *"hevel hayofi,"* vanity has beauty, standing apart is a challenge. Therefore, *"isha yiras Hashem hee tis'halal"* — a woman who embodies awe of G-d and true Torah values certainly earns praise.[1]

This is her true, inner beauty, which her husband applauds in a continuation of his praise from the previous verse.[2] An *Aishes Chayil* is also recognized for her children — and anyone whom she teaches — who emulate her by fulfilling Torah and mitzvos with joy, love and reverence.[3]

How did the Lubavitcher Rebbe explain this verse?

In 1991, Miri Goldfarb, a winner of the "Miss Israel" beauty contest, visited the Rebbe for a blessing and a dollar for charity. He remarked: "The Torah says 'Beauty is false,' but continues, 'a G-d-fearing woman is to be praised.' The commentaries explain that if a woman is G-d-fearing, she uses her beauty for beautiful endeavors in Torah and mitzvos. Give this message to your friends, also to the organizer and the entire group. Good tidings!"

And to the organizer of the visit, the Rebbe said: "You brought the beautiful women… May they be beautiful in Torah and mitzvos."

1 Rashi
2 Alshich
3 Chomat Anach

At the Splitting of the Sea, the children proclaimed, *"Zeh Keili v'anveihu* — This is my G-d and I will glorify Him!"[4] Our Sages relate *"anveihu* (אנוהו) — I will glorify Him" to *noi* (נוי), meaning "beauty" or "decoration," and interpret this verse to mean: Beautify yourself before G-d in Mitzvos.[5] Even if one fulfills the mitzvah by performing it simply, it is proper to do so as beautifully as possible.

What guides an Aishes Chayil to create a home filled with awe of G-d?

She is guided by the mission of the Jewish people to create a dwelling place for G-d in the physical world. Through continuous learning, she acquires a deep understanding of G-d's directives and how to translate them into action. King Shlomo said, "A woman's wisdom builds her home."[6]

Furthermore, we see in the story of the creation of the first woman, Chava, that the word *binah*, "understanding," shares a root with *"vayiven* — and He built." G-d endowed women with an extra measure of understanding.[7]

What is the connection between understanding and building?

The Rebbe Maharash explains that every Jewish woman is innately G-d-fearing because G-d endows her with a special understanding in order to build a Divine dwelling, an everlasting edifice based on Torah and mitzvos, in which children will be raised in the spirit of Judaism.

4 Shemos 15:2.
5 Talmud, Shabbos 133b
6 Mishlei 14:1
7 Talmud, Niddah 45b

A Jewish woman's staunch devotion to her Divine mission will ultimately illuminate the entire world, making it a fit abode for G-d.[8]

Which word hints to a G-d-fearing woman's true beauty?

"*Hachein* (החן)" — the Hebrew term for "charm, grace, beauty" is an acronym for the three fundamental mitzvos entrusted to every Jewish woman and girl, which reveal her true beauty:

ה *Hadlokas Haneiros* — kindling the Shabbos candles

ח *Challah* — setting aside a portion of one's dough

נ *Niddah* — sanctity of the family

Torah and mitzvos are the foundation of every Jewish household, and the three most fundamental mitzvos of Jewish family life were entrusted to the Jewish woman, as she is the solid pillar of the home. The name Chana (חנה) also serves as an acronym for the Hebrew names of these three mitzvos (חלה, נדה, הדלקת הנרות), for the prophetess Chana serves as a paradigm for Jewish women.

How do the three mitzvos entrusted specifically to Jewish women reflect our mission as Jews?

Our Sages compare the bond between G-d and the Jewish people to a marriage, and our world serves as the home for this ultimate couple. G-d created the raw materials, but delegated to the Jewish people — His wife — the responsibility of infusing them with spiritual purpose.

Here is how these three mitzvos serve as a blueprint for weaving together the physical and spiritual fabric of the Jewish home, connecting generations, and illuminating the world:

8 Lubavitcher Rebbe, Convention of N'shei Ubnos Chabad, 25th Day of Iyar, 5744/1984

1. Challah: The act of setting aside a portion of one's dough and dedicating it to G-d elevates the entire dough from the physical to the spiritual realm. It also extends to the preparation of kosher food, where even the simple acts of eating and drinking are carried out in a manner that reflects one's connection with G-d.

Prayer: May G-d bless the family with ample livelihood so that they can support and contribute generously to charitable causes.

2. Niddah — Family Purity: The observance of the Torah's guidelines for maintaining the holiness of marital life. This includes purification in a mikvah. Here, too, a basic physical activity draws down the highest spiritual energies.

Prayer: May Hashem bless the family with healthy children who will grow up to be pious and upstanding men and women.

3. Hadlakas Haneros — Kindling the Shabbos Candles: This mitzvah involves lighting candles to welcome the Shabbos and festivals into our homes. Women are uniquely gifted with the ability to generate light, and the candles symbolize all the mitzvos that add light to the world. King Solomon said, "A mitzvah is a candle, and the Torah is light."[9]

Prayer: May G-d illuminate the home with Shalom Bayis and with children radiating nachas.

We have G-d's promise: "If you cherish the lights of Shabbos, I will show you the lights of Zion."[10] Shabbos is a foretaste of "the Day which is entirely Shabbos."[11]

Kindling Shabbos candles brings the future era of Moshiach.

When does Jewish education begin and at what age should a girl light candles?

Education in the mitzvos begins at a young age, since a Jew inherits the entire Torah at birth, as it is written: "The Torah which Moshe commanded us is the inheritance of the congregation of Yaakov."[12] As a child grows, so does their soul, and once they begin to speak, they are taught the above verse.

When a girl reaches the age that she can understand the difference between light and darkness and that kindling a candle adds light to the home, she is taught to kindle the Shabbos and festival lights. Her education in all aspects of Judaism prepares her to carry out her sacred mission as an ambassador of light.[13] [14]

WOMEN IN THE TORAH

Rus

The Midrash attributes the final three verses of "*Aishes Chayil*" to Rus for her noble ways. She was committed to observing the three special mitzvos entrusted to Jewish women (see above). She surpassed all women when she left her wealthy mother and father and

---

9 Mishlei 6:23
10 Yalkut Shimoni, Parshas Behaalos'cha, sec. 719
11 Tamid 7:4
12 Devarim 33:4
13 Based on a talk of the Lubavitcher Rebbe at the Convention of N'shei Ubnos Chabad, 25th of Iyar, 5744/1984
14 For further reading on the Jewish understanding of true beauty: https://jewishaction.com/religion/shabbat-holidays/sukkot/the-etrog-jewish-beauty-and-the-beauty-of-jewishness

departed to Israel with her mother-in-law, Naomi, to accept the mitzvos. She valued a life of Torah and her inner, spiritual wealth radiated true beauty.

How did Rus communicate her devotion to the mitzvos?

When Naomi instructed Rus to return to her family in Moav, she replied with these words:

"Where you will walk, I will walk." I accept the laws of Shabbos [when the distances we may walk are limited].

"Where you will lie, I will lie." I accept the prohibitions on being alone with a man.

"Your people are my people." I accept the six hundred and thirteen mitzvos.

"Your G-d is my G-d." I accept belief in one G-d and will give up idol worship.

"And in that which you will die, I will die, and there I will be buried." I accept the four death penalties of the Jewish court.[15]

What was Rus's reward?

She merited to become the great-grandmother of King David, who gave pleasure to the Holy One, blessed be He, with songs and praises. In the future, our redeemer Moshiach will also descend from her.[16]

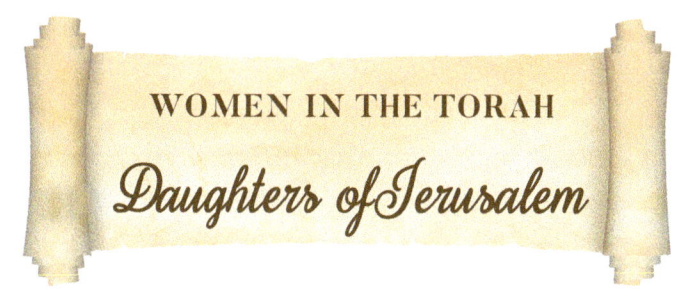

WOMEN IN THE TORAH
Daughters of Jerusalem

King Shlomo emphasized the importance of reverence for G-d, as shown by the following Talmudic tradition where young men sought proper brides:

There were no greater festivals for Israel than the 15th of Av and Yom Kippur. On these days, the daughters of Jerusalem would go out in borrowed white garments in order not to shame anyone who had none. They would dance in the vineyards. And what would they say? "Young man, raise your eyes and see which you choose for yourself. Do not set your eyes on beauty… for 'Charm is false and beauty is vain; [but] a G-d-fearing woman, she should be praised.'"[17]

How can we apply this to our lives?

In our quest to find the *Aishes Chayil* within us, it is crucial to take care of our external appearance and well-being while also aligning it with our soul's mission.

G-d chooses us and sees our true, inner beauty. When we recognize our value and utilize the gifts He has given us, we choose Him as our Divine partner.

G-d witnesses our kindness, compassion, imperfections, and struggles to grow through challenges to live a life of Torah values. As a result, we radiate from the inside out as G-d's *Aishes Chayil*.

---

15 Midrash Shachar Tov
16 Midrash Shachar Tov

17 Talmud, Taanis 26b

THE "MAKE-UP" OF A JEWISH HOME

When applying makeup to the face, it might take just a few minutes. However, applying the makeup of the Jewish home takes a lifetime, as we constantly seek ways to improve it. The manner of physical beautification can serve as a reminder for spiritual beautification.

Foundation: Foundation is foremost in the makeup of a Jewish home, which sets the tone with shades like Shabbos and holiday observances, Jewish art and music, and the Jewish feelings we imbue in our family.

Blush: When it comes to the makeup of the Jewish home, there is no need for the blush of embarrassment about being Jewish! Rather, we should allow our inherent Jewish pride to shine naturally.

Eyeliner: Just as a neat line defines our eyes, we should aim to carefully shape our perceptions of others, always seeking to judge them favorably, identify those who need our assistance, and view Torah and mitzvos in the proper light.

Eye Shadow: Eye shadow colors the eyelid, and in Judaism, we seek ways to add vibrancy to our heritage. By doing additional mitzvos, we add color to our family traditions!

Mascara: Mascara, though black, enhances beauty. Similarly, at first glance, Torah and mitzvos may seem plain or restrictive. However, if we look more closely, we can appreciate the beauty that each additional mitzvah adds to the home.

Lipstick: Just as lipstick enhances the lips, the words that emanate from our lips have the power to enhance the atmosphere in the Jewish home. Therefore, let us choose to speak positively, express gratitude and praise, and thank G-d for our home.

Matte: Matte is the final touch makeup looking fresh throughout the day. Just as makeup needs that finishing touch, our home can benefit from those finishing touches that make it truly remarkable. Whether it's the warmth in our interactions, or the traditions that add meaning, these 'final touches' are the secrets to creating a Jewish home that stands the test of time.

Mirror: One always needs a mirror to apply makeup. The Baal Shem Tov taught that we can learn a lesson in serving G-d from everything in life. Mirrors enable us to examine ourselves, and spiritually, we can reflect deeply within ourselves. When you look in the mirror each morning, you will find the person who can change the world — the choice is yours!

Reflect: "Is the me that I see the me I want to be?"

Reflect: "Which Women of Valor will I mirror today?"

Meaningful Melody

DEEP IN THE GROUND

Lyrics by Racheli Jacks

Deep in the ground
Yet to be found
A gemstone concealed
Waiting to be revealed

A polish, a shine
And before our eyes
A glittering diamond
In majesty it lies

Chorus:
Aishes Aishes Chayil
A precious woman who can find?
Gleaming in every facet
Revealing she's one of a kind

Through challah, lighting candles
And raising her family
Sheker Hachein
It's not appearance or fame
Unlocking her inner beauty

Meaningful Melody

ETERNALLY BRIGHT

By Basia Kahn and Chaya Bracha Rubin

A tiny flame ignited
Late Friday afternoon
Standing in front of her *lichtelach*
Shabbos is coming soon
Waving her hands gracefully
She brings Shabbos to her home
A light majestic
Full of *bracha* and shalom

Chorus:
So precious and so unique
The mitzvos of *Bnos Yisroel*
They fill us with *heilige* light
Shining eternally bright

My dear sisters
More than we know
The power we have to transform
Ourselves
And our homes
Into a *mikdash me'at*

A bowl of puffy challah dough
So warm, it grows
She pulls a small piece away
With a *bracha* focused and slow
Separated for *Hashem*
Giving her first and her best to Him

Making her food *Kadosh*
Instilling *kochos*

Her actions, speech, behavior and more
The Torah is her guide
Gracefully and modestly
Royalty full of pride
Bringing *nachas* to *Hashem*
More than you can
Imagine
Hashem pours *brachos*
More than you can fathom

I WILL GO WHERE YOU WILL GO

By Rivky Feld

I will go where you will go
And that is where I'll stay
I want to lead a Holy life
Not one of glitter and fame

To be a princess, Moabite
Is not my kind of life!
I'd rather stay with you always
In pain, hunger, or strife

Shabbos *Kodesh*, that is what I'll keep
I will go where you will go and that is where I'll sleep
Your people are my people now
Your G-d is my G-d!
Amech Ami, V'elokayich Elokai

Eretz Yisroel, the focus of G-d's eye
If death will make us separate
That is where I'll lie

I will go where you will go
And that is where I'll stay
I want to live a Jewish life
To be with you always
Please don't push me away

Pearls of Wisdom

"If a woman is G-d-fearing, she uses her beauty for beautiful endeavors in Torah and mitzvos."

-The Lubavitcher Rebbe to Miss Israel, 1991

Dedicated to all women and girls who perished. We will keep your flames burn-

Shabbos Candles — הדלקת נרות :החן

One Mitzvah Overcomes Total Darkness

Excerpted from I Shall Live *by Edith Davidovici*

It was miraculous that while in Auschwitz, I sometimes managed to focus on the spiritual when the physical was so overwhelmingly bleak. I was surrounded by women who had clearly lost their will to live. I prayed for Divine deliverance and that the flame within all of us, the will to survive, would continue to burn brightly within me. I turned to my sister-in-law with a plan to reinvigorate our spiritual senses.

"Would you be willing to sacrifice a ration of bread so that we can buy Shabbos candles?" I asked Eta.

The international currency of the camp was bread. One could buy lots of things if one was willing to give up one's bread. Eta agreed, so I managed to procure a candle for bread. I cut it in half so that I now had two candles. I was quite proud of my bargain, for I had been successful in getting this candle for one slice of bread, and not two, which was the "original" price.

After securing the candles, we anxiously waited for Friday to arrive so that we could secretly execute our plan. The work of that week seemed less harsh because we were focused on the arrival of Shabbos. We hardly felt the great pangs of hunger caused by sacrificing our precious bread ration to buy the candle. We were ready to welcome the Shabbos Queen in all her splendor and glory. We were ready to revel in the radiance of Shabbos.

> *"Would you be willing to sacrifice a ration of bread so that we can buy Shabbos candles?" I asked Eta.*

That Friday night, Eta and I each lit one half of the precious candle. We had lit Shabbos candles many times in our lives, but our prayers that evening were something special. Our tears flowed like fountains. We cried and cried long into the night. To accomplish this precious mitzvah, this ancient ritual, in the death camps was so very poignant.

The flickering flames were our light of hope for the future. They were affirmation of our faith and the bright shining lights of our souls, which no Nazi, even the cruelest and most brutal, can ever extinguish. My sister-in-law and I could not stop gazing at the flickering flames. They gave us hope that we would escape the confines of the barbed wire and reunite with our families.

The flickering flames were our light of hope for the future. They were affirmation of our faith and the bright shining lights of our souls, which no Nazi, even the cruelest and most brutal, can ever extinguish.

Aishes Chayil Story

Challah — חלה ׃ החן

Bubbe's Challah

A TRIBUTE TO

Bubbe Muriel – Marnina Leah bat Aharon OB"M

by Susan Axelrod

When my in-laws moved into an assisted living residence, we knew that we had seen the last year with homemade '*challey*' from *Bubbe*.

For 30 years of my life, I had the pleasure of celebrating Rosh Hashanah with home-baked challah from my mother-in-law, Muriel Goldenberg Axelrod. It was always a source of pride for her, and we felt blessed to spend the High Holy Days with either my family or my husband's family. When we were not with her, she made sure we had *challey* wherever we were.

When my husband was a young man, he became the High Holiday *chazan* for his home synagogue, and every year we would go there and I would gorge myself on 'Mum's' challah and honey. When I became president of my congregation, we had to decide whether to be apart for the holidays or if he would give up his contract

Nechama's Challah on the Axelrods' Rosh Hashanah table

for those years. Fortunately, he was recruited to become the High Holiday *chazan* at our congregation and my in-laws started coming to us and Mum brought her *challey* with her.

The year that my beloved in-laws entered the last chapter of their lives, we knew home-baked challah was a tradition of the past. Neither my husband nor I had ever learned to bake challah.

That year, the day of *Erev* Rosh Hashanah, I got a call from Nechama Laber saying she had challah for me and asking when she could bring it over. Though both of us were so busy, we managed to meet at her home just long enough for her to hand me a bag with five round challahs in it for the holidays.

Though Nechama had no idea about it, I knew immediately of the importance of this to me and to my family. Over those holiday meals, time and again we

> *The year that my beloved in-laws entered the last chapter of their lives, we knew home-baked challah was a tradition of the past. Neither my husband nor I had ever learned to bake challah.*

told the story of how we didn't think that we would have home-baked '*challey*' that year, but we did thanks to Nechama Laber, and the work she does helping others.

The first bite of challah was an 'event' at our *Yom Tov* table because we were, of course, such homemade challah mavens. Though unspoken, we were all thinking the same thing, "How good can this be? It can't be as good as Mum's. My father-in-law, Saul Axelrod, was the one who said "Mur, this is good." And we all agreed.

We delighted in the sweet honey from Rabbi Laber's own beehives, and I was elated to have delicious home-baked honey cakes that Nechama also provided for us. While we did not know what *Hashem*'s plans were for my mother-in-law, that year was undoubtedly a good celebration with Nechama's challahs. Sadly, Mum passed away a few months later.

Was challah the binding ingredient for my relationship with Nechama and JGR (the Jewish Girls Retreat)? Founded a decade earlier, JGR is a program for young Jewish girls from the heart of a premier Jewish educator, Nechama Dina Wasserman Laber. I had been on my own spiritual journey and we bonded over a shared interest, helping our Jewish daughters become Jewish mothers. It was in that year of *Bubbe's challey*, 2014, that we started working together to envision a global online platform for Jewish girls; our shared mission was to create a global community of empowered Jewish girls and women, using innovative approaches in education and technology.

Together, we envisioned creating a permanent home for the Jewish Girls Retreat and the global headquarters for Jewish Girls Unite (JGU). Today, JGR is located at the beautiful Jewish Greenbush Retreat in the Southern Adirondacks. JGU is an established global institution spreading love of *Hashem* and love for all of our Jewish daughters (of all ages!). It's heaven on earth, a place to learn to bake challah now that *Bubbe* can no longer do it.

I weep with love for my own precious Jewish daughters, Rebecca and Sarah and am grateful to be part of creating something that binds them to their *Bubbe* and is part of their lasting legacy.

That year, the day of Erev Rosh Hashanah, I got a call from Nechama Laber saying she had challah for me and asking when she could bring it over.

I'm **Grateful** for coming together with Nechama Laber; I **Recognize** the power of conscious commitment to our world; in **Oneness** with *Hashem*, I pray for love and grace for all of our Jewish daughters, and I **Wish** for ongoing impact in this space.

Women and girls, keep baking your challahs!

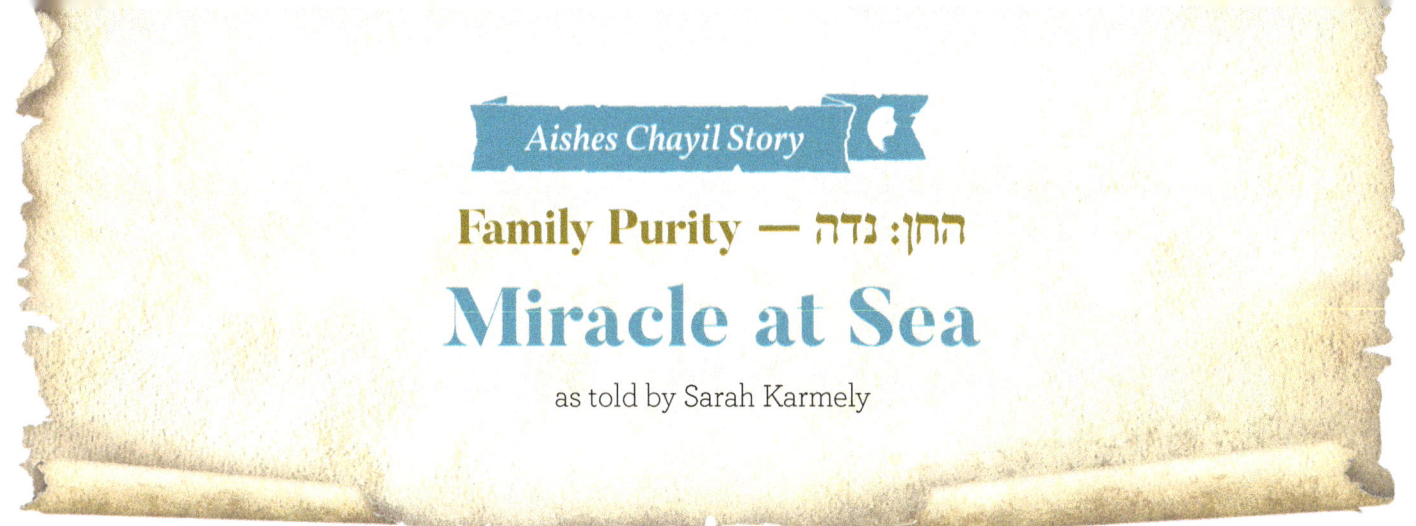

Aishes Chayil Story

Family Purity — החן: נדה

Miracle at Sea

as told by Sarah Karmely

I was in Bangkok, Thailand when Ronit, my husband's cousin, told me her personal story. Before there was a *Mikvah* in Bangkok, women would have to travel down to the seaside and immerse themselves in the sea. Over twenty years ago, the Lubavitcher Rebbe had instructed the four Jewish families living in Thailand to construct a *Mikvah*.

They took a long time to fulfill his wishes because they reasoned, "Who would want to go to the *Mikvah* in this foreign country?" Currently, thank G-d, the small *Mikvah* in the Chabad House in Bangkok is used by immigrants, Jewish visitors and many Israeli families.

Anyway, returning to Ronit's story, she had to prepare herself at home and travel with her husband to the nearest seaside town, Pattaya, about two hours away. Her husband would drive the "water-scooter," and they would go out into the sea where Ronit would immerse herself. They would then make the two-hour return journey.

After a couple of years, something amazing happened. One day, when it was time for Ronit to go to the *Mikvah*, she and her husband prepared as usual and drove to the seaside town. They rented a water-scooter and went out to sea, far enough for privacy.

Ronit immersed herself in the sea, and then mounted the scooter. Her husband turned the key in the ignition, but the engine did not take. He tried again and yet again, many times, until they both realized — the motor was dead, totally! Ronit and her husband swam towards the shore with apprehension, as the current in the Andaman Sea is notoriously strong and can sweep swimmers out to sea without their realizing it. However, they found themselves being driven towards a big, craggy rock-formation in the sea, and they both realized that it was essentially all

> "Who would want to go to the Mikvah in this foreign country?"

They both lifted up their faces, raised their voices, and together they instinctively cried out to Hashem: "Save us, Hashem! Don't let people say that we were killed while performing your mitzvah!"

over for them. Despite this, Ronit said matter-of-factly that it still did not register with them that they were going to die. She only thought about how her mother would react when she found out that her daughter was smashed to pieces on the rocks.

Faced with certain death, they both lifted up their faces, raised their voices, and together they instinctively cried out to *Hashem*: "Save us, *Hashem*! Don't let people say that we were killed while performing your mitzvah!"

Suddenly, a strong wave came out of nowhere and swept them safely back to shore! *Hashem* listened to their cries and saved them! "That was the month I conceived," Ronit said quietly and emotionally. "After two agonizing years of trying to have a baby, that month *Hashem* finally granted me my wish. The son I gave birth to, we called Doron, which means 'gift'."

Thankfully, today we don't have to endanger ourselves by going into unknown waters or travel long hours each month to fulfill *Hashem*'s will. We can go to a warm, clean, and safe Mikvah with modern conveniences and even luxurious surroundings. However, even if we had to go to a muddy hole in the ground, we would still do it to fulfill *Hashem*'s will because He is our Creator and knows what benefits us, our relationship with our spouse, our children, and Him.

GROW as an *Aishes Chayil*

Gratitude: I am grateful for my beautiful self because...

I'm grateful for the mitzvah of...

Recognition: How can you elevate your physical beauty by using it for a mitzvah?

Write a poem recognizing why you cherish and how you beautify one of the three special mitzvos entrusted to Jewish women.

Oneness: How can you beautify a mitzvah?

Wish: Inspired by this verse, what is your wish from G-d?

תְּנוּ לָהּ מִפְּרִי יָדֶיהָ וִיהַלְלוּהָ בַשְּׁעָרִים מַעֲשֶׂיהָ.

ת

A Thread of Redemption

*"Give her the fruit of her hands,
and let her deeds praise her at the gates."*

Digging Deeper

Why does King Shlomo conclude "Aishes Chayil" by saying, "...let her deeds praise her..."?

She is praised for her actions and the character she develops rather than the gifts G-d endowed her with at birth.[1]

Her lifelong deeds speak for themselves, earning her the praise of all who pass by the city gates.[2]

Alternatively, "the gates" refer to the Gates of Redemption.

Why are the accomplishments of an Aishes Chayil compared to fruits?

Some people grow like wheat, which ripens in a single season. Others grow like dates, which may take seventy years to blossom. However, before wheat can provide nourishment, one must harvest, thresh, grind and knead it into bread and dispose of the waste. Once dates finally mature, their sweetness offers instant delight and the entire palm tree has value.

An *Aishes Chayil* understands that true satisfaction comes after years of effort and dedication. She prioritizes her personal growth while also being a positive influence on others, helping them to grow, even when progress is slow. Eventually, she reaps the sweet fruits of her labor.

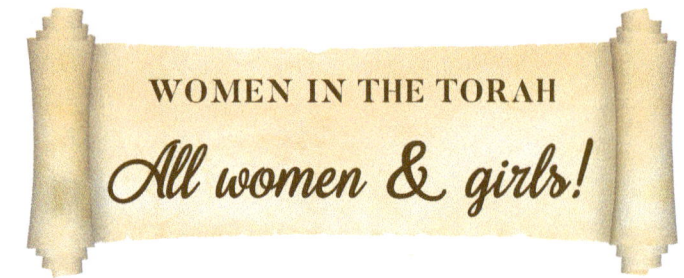

WOMEN IN THE TORAH
All women & girls!

The concluding verse of the "*Aishes Chayil*" is the third verse attributed to Rus. Learn from her to be strong in ethical behavior, keep the Torah, and be rescued from the evil inclination.[3]

In addition to Rus, we dedicate this verse to all girls and women who are bringing the redemption today.

What kind of attitude will pave the way for us to achieve our goals and ultimately reap the fruits of Redemption?

"The sweetest fruits of life take the longest to mature."
-Tzvi Freeman

Every moment of your journey is precious. It may be that you cannot see a reason or cannot fathom the plan of your Creator. Nevertheless, when you "work your land" with trust in G-d, He will bless you and cause the fruits of your labor to grow.

Together, we will transform this physical realm into G-d's garden and sanctuary, and reveal the inner purpose of creation. We will reap the spiritual harvest by 'sowing our fields' with seeds of light, 'pruning our vineyards' to remove negative habits, and 'branching out' with good deeds, always striving toward the ultimate goal of tasting the sweet fruits of Redemption.[4]

---

1 Rabbeinu Bachya
2 Rashi, Metzudas Dovid

3 Midrash Shachar Tov
4 Based on a talk of the Lubavitcher Rebbe for Parshas Behar, 5735/1975; see the introduction to this book for more

In a letter, the Lubavitcher Rebbe calls upon all Jewish women, mothers and daughters:

"Follow the example of your mothers of old and keep alive the great tradition of Jewish womanhood. Remember, the future of our people is largely your responsibility!"

In YOUR merit, we will be redeemed and the fruits will be truly sweet. Your good deeds will complete the tapestry of creation, bringing us to the Gates of Redemption and rebuilding the third *Beis Hamikdash* in the Holy Land. May it be now!

THE SECRET

By 8th Day

My grandmother whispered a secret to me
And placed something soft in my hands
I crafted this scarf for you my dear child
And my love for you is in every strand
But setting each stitch and knitting the rows
With patterns to form a design
Takes passion and skill, the will to create
And hours and hours of time

Hazorim b'dimah b'rinah, b'rinah yiktzoru
B'rinah, na, na, na, na
Hazorim b'dimah b'rinah, b'rinah yiktzoru
Oh oh oh oh
B'rinah yiktzoru

WELCOME TO OUR GARDEN

by Racheli Jacks

Welcome to our garden
Its beauty so divine
The grass is green, the flowers thrive
Each plant its own design

Come and join our team
Where we each do our part
Bringing heaven down to earth
A stunning piece of art

To make this happen, we must have a plan
With each of our good deeds
We're planting little seeds
Our souls we're nurturing
Making this world evergreen
Where G-dliness is seen

Now look
The trees are starting to bear fruit
With each of our good deeds
Removing all the weeds
Our world we are nurturing
Geula revealed soon
Our garden in full bloom

Second time:
With Hashem's help
plow and sow
Ready Set GROW!

Pearls of Wisdom

הזורעים בדמעה
ברנה יקצרו

"Those who sow with **tears** will reap with **song**."

—Tehillim 126:5

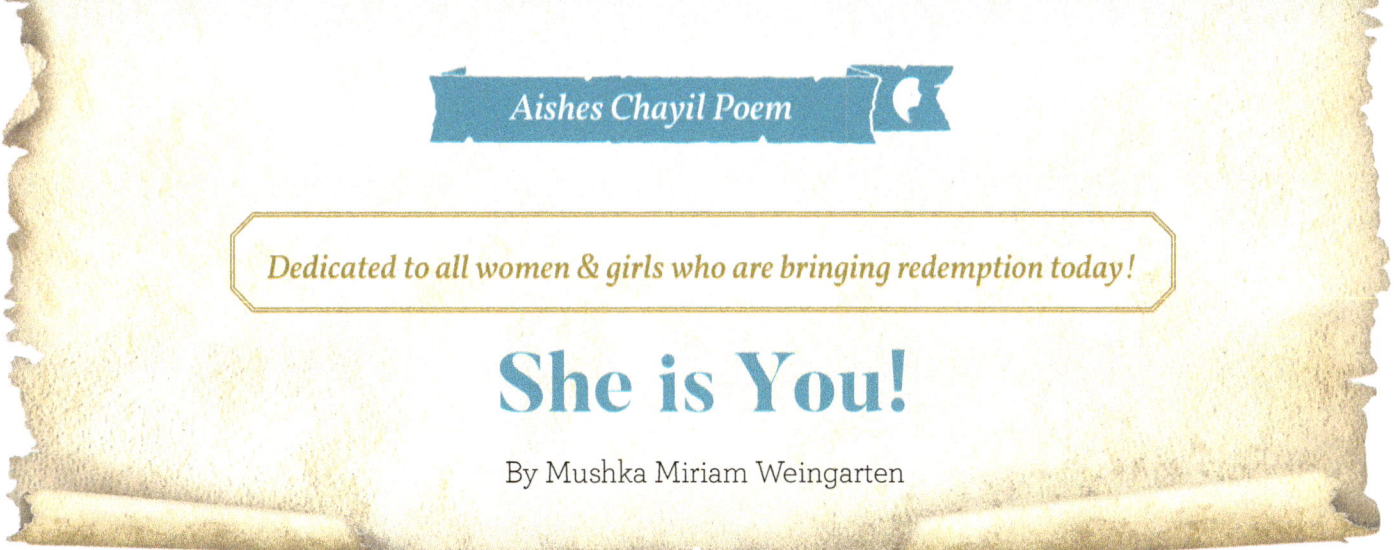

Aishes Chayil Poem

Dedicated to all women & girls who are bringing redemption today!

She is You!

By Mushka Miriam Weingarten

Sarah, Rivkah, Rochel
Michal, Rachav and Rus
They share common threads
Although different textures
   and colors
Some vibrant
Some light and soft
Woven together
They create an elaborate
   tapestry

With threads of hope
Threads of care
Threads of compassion and
   nurture

With threads of strength
Threads of faith
Threads of courage and
   endurance

With threads of modesty
Threads of royalty
Threads of joy and
   understanding

Woven together to create a
   tapestry
A tapestry that is more than an
   ornament
   or design

It is an ever-growing tapestry
That grows bigger
Stronger
With each generation
With each woman

Not an ordinary woman
A superwoman
A woman who
Through painting and art
Through decorating and
   design
Through writing and an open
   heart
Through cooking and baking
Through dressing and
   nurturing
Has the power to change
and transform
Herself
Her home
The world
For good

Who is she?

She is YOU!
The Jewish woman
G-d's *Aishes Chayil*
You have the power
And you make a difference!

GROW as an *Aishes Chayil*

Gratitude: **What is an accomplishment of which you are proud and grateful?**

_____
_____
_____
_____

Oneness: **How can you impact others and produce the fruits of your redemption?**

_____
_____
_____
_____

Recognition: **Recognize an Aishes Chayil's accomplishment (yours or someone else) and compare it to harvesting fruits?**

_____
_____
_____
_____
_____
_____

Wish: **Express your wish for redemption. Write a personal letter to G-d.**

_____
_____
_____
_____
_____
_____

We are *Grateful* to you for growing with us as an Aishes Chayil. We are grateful for Jewish women throughout history and especially today, who are weaving the Divine into countless fields and areas of expertise with a distinct feminine touch.

We *Recognize* that women are mothers, wives, homemakers, authors, artists, educators, coaches, entrepreneurs, healthcare providers, scientists, judges, public servants, speakers, performers, producers, and so much more.

In *Oneness* with Hashem, we are "Weaving the Tapestry" of creation through combining our various gifts to beautify Hashem's home on earth. Together we unite our strengths. Together, we are G-d's bride, Aishes Chayil, preparing to celebrate the grand wedding with our Divine Partner.

Together we are ONE!

We *Wish* to rejoice and dance with our tambourines in G-d's home, the 3rd Holy Temple in Jerusalem! May this be speedily in our days!

Aishes Chayil Story

My Aishes Chayil Story

Aishes Chayil verse _____

GLOSSARY

Heb. — Hebrew; Yid. — Yiddish; Ara. — Aramaic

Alef-Beis – *Heb.* The Hebrew alphabet

Alter – *Yid.* Elder

Avinu – *Heb.* Our Forefather

Bais Lechem – *Heb.* Bethlehem

Bar Mitzvah – *Heb.* Literally, "Son of the Commandment"; a Jewish boy who has reached the age of thirteen, becoming an adult in terms of Jewish Law and Divinely responsible for his own conduct; also refers to the celebration marking this occasion

Baruch Hashem – *Heb.* Literally, "Blessed is G-d"; also commonly used to mean, "Thank G-d"

Bashert – *Yid.* Literally, "destined; intended"; one's soulmate

Bat Mitzvah (or Bas Mitzvah) – *Heb.* Literally, "Daughter of the Commandment"; a Jewish girl who's reached the age of twelve, becoming an adult in terms of Jewish Law and Divinely responsible for her own conduct; also refers to the celebration marking this occasion

Beis Hamikdash – *Heb.* The Holy Temple in Jerusalem

Benching Licht – *Yid.* Literally, "blessing light," a reference to kindling Shabbos candles with a blessing

Bereishis – *Heb.* Literally, "in the beginning"; Genesis, the first of the Five Books of Moses

Bikkurim – *Heb.* The first fruits of the harvest brought by ancient Israelite farmers to the *Mishkan* or *Beis Hamikdash* as an offering to G-d

Binah Yeteirah – *Heb.* An "additional measure of understanding" that G-d endows to women, according to our tradition

Bitachon – *Heb.* Trust, usually referring to trust in G-d Almighty

Blintzes – *Yid.* A crepe often stuffed with fruit or cheese, rolled into a cigar shape, then fried or baked

Bnai Yisroel – *Heb.* The Children of Israel, i.e. the Jewish nation

Bracha – *Heb.* Blessing

Bris – *Heb.* – Literally, "covenant"; a shortened form of the expression "bris milah — the covenant of [ritual] circumcision" performed on Jewish males, usually at eight days old; the celebration marking this occasion

Bubby/Bubbe – *Yid.* Grandmother

Chabad (or Chabad-Lubavitch) – *Heb.* Acronym for "chochmah [wisdom]," "binah [comprehension]" and "daas [knowledge]," the soul's three intellectual faculties; a movement within Chassidus founded by Rabbi Shneur Zalman of Liadi in the later 1800s, centered in the Russian village of Lubavitch for over a century, emphasizing application of one's mind to recognize G-d's Oneness, the Divine purpose of creation, and how to elevate every experience with this consciousness; of or relating to the Chabad-Lubavitch movement, a network of emissaries with centers stationed around the globe to disseminate Judaism

Challah – *Heb.* Literally "loaf"; the portion separated from one's dough, given through the priest as a gift to G-d in Temple times; the traditional, often-braided bread made for Shabbos, festivals and other celebrations

Chanukah – *Heb.* Literally, "[re]dedication"; the eight-day winter holiday of beginning on Kislev 25, celebrated with thanksgiving and kindling a menorah's lights to commemorate the miracles G-d performed for us in Israel under pagan Syrian-Greek oppression

Chassid (pl. chassidim) – *Heb.* A practitioner of Chassidus

Chassidus – *Heb.* Literally, "piety" (also "kindness"); Hasidism; the eighteenth-century movement based on Jewish mysticism, founded by the Baal Shem Tov in Eastern Europe; the teachings of the movement

Chayil – *Heb.* Soldier; valor

Chessed – *Heb.* Kindness

Chumashim – *Heb.* Copies of the Five Books of Moses

Chuppah – *Heb.* A canopy; usually in

reference to a wedding canopy under which the bride and groom are married during the ceremony

Davening – Yid. A slightly-Anglicized term meaning "prayer" or "to pray"

Devarim – Heb. Literally, "words" or "things"; the fifth of the Five Books of Moses

Emes – Heb. Truth

Emunah – Heb. Faith

Eretz Yisroel – Heb. The Land of Israel

Erev – Heb. Eve; the eve of

Farbrengen – Yid. Either an informal gathering with words of Torah, inspiration and song, or a formal gathering of *chassidim* addressed by a Rebbe

Frum – Yid. Pious; religiously observant

Gan Eden – Heb. The Garden of Eden

Geulah – Heb. Redemption

Golus – Heb. Exile

Hafrashas Challah – Heb. Literally, "Separation of the Challah"; the mitzvah-act of separating a portion of one's dough as a gift for G-d, which we burn today but gave to a priest when the Temple stood in Jerusalem

Haftarah – Heb. A portion from the Prophets read weekly on Shabbos and on holidays

Halacha (pl. Halachos) – Heb. Literally, "way"; Jewish law, which teaches the ways G-d wants us to conduct our lives

Haneviah – Heb. "The Prophetess"

Hashem – Heb. G-d

Heilige – Yid. Holy

Histalkus – Heb. Passing; death

Holishkes – Yid. Stuffed cabbage rolls

Ima – Heb. Mother

Imahot – Heb. Matriarchs

Imeinu – Heb. Our Foremother

Kabbalah – Heb. Jewish mysticism (passed down from a reliable Torah source)

Kashrus – Heb. The state of being Kosher

Kedusha - Heb. Holiness

Kesiva Vechasima Tova - Heb. "[May you be] written and sealed for [a] good [judgment]," a traditional greeting extended to one another before and during Rosh Hashanah

Kiddush – Heb. Literally, "sanctification"; the blessing(s) recited, typically over wine, declaring the holiness that endow the days of Shabbos and festivals

Knish (pl. Knishes) – Yid. A doughy sort of dumpling stuffed with mashed potato, vegetables, grains, meat or cheese, which is baked or fried

Kohain Gadol (pl. Kohanim Gedolim) – Heb. The "High Priest" or chief of the Kohanim

Kohanim – Heb. "Priests," descendants of Aaron who are designated to serve in the Holy Temple

Kohelet – Heb. Ecclesiastes, a book of the Tanakh that contains King Solomon's wise and solemn observations on life

Korban – Heb. Sacrificial offering

Kosher – Heb. Literally, "proper," or "fit"; foods permitted for a Jew to consume; of or relating to the Kosher dietary laws

Kugel – Yid. An ethnic Jewish pudding or casserole, often made primarily of noodles, potatoes, or other vegetables

Latkes – Yid. Potato pancakes, traditionally eaten on Chanukah

Lichtelach – Yid. Candles

Likutei Sichot – Heb. The transcribed, edited and published collection of the Lubavitcher Rebbe's talks

Melachim – Heb. Literally, "kings"; the two-part book of Tanakh recounting the history of the Jewish People and their kings, from David's passing until the Babylonian Exile

Mesiras Nefesh – Heb. Literally, "surrendering the soul"; self-sacrifice

Mezuzah – Heb. A parchment scroll (usually placed in a narrow case) containing Torah-passages, affixed to the doorposts of Jewish homes and businesses as a sign of G-d's protection

Midbar – Heb. Desert; wilderness

Middah – Heb. Literally, "measure"; a quality or character trait

Midrash – Heb. The classical, homiletic teachings (individually or collectively) of our Sages on the Torah

Mikdash Hashlishi – Heb. The third Holy Temple, to be reestablished when Moshiach comes

Mikvah – Heb. A ritual bath in which people immerse as a step to spiritual purity, such as in marriage, preparation for holy days, and conversion to Judaism

Mishkan – Heb. The Tabernacle that traveled with the Jews for forty years in the Wilderness and for a period afterwards in Israel

Mishlei – *Heb.* Proverbs, a book of Tanakh by King Solomon containing his wise parables and advice

Mishneh Torah – *Heb.* Maimonides's classic, fourteen-volume work of Jewish law

Mitzrayim – *Heb.* Egypt

Mitzvah (pl. Mitzvot, or Mitzvos) – *Heb.* Literally, "commandment"; one of G-d's 613 commandments in the Torah, and their derivatives; also stems from the root "tzavsa," meaning "connection," since engaging in a mitzvah binds you to G-d

Modeh Ani – *Heb.* Literally, "I give thanks"; the short prayer we say immediately upon awakening in the morning, to thank G-d for restoring our soul and granting us a new day of life

Moshiach – *Heb.* The Messiah; a shortened way of saying "Yemos HaMoshiach — The Days of Moshiach," or the Messianic Era

Motzei Shabbos – *Heb.* The departure of Shabbos on Saturday night

Nachas – *Heb.* Joy, satisfaction (often in the context of parents from their children)

Navi – *Heb.* Prophet

Nazir – *Heb.* An individual who 'separates' him/herself for a very holy and strict level of Divine service by abstaining from certain activities and physical pleasures

Neshama – *Heb.* Soul

Niftar – *Heb.* Passed away

N'shei Chabad – *Heb.* The global organization of Chabad women promoting Jewish education and awareness

Ob"m – Abbreviation for "of blessed memory"

Pasuk – *Heb.* Verse

Pesach – *Heb.* Passover; the seven-day festival (eight outside of Israel) beginning on Nissan 15, commemorating our miraculous liberation from Egyptian bondage; the name of the special offering brought up in the Holy Temple on Erev Pesach

Pirkei Avos – *Heb.* Literally, "chapters of the fathers"; another name for the tractate of the Oral Torah called "Avos", containing ethical teachings of our Sages

Rabbeinu – *Heb.* Our Teacher

Rebbe – *Yid.* A Yiddish form of the word "Rabbi," especially a head of a Chassidic community; often used simply in reference to the seventh Lubavitcher Rebbe, Rabbi Menachem Mendel Schneerson, of righteous memory

Rebbetzin – *Yid.* A Rabbi's wife

Rosh Chodesh – *Heb.* Literally, "head of the month"; the mini festival marking the beginning of each new Hebrew month, when the moon is almost invisible and restarts its cycle

Rosh Hashanah – *Heb.* Literally, "head of the year"; the Jewish New Year occurring on Tishrei 1-2, initiating the Ten Days of Repentance; the anniversary of Adam and Eve's creation, when the universe was completed and is renewed, when we coronate G-d as our King, when we are Divinely judged for our conduct in the past year and our future for the coming year is decreed

Sephardic – *Heb.* Of or relating to Jews of Spanish descent ("Sepharad" is Hebrew for "Spain") and their customs

Shabbos (or Shabbat) – *Heb.* The Sabbath

Shechinah – *Heb.* The Divine Presence; G-d as He fills and is manifest with the world

Shekel (pl. Shekalim) – *Heb.* An ancient Hebrew coin, a newer version of which is still used in Israel today

Shemos – *Heb.* Literally, "names"; Exodus, the second of the Five Books of Moses

Shevet Levi – *Heb.* The Tribe of Levi, the third-eldest son of Jacob and of the Twelve Tribes

Shevet Reuven – *Heb.* The Tribe of Reuben, the eldest son of Jacob and of the Twelve Tribes

Shira – *Heb.* Song of praise

Shir Hashirim – *Heb.* "The Song of Songs", a book (in the Tanakh) by King Solomon, expressing the love between G-d and the Jewish people, using the metaphor of marriage

Shiva – *Heb.* Literally, "seven"; the week-long mourning period after the burial of an immediate relative

Shliach (pl. Shluchim) – *Heb.* Male (Chabad) emissary

Shlichus – *Heb.* Mission

Shlucha (pl. Shluchos) – *Heb.* Female (Chabad) emissary

Shmitta – *Heb.* A Sabbatical year; the final year in a seven-year agricultural cycle, when the land of Israel is left to "rest" uncultivated, all resulting produce is free for public consumption, and any outstanding monetary debts between Jews are waived

Shofar – *Heb.* A ram's horn, traditionally blown during the month of Elul, Rosh Hashanah, and the end of Yom Kippur

Shoftim – *Heb.* Literally, "judges"; a book of the Tanakh recounting the historical period when judges ruled the Jewish People in Israel

Shul – *Yid.* Synagogue

Sicha – *Heb.* Talk; often used especially in reference to am address given by the Lubavitcher Rebbe, of righteous memory

Siddur (pl. Siddurim) – *Heb.* Literally, "order"; a prayer book

Simcha – *Heb.* Joy; joyous occasion

Simchas Torah – *Heb.* Literally, "joy of the Torah"; a festival immediately following Sukkot to restart the annual, public Torah-reading cycle with great celebration

Sukkah – *Heb.* Literally, "booth"; the temporary structure in which we celebrate and dwell for the weeklong festival of Sukkot, reminiscent of our ancestors' nomadic dwellings during their forty-year journey through the wilderness

Talmud – *Heb.* The main body of Jewish law and thought, divided into tractates, comprising the basic teachings of Oral Torah and their elaboration; the unspecified term usually refers to the edition of Babylonian Talmud rather than the Jerusalem Talmud that was later developed

Talmud-Torah – *Heb.* An elementary school for Torah study

Tanakh – *Heb.* An acronym referring to the Jewish Bible, comprised of "Torah" (the Five Books of Moses), "Nevi'im" (the Prophets) and "Kesuvim" (the Scriptures)

Tefillah (pl. Tefillos) – *Heb.* Literally, "attachment" or "to judge"; prayer

Tehillim – *Heb.* (King David's) Psalms

Teshuvah – *Heb.* "Repentance" or "return," particularly to one's essence and Jewish observance

Tzedakah – *Heb.* Literally, "righteousness," but commonly used to mean "charity"

Vayikra – *Heb.* Literally, "and He called"; Leviticus, the third of the Five Books of Moses

Yam Suf – *Heb.* The Sea of Reeds

Yahrtzeit – *Yid.* Anniversary of a passing

Yerushalayim – *Heb.* Jerusalem

Yeshiva (pl. Yeshivos) – *Heb.* An academy of Torah study

Yiddishe Mama – *Yid.* A Jewish mother

Yiddishkeit – *Yid.* Judaism; one's essential Jewishness

Yom Kippur – *Heb.* Literally, "the Day of Atonement"; the solemn fast day and holiest day of the year, occurring on Tishrei 10, when we repent for sins and reconnect to our pure soul-essence, and G-d determines our judgment for the coming year

Yom Tov – *Heb.* One of the Biblically-mentioned Festivals

Zuidy – *Yid.* Grandfather

ACKNOWLEDGMENTS

We express our heartfelt gratitude to **Hashem** for the precious gift of life and for uniting us in the beautiful endeavor of *Weaving the Tapestry*.

With gratitude to **the Lubavitcher Rebbe** whose teachings permeate the pages of this book and empower us to be lamplighters.

Special thanks to the following individuals who have played a crucial role in the creation of this book. Their unwavering support and valuable contributions ensure that it inspires generations of Jewish women and girls. We recognize that great achievements are accomplished through collective unity, and together as one, we are Weaving the Tapestry.

With thanks to my beloved family:

My dear Tatty, **Rabbi Azriel Yitzchok Wasserman** ob"m, for instilling in me a lifelong foundation of faith and a passion for teaching.

My dear mother, **Daniella Katzenberg** Shtichye, for exemplifying the qualities of an Aishes Chayil and creating a beautiful Jewish home.

My late Daddy, **Yitzchok Levi Hacohen Katzenberg** ob"m, a man of integrity and a loving father and grandfather to my children.

My husband, **Rabbi Avraham Laber**, for his invaluable edits, guidance, research, and unwavering support throughout the creation of this book.

My five precious daughters: **Chaya Shepherd, Chana, Shaina, Raizel, and Rivkah Laber**. Your dedication and collaboration make us a formidable team, welcoming many more spiritual daughters into our extended family.

With deep gratitude to our JGU Press Team & Contributors:

Global Advisor: **Susan Axelrod**, whose visionary leadership founded and guided JGU for a decade, laying the foundation for our mission.

Writer: **Tzipporah Prottas**, who devoted endless hours to learning, researching, writing, revising, and proofreading this manuscript, as well as creating the glossary.

Design: **Leah Caras** of Carasmatic Design, whose artistic talent beautifully crafted the graphic design of this book. Leah's journey began as a teen camper at Bat Mitzvah Camp in 2005, and since 2006, she has been a valuable member of our staff. Together, we founded the Jewish Girls Retreat and Jewish Girls Unite.

Susannah Levin for your assistance with typesetting and layout.

Chief Editor: **Chana Shloush**, whose meticulous editing and proofreading contributed immensely to the quality of this book.

Editors: **Rabbi Avraham Laber** and **Gittel Laber**, for their invaluable contributions as part of the editorial team for this final version of the book.

Yael Jacobs and **Malka Bracha Finkler**, who played pivotal roles in editing earlier drafts of this book, which ultimately led to the creation of this final version.

Artist: **Chana Cotter**, whose detailed illustrations for each verse have added visual depth and character to the book.

Cover Art: **Miriam Leah Herman**, for granting permission to use her stunning artwork for the cover.

Song Artists: The chapters of this book are enriched by Meaningful Melodies, with some composed specifically for JGU and JGR, while others are powerful songs that resonate with the book's themes. We extend our gratitude to the following talented individuals for sharing their gifts:

Racheli Jacks
Chaya Bracha Rubin
Mali New
Rivka Leah Popack
Sarah Leah Eber
Rivkie Feld
Tzirel Liba Greenberg
Sarah Hecht
Rivkah Krinsky
Chavie Rappaport

Contributing Writers: With thanks to the many writers who contributed to the stories in this book:

Susan Axelrod
Chana Burston
Edith Davidovici
Rishe Deitsch
Chedva Federman
Shoshana Fox
Zalman Goldstein
Shea Hecht
Ed Jacobs
Sarah Karmely
Terri Klein
Gittel Laber
Rabbi Laber Avraham
Shmuel Marcus
Dovid Margolin
Malkie Marrus
Rabbi New Ruvi
Tzipporah Prottas
Goldy Rosenberg
Eli Rubin
Chana Sirota Zobin
Esther Sternberg
Mendel Super
Rachael Tahir
Avraham D. Vaisfiche
Mushka Miriam Weingarten
Blumah Wineberg
Rabbi Yosef Wolvovsky

Chabad.org Team: **Chana Weisberg**, Editor of Chabad.org, we express our gratitude for your inspiring articles, books, and invaluable encouragement. Thank you to **Chabad.org**, for granting permission to include stories and for serving as a valuable resource, allowing readers to learn more about any of the topics in this book.

We are grateful to **Rabbi & Mrs. Israel Rubin** for warmly welcoming us as Chabad Shluchim to the Capital Region in 1996. We also want to acknowledge Maimonides Day School and Bnos Chaya High School of Albany, where I had the opportunity to teach the Aishes Chayil.

With deep appreciation to our tribute page sponsors for their support and partnership in this important endeavor.

Thank you for sharing your cherished memories!

Special thanks to:
Susan Axelrod
Michael & Leah Caras
Yocheved Daphna
Ben & Rachel Federman
Federman Family
Sarah Freedman
Yitzchok & Leah Gniwisch
Shoshana Fox
Dr. Edward & Laura Jacobs
Terri Klein
Gittel Laber
Laber Family
Levin Family
Loren Lichtenstein
Norman & Micki Massry & Family
Sholom & Chana Zeldy Minkowitz
Kim Ritz
Eda & David Schottenstein
Rachael Tahir
Goldie Tennenhaus
Azriel & Chana Wasserman

To the JGR & JGU Staff & Girls:

Since 1999, we have been educating the Bat Mitzvah Club of the Capital Region about remarkable women from the past. We shared early drafts of this book at the Jewish Girls Summer Retreat in 2004 and 2010, as well as during the JGU Creative Online Camp in 2020.

Each woman and girl who has cherished moments of learning from this curriculum serves as a catalyst, inspiring generations of women and girls through the pages of this book.

Together, we celebrate the strength and purpose of Jewish women as we continue to Weave the Tapestry and inspire countless others. So many were involved in creating this book, this glorious tapestry, that it's possible that we might have left someone out. If we did, we ask for your forgiveness and to inform us so we may revise in the next edition.

With gratitude,

Nechama Dina Laber

ABOUT THE AUTHOR

Nechama Dina Laber experienced a profound loss in her childhood when her beloved father, Rabbi Azriel Yitzchok Wasserman ob"m, passed away. However, she drew strength from the stories of resilient women throughout history, which became a guiding force in her life. Alongside her supportive husband, Rabbi Avraham Laber, and their 11 children and grandchildren, Nechama has been dedicated to serving as a Chabad *Shlucha* since 1996. She co-directs Chabad of Southern Rensselaer County at the Jewish Greenbush Retreat Campus, where she also directs retreats.

As a mother to Yosef Chaim, her 11th child born with Down syndrome, Nechama finds inspiration from the women of valor, both past and present. Their examples grant her the strength and determination to accept her mission from G-d with love.

Nechama's passion lies in empowering girls and women to build joyous Jewish homes. She firmly believes that the future of the Jewish people greatly depends on the daughters of Israel, as their inherent strengths hold tremendous potential. For over three decades, Nechama has passionately served as an educator and *shlucha*. She is a life coach, mentor for the Bat Mitzvah Club, the director of the Jewish Girls Retreat, and the driving force behind Jewish Girls Unite. Through these roles, she shares inspiring stories of women of valor, instilling their significance in the hearts of countless individuals.

Additionally, Nechama is the founder of the GROW Method™ of Prayer, which provides training for educators and leaders worldwide through the GROW Connection Network. This program focuses on growing meaningful connections to one's core, creator, and community.

Furthermore, Nechama established the JGU Press and has authored several publications, including *One More Light*, *Finding Song in Sorrow*, *Seven Voices of Leadership Bat Mitzvah Journal*, *GROW Through Prayer*, *GROW Planners*, and *GROW through the Haggadah*, as well as educational curricula and resources that are utilized around the world.

Ready, set...
GROW
gratitude · recognition · oneness · wishes

Here are the steps to grow a connection to your core, your Creator, and community using the structure of the Siddur.

G is for *Gratitude*, corresponding to the **morning blessings**, as we realize our dependence on G-d for our existence and thank Him for all our blessings.

R is for *Recognition*, corresponding to the **verses of praise**, as we recognize G-d through His creations and miracles in our lives.

O is for *Oneness & Ownership*, corresponding to the **Shema** that declares our faith in the One G-d, as we embrace the gifts and experiences He gives us to accomplish our mission in life, and recall that we are always one with Him.

W is for *Wants or Wishes*, corresponding to the **Shemoneh Esrei/Amidah** prayer, as we request our desires from Hashem to fulfill our mission to increase goodness and holiness in our world!

For more information and resources on the GROW Method, visit GROWconnectionNetwork.com

MORE FROM JGU PRESS

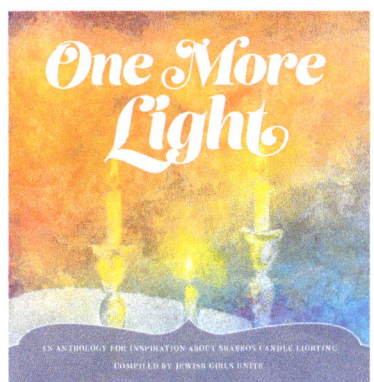
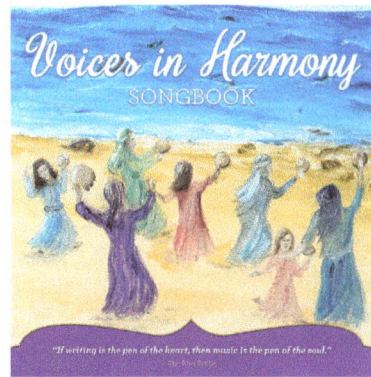
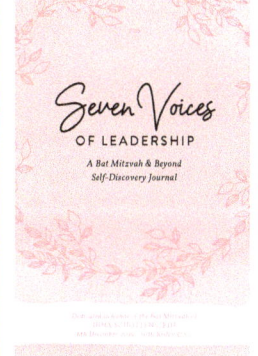
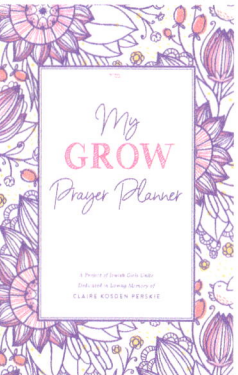
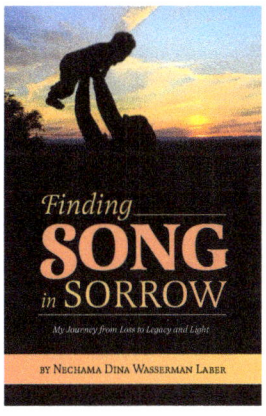

To purchase any of these books or curricula downloads and resources visit JewishGirlsUnite.com.

www.ingramcontent.com/pod-product-compliance
Lightning Source LLC
Chambersburg PA
CBHW061810290426
44110CB00026B/2842